PHONETIC LINGUISTICS
Essays in Honor of Peter Ladefoged

Peter Ladefoged

PHONETIC LINGUISTICS

Essays in Honor of Peter Ladefoged

Edited by

Victoria A. Fromkin

Department of Linguistics
University of California, Los Angeles
Los Angeles, California

1985

ACADEMIC PRESS, INC.

(Harcourt Brace Jovanovich, Publishers)

Orlando   San Diego   New York   London
Toronto   Montreal   Sydney   Tokyo

All royalties from the sale of this book accrue to the
Linguistic Society of America.

ACADEMIC PRESS, INC.
Orlando, Florida 32887

United Kingdom Edition published by
ACADEMIC PRESS INC. (LONDON) LTD.
24-28 Oval Road, London NW1 7DX

LIBRARY OF CONGRESS CATALOGING IN PUBLICATION DATA

Main entry under title:

Phonetic linguistics.

"Bibliography of Peter Ladefoged":p.
Includes index.
1. Phonetics—Addresses, essays, lectures.
2. Ladefoged, Peter.   I. Ladefoged, Peter.   II. Fromkin,
Victoria.
P221.P47   1985   414   84-18568
ISBN 0-12-268990-9 (alk. paper)

PRINTED IN THE UNITED STATES OF AMERICA

85 86 87 88   9 8 7 6 5 4 3 2 1

Contents

8
Universal Phonetics and the Organization of Grammars
Patricia A. Keating

9
Computation of Mapping from Muscular Contraction Patterns to Formant Patterns in Vowel Space
Yuki Kakita, Osamu Fujimura, and Kiyoshi Honda

10
Rhythm of Poetry, Rhythm of Prose
Ilse Lehiste

15
Around *Flat*
John J. Ohala

16
Evidence for the Role of Acoustic Boundaries in the Perception of Speech Sounds
Kenneth N. Stevens

Contributors

Numbers in parentheses indicate the pages on which the authors' contributions begin.

DAVID ABERCROMBIE (15), 13 Grosvenor Crescent, Edinburgh EH12 5EL, Scotland

ARTHUR S. ABRAMSON (25), Department of Linguistics, University of Connecticut, Storrs, Connecticut 06268, and Haskins Laboratories, New Haven, Connecticut 06511

CATHERINE P. BROWMAN (35), Haskins Laboratories, 270 Crown Street, New Haven, Connecticut 06511

GUNNAR FANT (55), Department of Speech Communication, Royal Institute of Technology, Stockholm 100 44, Sweden

ELI FISCHER-JØRGENSEN (79), 2830 Virum Kongestien 45, Denmark

VICTORIA A. FROMKIN (1), Department of Linguistics, University of California, Los Angeles, Los Angeles, California 90024

OSAMU FUJIMURA (133), AT&T Bell Laboratories, Murray Hill, New Jersey, 07974

LOUIS M. GOLDSTEIN (35), Department of Linguistics and Psychology, Yale University, New Haven, Connecticut 06520, and Haskins Laboratories, New Haven, Connecticut 06511

MORRIS HALLE (101), Department of Linguistics, Massachusetts Institute of Technology, Cambridge, Massachusetts 02139

KIYOSHI HONDA (133), Faculty of Medicine, RILP, University of Tokyo, Tokyo 113, Japan

YUKI KAKITA[1] (133), Department of Otolaryngology, Kurume University, Kurume 830, Japan

PATRICIA A. KEATING (115), Department of Linguistics, University of California, Los Angeles, Los Angeles, California 90024

[1] Present address: Department of Electronics, Kanazawa Institute of Technology, 7-1 Ohgigaoka, Kanazawa-Minami [921], Japan.

ILSE LEHISTE (145), Department of Linguistics, Ohio State
    University, Columbus, Ohio 43210
MONA LINDAU (157), Department of Linguistics, University of
    California, Los Angeles, Los Angeles, California 90024
BJÖRN LINDBLOM (169), Department of Phonetics, Institute of
    Linguistics, University of Stockholm, Stockholm 106 91, Sweden
LEIGH LISKER (25), Department of Linguistics, University of
    Pennsylvania, Philadelphia, Pennsylvania 19104, and Haskins
    Laboratories, New Haven, Connecticut 06511
JAMES LUBKER[2] (169), Department of Phonetics, Institute of
    Linguistics, University of Stockholm, Stockholm 106 91, Sweden
PETER F. MacNEILAGE (193), Departments of Linguistics and
    Psychology, University of Texas at Austin, Austin, Texas 78712
IAN MADDIESON (203), Department of Linguistics, University of
    California, Los Angeles, Los Angeles, California 90024
JOHN J. OHALA[3] (223), Department of Linguistics, University of
    California, Berkeley, California 94720
KENNETH N. STEVENS (243), Department of Electrical
    Engineering and Computer Science, Massachusetts Institute of
    Technology, Cambridge, Massachusetts 02139

[2] Present address: The University of Vermont, Department of Communication Science
and Disorders, Burlington, Vermont 05405.
    [3] Present address: Institute of Phonetics, University of Copenhagen, DK-2300 Copenhagen
S, Denmark.

Preface

This book was conceived out of a recognition of the important role played by Peter Ladefoged in the development of phonetic linguistic theory and the desire to publicly acknowledge our debt to him. Had all those who have contributed significantly to phonetics and who have studied or worked with Peter Ladefoged been included, many volumes would have had to be published. The authors of the 16 chapters, therefore, represent a small but significant subset of all those individuals throughout the world whose research has added to our knowledge of the perception and production of speech and of the acoustic and articulatory parameters of linguistic phonetic units. Among the writers are phoneticians who have taught or been taught by Peter Ladefoged, as well as research colleagues who have both argued against and agreed with his views. To a large extent, these chapters represent the "state of the art" in linguistic phonetics.

The topics covered are broad in scope and are both historical and contemporary in content. They will be of interest to those whose research interests lie in the areas of acoustics, articulatory motor controls of production, perception, the interface between articulation and acoustic output, the phonetic representation of linguistic units, universal phonetic theory, segments and prosodies, phonetic aspects of poetry and prose, individual phonetic features, and larger phonetic units.

All of the chapters reflect the substantive and innovative work of Peter Ladefoged. Yet even the complete listing or reading of his many books and publications that follows cannot reveal the profound influence he has exerted on all of us who have had the opportunity of working with him and knowing him personally. His commitment to the highest standards of scholarship, his meticulous methods, and his devotion to finding the "truth," even though it might destroy his own hypotheses, are bywords of his own scholarly research and attest to his personal and scientific integrity. But even they do not portray Peter, who with the zeal of an explorer discovering a new continent, went forth into the bush in Africa or the jungles of New Guinea or the mountains of Tibet and Nepal, his suitcases filled with phonetic equipment, often accompanied by Jenny Ladefoged, also loaded down with FM recorders and fiber-optic tubes, in order to record speech from more people speaking more languages than any other phonetician has ever done. These recordings and his analyses of the articulatory and acoustic parameters of these sounds provide the empirical basis of current theoretical hypotheses.

As a student of Peter Ladefoged—in fact his first doctoral student—I feel confident that I speak for all his students who have discussed and argued with him and who have been taught, supported, fed, criticized, and continually helped by him. This book is, therefore, from us all, Peter, on your sixtieth birthday, as an expression of our deepest gratitude to you as a teacher, a scholar, a friend, and the most human of human beings.

Curriculum Vitae of Peter Ladefoged

Birthdate: September 17, 1925
Place of birth: Sutton, Surrey, England

Education

1938–1943	Haileybury
1943–1944	Caius College, Cambridge University
1944–1947	Royal Sussex Regiment
1951	M.A., University of Edinburgh, Scotland
1959	Ph.D., University of Edinburgh, Scotland

Honors

President, Linguistic Society of America, 1978
President, Permanent Council for the Organization of
  Congresses of Phonetic Sciences
Fellow, Acoustical Society of America
Fellow, American Speech, Language and Hearing
  Association
Fellow, International Society of Phonetic Sciences
  Council of the International Phonetics Association
Distinguished Teaching Award, UCLA

Academic Positions

1965–present	Professor of Phonetics, Department of Linguistics, UCLA
1977–1980	Chair, Department of Linguistics, UCLA
1961–1962	Field Fellow, West African Languages Survey
1961 (summer)	Guest Researcher, Speech Transmission Laboratory, Royal Institute of Technology, Stockholm, Sweden
1960 (summer)	Guest Researcher, Communication Sciences Laboratory, University of Michigan
1959–1960	Lecturer in Phonetics, University of Ibadan, Nigeria
1960–1961; 1953–1959	Lecturer in Phonetics, University of Edinburgh

Publications of Peter Ladefoged

1956   • D. Broadbent, P. Ladefoged, & W. Lawrence. Vowel sounds and perceptual constancy. *Nature, 178,* 815–816.
- P. Ladefoged. The classification of vowels. *Lingua, 5*(2), 113–128.
- P. Ladefoged. Recording and listening techniques. *Speech, 20*(1), 23–29.

1957   • D. E. Broadbent & P. Ladefoged. On the fusion of sounds reaching different sense organs. *Journal of the Acoustical Society of America, 29,* 708–710.
- M. Draper, P. Ladefoged, & D. Whitteridge. Expiratory muscles involved in speech. *Journal of Physiology, 138,* 17–18.
- P. Ladefoged. The function of a phonetics laboratory. *Orbis, 5*(1), 211–219.
- P. Ladefoged. Use of palatography. *Journal of Speech and Hearing Disorders, 22,* 764–774.
- P. Ladefoged & D. Broadbent. Information conveyed by vowels. *Journal of the Acoustical Society of America, 29,* 98–104.

1958   • P. Ladefoged, M. Draper, & D. Witteridge. Syllables and stress. *Miscellanea Phonetica, 3,* 1–14.

1959   • P. Ladefoged. The perception of speech. *Proceedings of the symposium on the mechanisation of thought processes* (pp. 1–13). London: H.M.S.O.
- P. Ladefoged, M. Draper, & D. Witteridge. Respiratory muscles in speech. *Journal of Speech and Hearing Research, 2*(1), 16–27.

1960   • D. Broadbent & P. Ladefoged. Vowel judgements and adaptation level. *Proceedings of the Royal Society, 151,* 384–399.
- M. Draper, P. Ladefoged, & D. Witteridge. Expiratory pressures and airflow during speech. *British Medical Journal,* 1837–1843.
- P. Ladefoged. The regulation of subglottal pressure. *Folia Phoniatrica, 12*(3), 169–175.

- P. Ladefoged. The value of phonetic statements. *Language, 36,* 387–396.
- P. Ladefoged & D. Broadbent. Perception of sequence in auditory events. *Quarterly Journal of Experimental Psychology, 12*(3), 162–170.

1961
- T. O. Howie, P. Ladefoged, & R. E. Stark. Congenital subglottal bars found in 3 generations of one family. *Folia Phoniatrica, 13,* 56–61.

1962
- P. Ladefoged. *The nature of vowel quality.* Monograph supplement to Revista do Laboratorio de Fonetica Experimental da Faculdade de Letra da Universidade de Coimbra.
- P. Ladefoged. Subglottal activity during speech. *Proceedings of the 4th International Congress of Phonetic Sciences* In Sovijarvi, A., and Alto, P. (Eds.), The Hague: Mouton, 73–91.

1963
- P. Garvin & P. Ladefoged. Speaker identification and message identification in speech recognition. *Phonetica, 9,* 193–199.
- P. Ladefoged. Review of *English phonetics* by Yao Shen. *Language, 39,* 581–584.
- P. Ladefoged. Some physiological parameters in speech. *Language and Speech, 6*(3), 109–119.
- P. Ladefoged & N. McKinney. Loudness, sound pressure, and subglottal pressure in speech. *Journal of the Acoustical Society of America, 35,* 454–460.
- P. Ladefoged. La base phonétique de langues de l'Afrique. *Occidental Actes du Second Colloque International de Linguistique Negro–Africaine,* 3–21.

1964
- P. Ladefoged. Comment on "Evaluation of methods of estimating subglottal air pressure." *Journal of Speech and Hearing Research, 7,* 291–292.
- P. Ladefoged. Igbirra notes and word-list. *The Journal of West African Languages, 1*(1), 27–37.
- P. Ladefoged. *A phonetic study of West African languages.* Cambridge: Cambridge University Press.
- P. Ladefoged. A phonetic study of Western African language. *West African Language Monograph 1.* London: Cambridge University Press.
- P. Ladefoged. Review of *Manual of articulatory phonetics* by William A. Smalley. *International Journal of American Linguistics, 30,* 424–427.
- P. Ladefoged. Some possibilities in speech synthesis. *Language and Speech, 7,* 205–214. Also in *UCLA Working Papers in Phonetics 1,* 2–9 (1964).

1965 • P. Ladefoged. The nature of general phonetic theories. *Georgetown University Monograph—Language and Linguistics, 18,* 27–42.
• P. Ladefoged. Review of *Acoustic characteristics of selected English consonants* by Ilse Lehiste. *Language, 41,* 332–338.
• P. Ladefoged. Review of *Phonetics: History and interpretation* by Elbert R. Moses, Jr. *International Journal of American Linguistics, 31,* 182–183.
• P. Ladefoged & C. Kim. Human, replica, and computer generated formants. *UCLA Working Papers in Phonetics, 2,* 18–26.

1966 • P. Ladefoged. New research techniques in experimental phonetics. *Study of sounds.* Phonetic Society of Japan, *12,* 84–101.
• N. McKinney, M. Tatham, & P. Ladefoged. Terminal analog speech synthesizer. *UCLA Working Papers in Phonetics, 4,* 10–18.

1967 • V. Fromkin & P. Ladefoged. Electromyography in speech research. *Phonetica, 15,* 219–242.
• R. Harshman & P. Ladefoged. The LINC–8 in research on speech. *DECUS Proceedings.* Also in *UCLA Working Papers in Phonetics, 7,* 57–68.
• P. Ladefoged. Linguistic phonetics. *UCLA Working Papers in Phonetics, 6.*
• P. Ladefoged. Research possibilities in phonetics. *Research Institute of Logopedics* and *Phoniatrics Annual Bulletin, 1,* 31–34.
• P. Ladefoged. *Three areas of experimental phonetics.* London: Oxford University Press.
• P. Ladefoged & R. Vanderslice. The 'voiceprint' mystique. *Journal of the Acoustical Society of America, 42,* 1164 (abstract). Also in *UCLA Working Papers in Phonetics, 7,* 126–142.

1968 • J. Catford & P. Ladefoged. Practical phonetic exercises. *UCLA Working Papers in Phonetics 11.*
• P. Ladefoged. Linguistic aspects of respiratory phenomena. In A. Bouhuys (Ed.), *Sound production in man. Annals of the New York Academy of Sciences, 155,* 141–151.
• P. Ladefoged. *A phonetic study of West African languages.* (second ed.). London: Cambridge University Press.
• P. Ladefoged & V. Fromkin. Experiments on competence and performance. *IEEE Transactions on Audio and Electroacoustics,* AU–16, 130–136.

1970 • P. Ladefoged. Clicks. *Encyclopaedia Britannica,* 911. Chicago, IL.

• P. Ladefoged. The measurement of phonetic similarity. *Statistical Methods in Linguistics, 6*, 23–32.
• J. Ohala & P. Ladefoged. Subglottal pressure variations and glottal frequencies. *Journal of the Acoustical Society of America, 47*, 104 (abstract). Also in *UCLA Working Papers in Phonetics, 14*, 12–24, *as* Further investigation of pitch regulation in speech.

1971   • G. Allen & P. Ladefoged. Syllable structure and sentence rhythm—a cross language study. In Andre Rigault & Rene Charbonneau (Eds.), *Proceedings of the 7th International Congress of Phonetic Science* (pp. 833–836). The Hague: Mouton. Also in *Journal of the Acoustical Society of America, 50*, 116 (abstract).
• C. Criper & P. Ladefoged. Linguistic complexity in Uganda. In W. H. Whiteley (Ed.), *Language use and social change* (pp. 145–159). London: Oxford University Press.
• P. Ladefoged. An alternative set of vowel shift rules. *UCLA Working Papers in Phonetics, 17*, 25–28.
• P. Ladefoged. A basic linguistic phonetics laboratory. *UCLA Working Papers in Phonetics, 17*, 95–103.
• P. Ladefoged. *Elements of acoustic phonetics.* Chicago: University of Chicago Press. Translated into Japanese, Taishukan Publishing Company (1976).
• P. Ladefoged. The limits of phonology. In Sprang-Thomsen, B. (Ed.), *Form and substance: Papers presented to Eli Fischer-Jørgensen* (pp. 47–56). Copenhagen: Akademisk Forlag. Also in *UCLA Working Papers in Phonetics, 14*, 25–32, as The phonetic framework of generative phonology.
• P. Ladefoged. An opinion on 'voiceprints.' *UCLA Working Papers in Phonetics, 19*, 84–87.
• P. Ladefoged. *Preliminaries to linguistic phonetics.* Chicago: University of Chicago Press.
• P. Ladefoged, J. Anthony, & C. Riley. Direct measurement of the vocal tract. *Journal of the Acoustical Society of America, 49*, 104 (abstract). Also in *UCLA Working Papers in Phonetics, 19*, 4–13.
• P. Ladefoged, J. DeClerk, & R. Harshman. Factor analyses of tongue shapes. *Journal of the Acoustical Society of America, 50*, 114 (abstract). Also in *UCLA Working Papers in Phonetics, 19*, 47.
• P. Ladefoged, J. DeClerk, & R. Harshman. Parameters of tongue shape. *UCLA Working Papers in Phonetics, 19*, 47.
• P. Ladefoged, R. Glick, & C. Criper. *Language in Uganda.* Nairobi, Kenya: Oxford University Press.

- M. Lindau, R. Harshman, & P. Ladefoged. Factor analyses of formant frequencies of vowels. *Journal of the Acoustical Society of America, 50,* 117 (abstract). Also in *UCLA Working Papers in Phonetics, 19,* 17–25.

1972
- P. Ladefoged. Phonetic prerequisites for a distinctive feature theory. In A. Waldman (Ed.), *Papers in linguistics and phonetics in memory of Pierre Delattre* (pp. 273–286). The Hague: Mouton.
- P. Ladefoged. Phonological features and their phonetic correlates. *Journal of the International Phonetic Association, 2,* 2–12. Also in *UCLA Working Papers in Phonetics, 21,* 3–12 (1971).
- P. Ladefoged. The three glottal features. *Journal of the Acoustical Society of America, 51,* 101 (abstract). Also in *UCLA Working Papers in Phonetics, 22,* 95–101.
- P. Ladefoged, J. DeClerk, & R. Harshman. The control of the tongue in vowels. In Andre Rigault & Rene Charbonneau (Eds.), *Proceedings of the Seventh International Congress of Phonetic Sciences* (pp. 349–354). The Hague: Mouton.
- P. Ladefoged, J. DeClerk, M. Lindau, & G. Papcun. An auditory–motor theory of speech production. *UCLA Working Papers in Phonetics, 22,* 48–75.
- M. Lindau, L. Jacobson, & P. Ladefoged. The feature advanced tongue root. *Journal of the Acoustical Society of America, 51,* 101 (abstract). Also in *UCLA Working Papers in Phonetics, 22,* 76–94.
- R. Vanderslice & P. Ladefoged. Binary suprasegmental features and transformational word-accentuation rules. *Language, 48,* 819–838. Also in *UCLA Working Papers in Phonetics, 17,* 6–24 (1971).

1973
- P. Ladefoged. The features of the larynx. *Journal of Phonetics, 1*(1), 73–83.
- P. Ladefoged, R. Silverstein, & G. Papcun. The interruptibility of speech. *Journal of the Acoustical Society of America, 54,* 1105–1108. Also in *UCLA Working Papers in Phonetics, 17,* 85–94 (1971).
- T. Vennemann & P. Ladefoged. Phonetic features and phonological features. *Lingua, 32,* 61–74. Also in *UCLA Working Papers in Phonetics, 21,* 13–24 (1971).

1974
- R. Harshman, P. Ladefoged, L. Goldstein, & J. DeClerk. Factors underlying the articulatory and acoustic structure of vowels. *Journal of the Acoustical Society of America, 55,* 385 (abstract).
- P. Ladefoged. Phonetics. *15th Edition of Encyclopaedia Britannica,* 275–283. Also in *UCLA Working Papers in Phonetics, 20* (1971).

1975 • P. Ladefoged. A *course in phonetics*. New York: Harcourt Brace Jovanovich.
     • P. Ladefoged. Respiration, layrngeal activity and linguistics. In Barry Wyke (Ed.), *Ventilatory and phonatory control systems* (pp. 299–314). London: Oxford University Press.
1976 • S. Disner & P. Ladefoged. Trill seeking. *Journal of the Acoustical Society of America, 60,* S45 (abstract).
     • P. Ladefoged. How to put one person's tongue inside another person's mouth. *Journal of the Acoustical Society of America, 60,* S77 (abstract).
     • P. Ladefoged, I. Kameny, & W. Brackenridge. Acoustic effects of style of speech. *Journal of the Acoustical Society of America, 59,* 228–231.
     • P. Ladefoged, K. Williamson, B. Elugbe, & A. A. Uwalaka. The stops of Owerri Igbo. *Studies in African Linguistics,* Supplement 6: 147–163.
     • P. MacNeilage & P. Ladefoged. The production of speech and language. In E. C. Carterette and M. P. Freidman (Eds.), *Handbook of perception VII: Language and speech* (pp. 75–120). New York: Academic Press.
     • G. Papcun & P. Ladefoged. Two 'voiceprint' cases. *Journal of the Acoustical Society of America, 55,* 463. Also in *UCLA Working Papers in Phonetics, 31,* 108–113 (1974).
     • L. Rice & P. Ladefoged. Uniqueness of articulations determined from acoustic data. *Journal of the Acoustical Society of America, 59,* S70 (abstract).
1977 • R. Harshman, P. Ladefoged, & L. Goldstein. Factor analysis of tongue shapes. *Journal of the Acoustical Society of America, 62,* 693–707.
     • J. Hombert & P. Ladefoged. The effect of aspiration on the fundamental frequency of the following vowel. *UCLA Working Papers in Phonetics, 36,* 33–40.
     • P. Ladefoged. The abyss between phonetics and phonology. *Proceedings of the Chicago Linguistic Society, 13,* 225–235.
     • P. Ladefoged. Some notes on recent phonetic fieldwork. *UCLA Working Papers in Phonetics, 38,* 14–15.
     • P. Ladefoged, A. Cochran, & S. Disner. Laterals and trills. *Journal of the International Phonetic Association, 7*(2), 46–54.
     • P. Ladefoged & L. Rice. Formant frequencies corresponding to different vocal tract shapes. *Journal of the Acoustical Society of America, 61,* S32 (abstract).
     • P. Ladefoged, R. Harshman, L. Goldstein, & L. Rice. Vowel

articulation and formant frequencies. *UCLA Working Papers in Phonetics, 38,* 16–40.

1978 • P. Ladefoged. Expectation affects identification by listening. *Language and Speech, 21,* 373–374. Also in *UCLA Working Papers in Phonetics, 41,* 41–42.

• P. Ladefoged. Phonetic differences within and between languages. *UCLA Working Papers in Phonetics, 41,* 32–40.

• P. Ladefoged. Review of *Speech physiology and acoustic phonetics* by Philip Lieberman. *Language, 54,* 920–922.

• P. Ladefoged, R. Harshman, L. Goldstein, & L. Rice. Generating vocal tract shapes from formant frequencies. *Journal of the Acoustical Society of America, 64,* 1027–1035.

1979 • V. Fromkin & P. Ladefoged. Early views of distinctive features. In R. A. Asher & E. J. Henderson (Eds.), *Towards a history of phonetics* (pp. 3–8). Edinburgh: Edinburgh University Press.

• P. Ladefoged. Phonetic specification of the languages of the world. *Revue de Phonetique Applique, 49/50,* 21–40. Also in *UCLA Working Papers in Phonetics, 31,* 3–21 (1976).

• P. Ladefoged & R. Harshman. Formant frequencies and movements of the tongue. In B. Lindblom & S. Ohman (Eds.), *Frontiers of speech communication* (pp. 25–34). New York: Academic Press. Also in *UCLA Working Papers in Phonetics, 45,* 39–52.

• P. Ladefoged & M. Lindau. Prediction of vocal tract shapes in utterances. *Journal of the Acoustical Society of America, 64,* S41 (abstract). Also in *UCLA Working Papers in Phonetics, 45,* 32–38.

• P. Ladefoged, M. Lindau, & P. Coady. Generating vocal tract shapes in continuous speech. *Proceedings of the 9th International Congress of Phonetic Sciences,* p. 198. Copenhagen: Institute of Phonetics, Univ. of Copenhagen.

• P. Ladefoged, W. Linker, & J. Wright. Where does the vocal tract end? *UCLA Working Papers in Phonetics, 45,* 53–59.

1980 • P. Ladefoged. Articulatory parameters. *Language and Speech, 23,* 25–30. Also in *UCLA Working Papers in Phonetics, 45,* 25–31 (1979).

• P. Ladefoged. What are linguistic sounds made of? *Language, 56,* 485–502. Also in *UCLA Working Papers in Phonetics, 45,* 1–24 (1979).

• P. Ladefoged & J. Ladefoged. The ability of listeners to identify voices. *UCLA Working Papers in Phonetics, 49,* 42–50. Also to appear in W. Lea (Ed.), *Voice analysis on trial.*

• P. Ladefoged & A. Traill. Instrumental phonetic fieldwork. *UCLA*

Working Papers in Phonetics, 49, 28–41. Also to appear in R. Thelwall & J. Higgs (Eds.), *Studies in experimental phonetics in honor of E. T. Uldall.*

• P. Ladefoged & A. Traill. Phonological features and phonetic details of Khoisan languages. In J. W. Snyman (Ed.), *Bushman and Hottentot linguistic studies* (papers of seminar held on 27 July 1979). Pretoria: University of South Africa.

1982 • P. Ladefoged. Postscript to 'Attempts by human speakers to reproduce Fant's nomograms.' *UCLA Working Papers in Phonetics, 54,* 109.

• P. Ladefoged & A. Bladon. Attempts by human speakers to reproduce Fant's nomograms. *Speech Communication, 3.* Also in *UCLA Working Papers in Phonetics, 54,* 40–56.

• P. Ladefoged. *A course in phonetics* (second ed.). New York: Harcourt Brace Jovanovich.

1983 • P. Ladefoged. Cross-linguistic studies of speech production. In P. MacNeilage (Ed.), *Mechanisms of speech production* (pp. 177–188). New York: Springer-Verlag. Also in *UCLA Working Papers in Phonetics, 51,* 94–104 (1980).

• P. Ladefoged. The limits of biological explanation in phonetics. In A. Cohen & M. P. R. van den Broecke (Eds.), *Abstracts of the Tenth International Congress of Phonetic Sciences* (pp. 31–37). Dordrecht, Holland: Foris Publications. Also in *UCLA Working Papers in Phonetics, 57,* 1.

• P. Ladefoged. The linguistic use of different phonation types. In D. Bless & J. Abbs (Eds.), *Vocal fold physiology: Contemporary research and clinical issues* (pp. 341–350). San Diego: College Hill Press. Also in *UCLA Working Papers in Phonetics, 54,* 28–39.

• P. Ladefoged & P. Bhaskararao. Non-quantal aspects of consonant production: A study of retroflex consonants. *Journal of Phonetics, 11,* 291–302. Also in *UCLA Working Papers in Phonetics, 57,* 11.

1984 • P. Ladefoged. Linguistic phonetic descriptions of clicks. *Language, 60,* 1–20. Also in *UCLA Working Papers in Phonetics, 49,* 1–27, as The phonetic inadequacy of phonological specifications of clicks (1980).

1

Introduction

Victoria A. Fromkin

Phonetics is concerned with describing the speech sounds that occur in the languages of the world. We want to know what these sounds are, how they fall into patterns, and how they change in different circumstances. Most importantly, we want to know what aspects of the sounds are necessary for conveying the meaning of what is being said. The first job of a phonetician is therefore trying to find out what people are doing when they are talking and when they are listening to speech.

(Ladefoged 1975:1)

1. A PROFESSOR OF PHONETICS

The title of this introduction was plagiarized from George Bernard Shaw's Preface to *Pygmalion* (1916). Shaw's professor of phonetics was Henry Sweet, who was, according to Shaw, "the best (phonetician) of them all" (p. 5). The "all" referred to such contemporaries of Sweet as Alexander Melville Bell, the inventor of Visible Speech, his son Alexander Graham Bell, the inventor of the telephone, and Alexander J. Ellis, who developed the glossic alphabet. Shaw might have changed his views had he been writing today instead of in 1919, for on September 17, 1925, a future phonetician, named Peter, was born to Niels and Marie Ladefoged.

This volume is dedicated to Peter Ladefoged because his 60 years have proved that the line of great phoneticians was to continue after Sweet. The volume is also dedicated to Jennifer MacDonald, who became Jenny Ladefoged in 1953 and who has supported Peter through all these years in the phonetics laboratory, in the bush, and at home; and to Lise, born in Edinburgh in 1957; to Thegn, born in Cornwall in 1959; and to Katie, born in Nigeria in 1961. They have withstood his glottal mirrors, his "funny sounds," and the yellow fever injections required to accompany

PHONETIC LINGUISTICS

Copyright © 1985 by Academic Press, Inc.
All rights of reproduction in any form reserved.
ISBN 0-12-268990-9

Peter to Africa, India, Nepal, Thailand, Papua New Guinea, Australia, and China, just a few of the more exotic places where he personally recorded the sounds of hundreds of languages, many of which had never been recorded before. The Ladefoged family has never learned to travel light; while they may pack only one change of clothes, their baggage consists of fm tape recorders, ink writers, pitch meters, fiber optic tubes to stick down their own and their subjects' noses, and various other lethal instruments that are suspiciously scrutinized by customs officials.

Shaw prophesied that "The future of phonetics [would] rest probably with his [Sweet's] pupils" (p. 6). Peter Ladefoged and most present-day phoneticians are to a great extent pupils of Sweet, because of the great influence of Sweet and the entire School of English Phonetics (Firth 1957; Jones 1948). Peter Ladefoged is, in fact, a direct academic descendant; his professor was David Abercrombie, who was a pupil of Daniel Jones, who was a student of Henry Sweet. While sharing many of Sweet's views, and while devoting the last 35 years to the science of phonetics, Peter Ladefoged probably would not go quite as far as Sweet who, according to Shaw, believed that "all scholars who were not rabid phoneticians were fools" (p. 6).

Peter Ladefoged's phonetic roots go back even farther than Sweet. He is part of a continuing tradition that can be traced back at least as far as the sixteenth century phoneticians Sir Thomas Smith, William Bollokar, John Hart, and Dr. Timothe Bright. Post-Renaissance England brought with it a strong emphasis on phonetic and linguistic studies. In 1662, a committee of The Royal Society was formed specifically to "improve the English tongue." An interest in spelling reform, orthography, and the development of universal languages was stimulated by a rise of nationalism and an increased awareness of international language barriers. The spread of printing and literacy and the demise of Latin as the language of scholarship, which paralleled the rise of secular governments, stimulated the study of modern languages. In addition, the dominance of philosophical empiricism and pragmatism brought an emphasis on the study of phonetics and the education of the deaf.

Because a basic principle underlying the education of the period was the relationship between theory and practice, particularly practice that would be of use to humanity, experimentation was encouraged. It was in this climate that the great seventeenth–century English phonetic and linguistic predecessors of Sweet and Ladefoged emerged—William Holder, John Wallis, Francis Lodwick, and John Wilkins to name just a few.

This short excursion into early English phonetic history is presented simply to exemplify how Ladefoged and those of us who are fortunate to have been or are his students are part of a continuing phonetic tradition that defines language as "the expression of thought by means of speech sounds" (Henderson 1971: 5) and is concerned with both the physical and psychological aspects of language, agreeing with Sweet that "phonetics and psychology do not constitute the science of language, being only preparations for it; language and grammar are concerned not with form and meaning separately, but with the connections between them, these being the real phenomena of language" (Henderson 1971: 1). Ladefoged also continues the concern of his phonetic ancestors for general phonetic laws and universal tendencies. His attempts to collect and analyze all the sounds of all the languages of the world are more than his giving vent to his own personal pleasures; he continues to search for evidence regarding a theory of phonetic universals. These and others of his views on the nature of phonetics are best expressed in his own words in the interview that follows.

The chapters included in this volume are written by phoneticians throughout the world and cover a wide range of topics. Six of the authors (Victoria Fromkin, Catherine Browman, Louis Goldstein, Mona Lindau, Ian Maddieson, and John Ohala) are his former doctoral students. Peter Ladefoged's own research, as shown in his bibliography (see Appendix B) has contributed to every issue raised in these papers. The honors he has received, ranging from the Distinguished Teaching Award at UCLA to the presidency of the Linguistic Society of America, attest to the regard his students and colleagues have for him (see Appendix A). Peter Ladefoged is the quintessential professor of phonetics.

2. INTERVIEW WITH PETER LADEFOGED

VF: Your first publication in phonetics was in 1956. Thus you have been a working phonetician for at least 30 years. How, when, and where did you first become interested in phonetics?

PL: I became interested in phonetics in 1950, my second year as an undergraduate at the University of Edinburgh, where I was reading English Literature. I myself was trying to write, and I was interested in how people said things, what particular words they used, and how one way of expressing things differs from another. But I found that people in English literature weren't really concerned with that sort of thing. They were interested in what was being said rather than how it was being said. A friend of mine suggested that we both take a course with David Abercrombie who talked about phonetics—how things were actually said. I was fascinated, and I went on from there.

VF: And what was that course?

PL: It mainly covered the content of what was to become David Aber-
      crombie's book, *Elements of General Phonetics*. Actually it covered
      quite a bit more than that. There was also a small section taught
      by Betsy Uldall on experimental phonetics where we made kymo-
      grams and palatograms. It wasn't until my third year in phonetics
      that we got a sound spectrograph. That was in 1952.

VF: David Abercrombie disusses the British tradition in phonetics in
      his paper on Daniel Jones in this volume. He mentions you as
      being part of this tradition. I also referred to it in the introductory
      section but never defined its characteristics. What actually is the
      British School of Phonetics and do you consider yourself part of
      it?

PL: A major characteristic of this school is the emphasis on the ability
      to produce sounds oneself as well as on being able to hear small
      differences in speech sounds. Daniel Jones was very good at this.
      Learning to produce and discriminate a wide variety of sounds
      was very much part of the first course I took at Edinburgh. In the
      British tradition, one is trained to become a practical phonetician
      in this sense.

VF: I think David Abercrombie might refer to the British School of
      Phonetics as having its roots with Ellis and Bell and Sweet. J. R.
      Firth, in his article "The English School of Phonetics" [1957] says
      that the title is taken from a paper of Henry Sweet's to the Philological
      Society in 1884 in which Sweet said "England may now boast a
      flourishing phonetic school of its own." Daniel Jones also wrote
      a paper entitled "The London School of Phonetics" [1948]. Would
      you agree that these early phoneticians and those in Britain who
      followed them all reveal a particular approach emphasizing the
      production as well as the description of speech sounds?

PL: Yes. It's quite plain that Ellis and more distinctly Bell, and then
      Sweet and Daniel Jones and, I think we might add, his pupils such
      as David Abercrombie himself, all form a school in which the
      major goal of phonetics is to be able to describe sounds. But they
      also would say—wording it slighty differently from each other—
      that speech sounds shoud be described within a linguistic framework.
      Or at least that describing sounds as part of language was what
      they were interested in.

VF: And therefore you would see yourself as continuing this tradition?

PL: Yes, very much so.

VF: Do you then agree with Abercrombie that there isn't a similar
      American tradition in phonetics?

PL: There have been some very great American phoneticians. For
      example, Kenneth Pike. But Pike didn't form nor is he part of
      what can be called a "School of Phonetics," although he is very
      eager to advance the science of phonetics within linguistics.

VF: In the earlier period of your own work, you worked specifically
      in the English tradition. For example, you were interested in the
      use of Jones' cardinal vowels as a descriptive tool. In Abercrombie's
      discussion on cardinal vowels, he suggests that the system of
      cardinal vowels as a technique for describing sounds was distorted
      by many people because they didn't realize that the aim was not
      only to learn to produce the sounds but also to feel where the
      tongue was and what the shape of the vocal tract was. This then
      enabled the phonetician to place the dot on the cardinal vowel
      diagram depending on kinesthetic feeling.

PL: Ian Catford has written papers saying the same thing. I don't think
      that's true. This approach is what Pike would call an imitation
      label; after you've used a term like tongue height—raise the tongue,
      lower the tongue, move it to the back or front—you begin to feel
      that that is what your tongue is actually doing. But you are kidding
      yourself. This is not really what one does in trying to produce a
      vowel.

VF: Abercrombie refers to the fact that in your study of the cardinal
      vowels [Ladefoged 1962, 1967] the phoneticians who acted as your
      subjects were quite successful in repeating the sounds they heard.

PL: But that doesn't show what they were actually doing with their
      tongues; it just shows they could hear things well, and from my
      point of view, that they could label the formant structure of the
      vowels they heard and imitated.

VF: Although you have discussed some of the characteristics of the
      British School of phonetics, you have not really defined in general,
      or even specific terms, the science of phonetics itself. How would
      you define it?

PL: God knows. That's a difficult question because, plainly, the science
      of phonetics is both within and outside of linguistics. There is a
      part of phonetics that is concerned with characterizing the sounds

of language or a language, that is to say, the phonetic component of a phonology. Over and above that, there are many aspects of phonetics that are not specifically concerned with language.

Part of my life I have been a pseudo-physiologist, working on such things as electromyography. I've also been a pseudo-psychologist, studying the perception of speech. As you know, I spend much of my time designing systems for computer modeling of speech processes, so I suppose I'm also a pseudo-computer scientist. In addition, I have done quite a bit of work in the anatomy lab, dissecting the speech apparatus; does this make me a pseudo-anatomist? I think all these activities are part of phonetics, but it will be some time before they contribute significantly to a formal theory of linguistics.

VF: Given the complexities of language and speech, it's understandable why one needs cross-disciplinary research to understand it, but we have still not come up with an overall definition of phonetics.

PL: I could look the definition up in the Encyclopaedia Britannica.

VF: No, I want your view.

PL: It would be my view, since I wrote the entry on phonetics in the 15th Edition of the Encyclopaedia Britannica [1974]. Incidentally, that's also part of the tradition. I can't recall who wrote all the preceding ones, but one of Henry Sweet's last publications was the article on phonetics in the 1911 Encyclopaedia Britannica.

VF: It would be interesting to compare your entry with Sweet's, since it is obvious that the field as well as the science and the discipline of phonetics has developed and changed greatly since 1950 when you first became interested in it. I know it's a very big topic, but can you tell us what you see as the major changes that have taken place.

PL: I think there are two principal areas of change. One is that the whole of linguistics has changed, and since, as I have already said, phonetics is part of linguistics, precisely because linguistics has changed, phonetics has changed. According to the earlier notions in the 1950s, the phonetician's job was to gather all the nitty–gritty data, and then the linguist would come along and organize it. In fact, for a major group of American linguists at that time, phonetic details were considered irrelevant once the classification of sounds was made. But Chomsky and Halle [1968] changed all that by talking of physical phonetics and phonetic-detail rules as the final stage of a linguistic description. So the phonetician's task in relation to linguistics is different now. That's one major change.

The other major change is quite a different kind of thing. It came about with the development of instrumental phonetics and experimental phonetics. Daniel Jones tells a story about how, when he was setting off on a field trip, somebody asked him what instruments he was taking. He simply touched his ears and said, "Only these." That was great in Jones' time. Today it is still important to have good ears and to be able to distinguish sounds; and I'm sure Jones would agree that one also needs to have a good sound-producing mechanism to go with those ears. You have to be able to say the sounds that you hear your language consultants say. But today, anybody who relies simply on ears is out of date. There are so many things you can find out with experimental techniques and new instrumentation.

VF: Doesn't it depend to some extent on the questions one asks. For example, at an earlier period in phonetics, some of the major questions dealt with how we could describe the sounds we were hearing and producing, the sounds of a particular language. Are those the questions phoneticians still ask? Are there others?

PL: Surely these are some of the questions one still asks. But I think one also asks—working from the other end in a generative approach—how these sounds are structured within a person's mind. What are people doing when they produce speech? What kind of units have they stored in their minds? And how are these units put together to produce speech? You and I have often discussed these questions. These questions are surely very much part of phonetics, which wouldn't have been true 30 years ago before the Chomskyan approach.

VF: Nor would anyone have asked what target is aimed at when someone is producing speech, a question you have been deeply concerned with in your own research. For example, is the speaker striving to produce a sound or a particular vocal tract position?

PL: Precisely. Such questions do not arise if one is primarily concerned with a taxonomic classification of speech sounds, working on the data from the physical sounds upward.

VF: Your phonetic research has changed considerably in the 35 years of your life as a phonetician, as is apparent just from what has been discussed in this interview. In fact, one might suggest that one can trace the changes in the field by looking at the changes in your own work; there does seem to be a common thread that connects the past to the present in your work—the importance of quantitative and qualitative description of the speech sounds of the languages of the world with the aim of constructing a viable theory of linguistic phonetics. What questions are you now concerned with in your own research?

PL: I'm still worried about the relation between phonetics and phonology, between the units of both. This to me is still a problem that nobody is even close to solving. How does one relate a systematic phonetic transcription to actual sounds? If one takes the view that the sounds of language (or the words of a language) are represented in the minds of the speakers, there are three different kinds of things that need to be related: the actual physical objects (what Firth would call the phonic substance), the abstract representations in the mind of the speaker, and the units of a linguistic description. As far as I can see, many linguists would say that the last two were the same. As you and I have discussed and argued so often, it is not clear to me whether the observable properties of the language are, in any real sense, in the mind of the speaker.

VF: Even if you are right that we do not yet have a viable theory, the question is whether the goal of linguistic description is to discover how language is represented in the mind and accessed in speaking and comprehending. That is certainly the goal of some linguists, including myself. I'm not sure whether it is yours or not.

PL: I think we are so far from knowing about what goes on in the mind that most speculation along these lines is irrelevant to what we are doing in the laboratory.

VF: I'm not sure what you mean by irrelevant. Doesn't the goal one has in mind dictate what one does or the questions one asks? Can these questions be irrelevant to the kind of work that's being done? Suppose someone is trying to model what is in the mind of the idealized speaker, a sort of conglomerate abstract speaker. Would the phonetic research be different or the questions and hypotheses proposed differ from another investigator who says "Well, I don't care whether it's in the mind of anybody or not, I just want to describe the constraints on phonetic production."?

PL: Yes, I think they would, because the person who is leaping to model what is in the mind of an idealized speaker has to disregard so many links in the chain. For example, we don't really know how the gross anatomy of the vocal organs differs from speaker to speaker and how we can reconcile these differences in an idealization. We don't even know why the vocal cords vibrate, and certainly don't understand the physiological mechanisms involved in the motor control of speech. Even if we knew the articulatory movements that occurred, we still would not be able to describe the physical acoustics involved in the production of many consonants. It is obvious that the perceptual psychologists are having great fun disagreeing with one another and with the auditory physiologists. So, all in all, I think it is vastly premature to try to describe a language in terms of what goes on in a speaker's or listener's mind. Let's go on doing more anatomy, physiology, and psychology first; and I would add, more computer modeling of each of these links in the chain. But you and I are still linguists, so we also have to go on describing the observable patterns of sounds in the languages we are analyzing. We can't give up describing languages just because phoneticians have still so much to learn.

VF: When I decided to call this book *Phonetic Linguistics*, I had two thoughts in mind; one, that the initials "PL" were also your initials, and two, that you have always seen phonetics as part of linguistics. Your last statement shows that I made a correct assumption. There are, however, many working phoneticians in some of the most important laboratories in the world that do not consider themselves linguists and do not see their work as primarily linguistic, although they would probably see it related. There are often only a few linguists present at the speech communication sections at meetings of the Acoustical Society of America, and yet the papers presented and discussed are considered to be reporting on phonetic research.

PL: That is true. There are two kinds of phonetics, the part which is within linguistics and the part which is without. An aspect of speech such as how one individual differs from another is not part of linguistics but is part of phonetics. How a person sounds when angry, or when laughing, or under stress, or relaxed are all practical questions that are of concern. Are such questions part of linguistics? I don't think so. It is not even clear whether such paralinguistic phenomena represent codified behavior. There are a lot of systems that language interfaces with. Language is only part of speech; that is the way I would like to think of it.

VF: That's a nice way of putting it: speech includes language and also other things. In a sense you're saying that what I would call linguistic performance includes the language system and the other systems with which it interacts, such as physiological systems, memory, motor systems, perhaps even the knowledge of the world that affects what and how we speak.

PL: You've summed that up very well, and all those things are part of phonetics.

VF: How about questions such as those concerned with universal constraints on the set of speech sounds, or why some sounds appear to be more marked than others, or the kinds of questions Bjorn Lindblom asks about why we find certain vowel configurations as opposed to others? These are of course questions that are directly linguistic.

PL: Yes, and they are very interesting. But what you call universal constraints I would rather call universal tendencies. There are universal constraints but they are usually pretty uninteresting— for example, physiological things that constrain absolutely what one can or cannot do. Except for these, however, I would think there are very few universal constraints regarding speech sounds.

VF: Your own work has made all of us a little more careful about declaring what sounds can or cannot be part of the inventories of speech sounds. I remember when we used to tell phonetics classes that although we could make bilabial trills, such a sound was never used contrastively or phonemically, and then you found that it did occur as a contrastive sound.

PL: We knew that there were bilabials and we knew that there were trills but until recently that particular conjunction hadn't been observed except in onomatopoeic words and ideophones. But I didn't discover the fact that some languages use bilabial trills as regular speech sounds; this was pointed out to me by people working in the field. Incidentally, this gives me an opportunity to thank those many people who have shown me all the extraordinary things that languages do. I have spent a considerable amount of time wandering around the world, peering over the shoulders of people who are doing detailed work on little-known languages. My wife Jenny always says that my ambition is to hear every speech sound that occurs in one or other of the world's languages. Thanks to lots of helpful people, I feel that I'm getting fairly close to that aim.

But I can't think of any way in which I can define—again paraphrasing Pike—what could or could not be a speech sound.

It's awfully difficult to say why a particular sucking or popping noise is or is not a speech sound except to say that it is comparatively unnatural, which means that it's a little more difficult to make in some kind of way. But think of all the speech sounds that are difficult to make, which shows that the difficulty criterion is not very helpful.

VF: Are some of these unusual sounds found in some languages more difficult than other sounds for the speakers of those languages?

PL: I don't know. Anybody can make a sound consisting of putting the tongue between the lips and moving it rapidly from side to side. It seems to be very easy to do. But no language—or none that has yet been found—has the sound produced in this way.

VF: Isn't that what we used to say about bilabial trills?

PL: Exactly. Another example is that anybody can whistle . . .

VF: Not anybody. I have a lot of trouble trying to whistle.

PL: But it's certainly possible for anybody to learn to whistle, even you, if you really worked at it. But no language that we know of uses a straightforward whistle as a speech sound. There are the so-called whistling fricatives in Shona, but they have a considerable fricative component in comparison with the pure tone of a simple whistle. So that's a perfectly possible sound that does not happen to turn up, presumably because of the difficulty of integrating such a sound into a sequence of sounds. But I find I can't draw a line between what is possible to produce with the vocal organs and what is a possible speech sound.

VF: Do you really think that the main reason is difficulty in production?

PL: Or perception.

VF: Would you say those are the two major criteria for determining whether a sound occurs in a language?

PL: Yes, but then what are those clicks doing in languages? They are obviously very difficult for non-native speakers to produce, particularly as part of a continuous utterance. We don't know how to measure difficulty, and that's another very interesting topic— trying to devise some way of measuring difficulty of articulation.

VF: In Lindblom's view, difficulty is just one parameter among those that create the basic sound units of language, one factor as to the likelihood of sounds becoming speech sounds in a language. Actually, we really don't have any fully developed viable theory on this, do we?

PL: We have an approach through the work of Lindblom and others, such as those working on the perceptual aspects of what is likely to be confused with what and therefore what pairs of sounds are unlikely to co-occur. But then we speakers of English speak a language that speakers of other languages have difficulty with, such as in hearing the difference between [f] and [θ]. These are pretty close acoustically and auditorally, and it is very rare to find them both in a single language.

VF: Questions such as why some sounds are found in so few languages, whereas others seem to occur in nearly all languages were not questions raised at the start of your phonetics career. Perhaps the new instrumentation that has developed makes it possible to ask such questions today. What do you consider some of the most important instrumental techniques that have developed in the 35 years that you have been in the field?

PL: There is absolutely no doubt that the sound spectrograph and the ability to represent sounds in some kind of three-dimensional way has had an enormous influence, specifically on our ability to characterize vowels and measure the duration of sounds more accurately than was previously possible. I was lucky to get an early start in this field, because David Abercrombie bought the first spectrograph in Britain; I think it must have been in 1952.

VF: I remember when you first came to UCLA in 1962. The only instrument for phonetic research in the Phonetics Lab was the sound spectrograph. Is it still as important?

PL: Yes it is, although for actually determining values of things such as formant frequencies and vowel durations we nowadays often use a computer. But the sound spectrograph provides by far the best first look at virtually all of the acoustic properties of an utterance.

VF: Do the instruments in the laboratory today represent the state of the art in phonetic research?

PL: I'm very impressed by some of the new computer analysis systems, such as the SPIRE system devised at MIT. I'm sure they will enable us to make great progress in the acoustic analysis of speech.

Of course we will still have to do all the hard work of going out into the field and getting good samples from groups of speakers. We now realize the impossibility of being able to describe a language without having data on a number of individual speakers. But good computer-analysis systems certainly make the task easier.

VF: What other instruments or techniques would you consider indispensable in the field?

PL: We need good ways of looking at physiological phonetic parameters. We have been getting data on aerodynamic parameters such as subglottal and oral air pressure and air flow for many years. Recent fiberoptic studies and acoustic-analysis techniques such as inverse filtering have now enabled us to better characterize laryngeal actions. Movement sensors and (to a far lesser extent) electromyography have helped us study articulations. New techniques such as the x-ray microbeam system may also be helpful in this respect, although it is far from clear to me that they will provide data on enough speakers to enable us to study more than a few major languages. And what is also indispensable, and we don't yet have, is as good a way of visualizing physiological parameters as is provided by the spectrogram for acoustic data. We need a convenient, readily interpretable way of summing up on a single sheet of paper all the data that are in an x-ray motion picture and high-speed pictures of the glottis, for two half seconds of speech. The current plots of the x locations and the y locations of a number of separate points on the tongue are certainly inadequate.

VF: What advances do you predict or speculate we will make in phonetic research in the next five or ten years?

PL: I would hope that we would come close to a reasonably good model of what speakers are doing when talking. We will understand at least something of the relation between the stored units that speakers can control and the resulting spoken utterances. We will also come closer to a reasonably good model of what listeners are doing when they are interpreting utterances. We might even be able to figure out the units involved in speech perception. Then will come the hard part, because I have no reason to believe that these two sets of units will coincide. Talking and listening may very well be organized in very different ways. The language is what lies between them. This is what is truly inside a speaker–listener's mind.

REFERENCES

Abercrombie, D. (1967). *Elements of general phonetics*. Edinburgh, Scotland: University of Edinburgh Press.

Chomsky, N., & Halle, M. (1968). *The sound pattern of English*. New York: Harper & Row.

Firth, J. R. (1957). The English School of phonetics. In *Papers in linguistics. 1934–1951* (pp. 92–120). London: Oxford University Press. (Reprinted from *Transactions of the Philological Society,* 1946).

Henderson, E. J. A. (Ed.). (1971). *The indispensable foundation: A selection from the writings of Henry Sweet.* London: Oxford University Press.

Jones, D. (1948). The London School of phonetics. *Zeitschrift fur Phonetik, 11,* 127–135.

Ladefoged, P. (1960). The value of phonetic statements. *Language, 36,* 387–396. (Reprinted in *Three Areas of Experimental Phonetics,* 1967. London: Oxford University Press.)

Ladefoged, P. (1974). Phonetics. *Encyclopaedia Britannica,* 275–283. Chicago, IL.

Ladefoged, P. (1975). *A course in phonetics.* New York: Harcourt Brace Jovanovich.

Shaw, G. B. (1916). Preface to Pygmalion: A Professor of phonetics. *Pygmalion.* Baltimore: Penguin Books (1951 edition).

Sweet, H. (1900). *The history of language.* London: The Temple Primers.

Sweet, H. (1911). Phonetics. *Encyclopaedia Britannica.*

2

Daniel Jones's Teaching

David Abercrombie

British phonetics has a long and impressive tradition that includes both my teacher, Daniel Jones, and my student, Peter Ladefoged. It seems fitting, therefore, in paying tribute to this living British phonetician, Peter Ladefoged, to also pay tribute to one of his predecessors, the great phonetician Daniel Jones.*

I feel most honoured to be asked to give this Daniel Jones Memorial Lecture, and I am grateful to be given this opportunity to pay tribute to a great phonetician and one of the most influential figures in British linguistics. I met Daniel Jones over fifty years ago, and continued to be in touch with him until he died in 1967, at the age of 86.

I would like to take a look at some of the points that characterised his teaching, and particularly at points which are controversial, but which have been influential in the development of linguistics in this country— though the importance of some of them is in danger of being forgotten nowadays. Jones was not a profound thinker, and he did not pretend to be; nevertheless he was an outstanding teacher, demanding but kind; and his teaching left an indelible impression on all who passed through his hands.

1. THE TEACHING OF PHONETICS

Let me start, though, by recounting how I first came to meet Jones, and as a consequence, rather unexpectedly, became his student; and eventually, I think I may say, his friend. At the time when I met him I was a postgraduate student here at Leeds University. I was registered for an M.A. in the English Department, but after completing my first degree I had gone to live with my parents in London. The thesis topic on which I was working was "The Phonetic Basis of *i*-Mutation", under the supervision of E. V. Gordon, author of *An Introduction to Old Norse*.

* This paper was delivered by the author as the Daniel Jones Memorial Lecture, at The University, Leeds, 18 March 1982. At the request of the author, it appears, except for the first paragraph, exactly as delivered.

PHONETIC LINGUISTICS

I spent my time in London working in the Reading Room of the British Museum.

My father and Daniel Jones knew each other because they were both members of the B.B.C. Advisory Committee on Spoken English. My father told Jones one day that he had a son who was very interested in phonetics, and Jones very kindly suggested that I should go and have a talk with him. So I made an appointment, and went one October morning in 1930 to Jones's house in Golder's Green. I think I was expecting to have an informal discussion which would give me some guidance about how an aspiring young phonetician, doing an M.A. in English Language, should plan his future in the academic world. However, it did not turn out like that at all. Jones answered the door himself, let me in, and said "How do you do? Come in and sit down. Would you please say a voiced bilabial implosive?" At that time I was not aware that he did not have much in the way of small talk. Fortunately I was able to produce the required implosive, and he then said "Thank you. Now will you please say a close back unrounded vowel." As it happened I could do so, and did; and the rigorous performance examination went on for some time. He put no theoretical questions to me at all. But eventually he said he thought I should not worry too much about my Leeds M.A., but that I should right away become a student in his department at University College. I followed his recommendation. I continued working at my thesis, but I was also a postgraduate student at University College over a period of seven years, during two of which I was also working at the Institut de Phonétique in Paris. They were probably the happiest days of my life; but I never got my M.A. finished.

Jones as a phonetician belonged to a tradition, one which still continues, and one which goes back a long way: a tradition of teaching methods, of descriptive techniques, of technical terminology, of notation, handed on from one generation to the next. Phoneticians in this tradition were brought up by other phoneticians; few phoneticians in this country have been self-taught. Jones's predecessors included Ellis, Bell, and Sweet, and many phoneticians in Europe such as Storm, Passy, Viëtor, Jespersen. This is in remarkable contrast with America. It was possible for G. L. Trager to say, in 1943, "Phonetics is so young a branch of science that it is still true that most phoneticians are self-taught" (1943:16). It would have been unthinkable to say such a thing in 1943 here; but it was true of America.

It is not easy to see why a tradition did not establish itself in America, as it did here. After all, they had a fine phonetician who was contemporary with our founding fathers, Ellis and Bell: S. S. Haldeman (1812–1880), author of *Analytic Orthography* (1860), a paper on phonetic notation. Originally a geologist, he became the first professor of Comparative Philology at the University of Pennsylvania. (Daniel Jones used to say that the only discipline with which phonetics had nothing at all in common was geology.) He published on Indian and many other languages, and became a fine self-taught phonetician, of whom Ellis and Bell thought highly. And there were others who might have started a tradition, including Alexander Melville Bell himself, who became an American citizen, and his son Alexander Graham Bell.

Jones was a superb teacher, and his staff in the department were all superb teachers. Great importance was attached in the department's teaching to *performance*—which perhaps explains the nature of my preliminary interview with Jones. *General* phonetics as such was hardly ever taught. Students were taught the pronunciation of specific languages; matters of general theory were discussed only if they arose in connexion with these. The languages whose pronunciation was taught were very varied phonologically, and provided a broad survey of human phonetic capabilities. Among the languages on whose pronunciation I had to work, I remember, were Urdu, German, Sechuana, Cantonese, Sinhalese, Russian and Danish, and I expect others. In addition, of course, to French— everybody in the department had to do French. In all these the very highest standards of performance were demanded of the students.

This way of teaching phonetics meant intensive training of the proprioceptive, i.e., the tactile and kinesthetic, senses concerned with the organs of speech, something that is not valued very highly by many other schools of phonetics. The proprioceptive senses, in the view of phoneticians in the Jones tradition, play an important part in the analysis and description of unfamiliar sounds. The phonetician, having learnt to make a sound of the language he is working on to the complete satisfaction of his native informant, then examines what he himself is doing with his vocal organs, and infers the informant is doing the same thing. I have met many phoneticians, both in America and on the Continent, who are not capable of doing this; who believe, in fact, that there is something wrong with it as a procedure. It has been called (by a postgraduate student at Edinburgh University) "analysis by performance". However, there was one topic of general phonetics which was taught in Jones's department, and that was the system of Cardinal Vowels.

2. THE SYSTEM OF CARDINAL VOWELS

The system of Cardinal Vowels constitutes a technique, not a theory. It is a technique of description, a technique for providing much more precise specifications of vowels than the traditional kind of taxonomic approach is able to do. It is a technique that is not used in America, and not much used by continental phoneticians; it belongs more or less exclusively to the British tradition, though, as we know, it was adopted by the I.P.A. The *idea* of cardinal vowels was put forward by Ellis, the *word* "cardinal" by Bell, and Henry Sweet, too, spoke of "cardinal vowel positions." But only Daniel Jones produced a fully worked out system. Sweet said that Phonetics is both a science and an art. It should be remembered that the Cardinal Vowel technique belongs to the art, and not to the science, side of the subject.

It is a technique which is time-consuming and difficult to learn. I was taught the Cardinal Vowels by Jones himself, and it was a lengthy and painful process. Cardinal Vowel Number One turned out to be the most difficult of all, rather unexpectedly, and it took a long time before Jones was satisfied with my version. I had trouble, too, with Cardinal Number Three, I remember. Once I had learnt the Cardinal Vowels from Jones, other members of staff, and especially Ida Ward, later to become Professor of African Languages in London University, taught me how to use them as a descriptive technique.

Recently, Cardinal Vowels have been the object of much criticism, arising from a widespread misunderstanding of how they should be used in description. I was taught to use them proprioceptively, and I think that is how everyone used them at the time. With practice, it is true, one learns to take short cuts from the auditory impression straight to the placing of the dot on the Cardinal Vowel figure, the trapezium. But the full procedure was to imitate the informant until one had the vowel perfect, and then to feel, by means of the tactile and kinesthetic senses, how the tongue posture compared with that of the nearest Cardinal Vowels, and the identifying dot on the figure was placed accordingly. The lip posture had to be stated separately, but it is, after all, easy enough to see.

Nowadays, however, it is claimed by many people that the Cardinal Vowel figure encloses, not an articulatory space, but an *auditory* space. In other words, a dot placed on the figure represents, not a tongue position, but a quality of sound. The difficulty of this view, though, is that some of this quality of sound must derive from the posture of the lips, which varies independently of the tongue posture; yet the two-dimensional space of the Cardinal Vowel figure can not accommodate what in effect are three variables affecting vowel quality. Hence the criticism that the set of eight Cardinal Vowels should not be a mixture of vowels with lip-rounding and vowels without. A curiously angry article on this subject appeared some while ago in the *Journal of the I.P.A.* (McClure 1972). It said that the fact that some cardinal vowels are rounded while others are unrounded means the system contains "a contradiction so basic that any attempt to make use of it as a descriptive technique would be completely impossible." It is not explained how such a basic contradiction has escaped attention up till now, nor how it is that the system has been used successfully as a descriptive technique during the last 70 or so years.

However, there is only a contradiction if it is supposed that the Cardinal Vowel figure represents an auditory space, and that vowels are placed on it auditorily. I do not know when and where such an idea started,

but it is now quite widespread. It is to be found, for example, in J. D. O'Connor's *Phonetics* (1973).

It follows that if one wishes to relate a speaker's vowels to the Cardinal Vowels, it is necessary to be able to *see* him: one needs to know what his lips are doing. Peter Ladefoged (1960) conducted an interesting and well-known experiment to investigate how well phoneticians would agree with each other in placing the vowels of a number of test-words in an unknown language on the Cardinal Vowel figure. On the whole, they did pretty well. But this particular language contained some unrounded back vowels of varying degrees of closeness, and on these agreement was rather poor. However, it must be noted that it was not a live informant that was being used in the experiment; the judgments were made from recordings. If the speaker's lip-posture had been visible, the tongue positions might have been judged very much more accurately. The same consideration applies to another interesting experiment, carried out by John Laver (1965), designed to test how consistent individual phoneticians were at assessing vowels over periods of time. Again, recordings were used, and moreover recordings which were of synthetic, not humanly produced, vowels.

There have been suggestions recently that the time has now come to produce a new set of cardinal vowels, or perhaps a new cardinal vowel figure. But there would be a problem in getting a new system generally accepted, and getting it consistently taught; there seems little chance of a successful attempt. Some new figures have been put forward, but they do not seem to have caught on.

A curious criticism concerns the division of Cardinal Vowels into "primary" and "secondary". No vowel, it is claimed, can be more primary than any other: all vowels are equal. I am sure there were no *theoretical* reasons for singling out some vowels rather than others. The eight primary Cardinal Vowels were ones which Jones said he found to be "convenient" and "in practice to give particularly good results." They are primary (though he never used that term for them, as I remember), only in that he established them first. The secondary (or "subsidiary" as he originally called them) Cardinal Vowels he thought of later. Jones was a bit vague about their exact purpose (there are now ten; originally there were fourteen). I do not remember them being used by anyone in descriptions. Jones, it is true, made a recording of them; but he did not teach them, as far as I know—certainly not to me anyway.

As a matter of fact, in principle almost any set of vowels could form a system of cardinal vowels. The only requirement is that they should be conveniently situated within the vowel area to act as location points. They do not have to be easy to learn: they are to be used by professional phoneticians, who are supposed to be able to learn anything. But once the vowels are decided on, they must thereafter be fixed and invariable, or they will not work as a technique of description.

Many people would think, though, that a system of cardinal vowels

provides much more accuracy as a descriptive technique than is needed
for most purposes. I am inclined to think so myself. The traditional
taxonomic categories are normally good enough.

However, the cardinal vowels have another use, in addition to providing
a descriptive technique: they provide an excellent basis for exercises for
beginners in phonetics, as target points for practice in performance classes.
In such exercises absolute perfection of performance is not insisted on,
as it must be if the vowels are being taught as a descriptive technique.
And here the secondary Cardinal Vowels come into their own—they
too are excellent for practice for beginners.

3. PHONETIC NOTATION

One of Jones's chief interests throughout his career was notation, with
which he experimented a great deal. He worked out in 1907, for example,
together with Paul Passy, an "Organic phonetic Alphabet." It was perhaps
meant to rival Sweet's Organic Alphabet, itself derived from Alexander
Melville Bell's Visible Speech. In all these the shapes of the letters were
intended to be self-interpreting. Jones and Passy published their alphabet
as a supplement to the *Maître Phonétique* at the end of 1907, but it was
hardly every heard of again. I never heard Jones talk about it. Jones
was also a very keen advocate of the reform of English spelling, and he
was an influential member of the Simplified Spelling Society, of which,
for a time, he was President. After the last war he went so far as to
write all his personal correspondence in Nue Speling. Another of his
notational interests was the problem of a roman-based national script
for India (it was an interest also of J. R. Firth, and this was one of the
few points on which they collaborated).

His best-known interest, however, was in the notation of the International
Phonetic Association, and in different types of transcription making use
of it. He had much to do with making the I.P.A. alphabet widely used
throughout the world. He took an especial interest in types of transcription
of English. He made famous one type of transcription which was used
in many of his books, and especially in all but the most recent edition
of the *English Pronouncing Dictionary*; it is often in consequence called
"the Jones transcription of English". However it was not Jones who
devised it; it was the way English was transcribed by many members
of the I.P.A. at the time that Jones became a member in 1905. It was
the type of transcription used in the *Phonetic Dictionary of the English
Language*, by Hermann Michaelis and Daniel Jones (1913), the second
in a series of phonetic dictionaries under the general editorship of Michaelis.
It came out in 1913, and in it the words are arranged according to their
pronunciation, the orthography coming afterwards. It was natural, when
Jones came to make his own more orthodox pronouncing dictionary four
years later, to continue with the same type of transcription. I have heard
Jones say, though, that he did not really like it.

But although what is often said to be *the* Jones transcription of English is in fact not his, he did work out several other types of transcription for English. There was, for example, the type he called "extra broad", which has been used by a number of phoneticians in their books, for example by N. C. Scott, E. L. Tibbitts, and others; and, in a slightly modified form, by P. A. D. MacCarthy. There was the so-called "narrow" transcription which Miss I. C. Ward and Miss L. E. Armstrong used in their various books, and which proved popular with many other writers. Jones made several other experiments in the transcription of English.

Like a number of other people in the I.P.A. early this century, Jones attached great importance to the general appearance and, above all, to the legibility of the printed page, and in consequence he believed great care should be taken over the design of letter shapes. It was ensured that new symbols added to the alphabet were typographically satisfactory; suggested symbols that were unsatisfactory were not officially accepted. This care for good design has given rise to misunderstandings. For example, the absence in the I.P.A. alphabet of distinct symbols for voiceless nasals, instead of using the symbols for voiced nasals with a devoicing diacritic added, has been taken by some to be theoretically motivated. It is claimed the I.P.A. has assumptions of "normality" and "abnormality" as regards sounds, and that the use of the diacritic shows the sound is regarded as "abnormal", a voiced nasal being more "normal" (Lyons 1968). But the I.P.A. has no such assumptions and conventions, and never has had. The plain fact is that no typographically acceptable symbols for voiceless nasals have yet been put forward, though there have been many suggestions. I do not think the I.P.A. has ever allowed contentious theoretical considerations—or rival phonological analyses—to influence its choice of symbols.

Jones's concern for typographical appearance is illustrated by the length of time that his book on *The Phoneme* took to appear after he had finished writing it. It is said that he considered the dot over the i in the Gill Sans typeface, which he was using in the book for phonetic notation, was too high above the stem, and time had to be spent on re-cutting it. It must be admitted, however, that the first two editions of his *Pronunciation of English* (1909 and 1914) were typographically hideous: at that date I do not think he was able to impose his will on his publishers as he could later.

In America phonetic notation has had a curious history. Bloomfield used I.P.A. notation in his early book *An Introduction to the Study of Language* (1914), and in the English edition of his more famous *Language* (1935). But since then, a strange hostility has been shown by many American linguists to I.P.A. notation, especially to certain of its symbols.

An interesting and significant story was once told by Carl Voegelin during a symposium held in New York in 1952 on the present state of anthropology. He told how, at the beginning of the thirties, he was being taught phonetics by, as he put it, a "pleasant Dane", who made him

use the I.P.A. symbol for *sh* in *ship,* among others. Some while later
he used those symbols in some work on an American Indian language
he had done for Sapir. When Sapir saw the work he "simply blew up",
Voegelin said, and demanded that in future Voegelin should use "s
wedge" (as š was called), instead of the I.P.A. symbol (Tax 1966).

I have no doubt that the "pleasant Dane" was H. J. Uldall, one of
Jones's most brilliant students, who was later to become one of the
founders of glossematics, with Louis Hjelmslev. Uldall did a great deal
of research into Californian languages, especially into Maidu or Nisenan.
Most of the texts he collected were not published during his lifetime. It
is ironic that when they were published, posthumously, by the University
of California Press (Uldall & Shipley 1966), the texts were "reorthogra-
phised", as the editor's introduction put it: the I.P.A. symbols Uldall
had used were removed and replaced by others.

What is strange is that the I.P.A. symbols seem so obviously preferable
to the Americanist alternatives, the "long s" to the "s wedge", for
example. As Jones often pointed out, in connected texts, for the sake
of legibility diacritics should be avoided as far as possible. Many Americanist texts give the impression of being overloaded with diacritics.

One may wonder why there should be such hostility in America to
I.P.A. notation. I venture to suggest a reason for this apparently irrational
attitude. The hostility derives ultimately from the existence, in most
American universities, of Speech Departments, which we do not have
in Britain. Speech Departments tend to be well-endowed, large, and
powerful. In linguistic and phonetic matters they have a reputation for
being predominantly prescriptive, and tend to be considered by some
therefore to be not very scholarly. In their publications and periodicals
the notation they use, when writing of pronunciation, is that of the I.P.A.
My belief is that the last thing a member of an American Linguistics
Department wants is to be mistaken for a member of a Speech Department;
but if he were to use I.P.A. notation in his writings he would certainly
lay himself open to the suspicion that he was.

4. THE PHONEME

The phoneme is a topic with which Jones was greatly concerned, and
I think he was disappointed that people did not have more regard for
what he had to say on the subject. His writings on the phoneme met
with little respect in America—and little respect even in parts of his
own Department. In a paper that I gave a while ago I recounted how,
when I first went to the Department, I found it was divided, geograhically
and ideologically, into two parts: upstairs and downstairs. Upstairs was
Daniel Jones and most of the lecturers. Downstairs, in the basement,
was the laboratory, presided over by Stephen Jones (no relation) and
much frquented by J. R. Firth and various postgraduate students. Downstairs was, on the whole, fairly critical of upstairs. While admiring the

expertise in practical phonetics to be found upstairs, downstairs thought the lack of interest in general theoretical matters upstairs to be deplorable. Jones's phoneme concept had the minimum of theory behind it. Jones always said there was no such thing as phonology as a subject separate from phonetics (he never used the word phonemics). His phoneme concept was unpretentious and unadventurous. Its purpose was to be of service to applied phonetics, especially the making of transcriptions for language teaching. As Jones wrote in 1931, "The main object of grouping the sounds of a language into phonemes is to establish a simple and adequate way of writing the language" (p. 78). Nothing more ambitious was expected of the concept. Jones took the idea of the phoneme in 1911 from the Russian phonetician Ščerba, as is well known. The idea, Jones has said, began to find a "regular place" in his Department's teaching from 1915. It underwent very little development afterwards.

By contrast, the phoneme idea came relatively late to America. In 1934, Morris Swadesh wrote, "It is only quite recently that the phonemic principle has had the serious attention of linguists" (p. 117). As a matter of fact the phonemic principle might have had attention in America very much earlier, for a now largely-forgotten linguist, J. P. Harrington,[1] adumbrated it in 1912. He proposed the adoption into English of the word "phonem" (without an e at the end), and he wrote (Harrington 1912:190) that in the language of the Tewa Pueblo Indians, ng and g, for example, are "two aspects of the same phonem, as is the case with Castilian g and levis g, d and levis d, b and levis b." Unfortunately nobody followed his suggestion, perhaps because although he was known as a talented phonetician and a gifted fieldworker, he was also a noted eccentric. Nevertheless he himself continued to use his term all his working life.

Incidentally, the form "phonem" is not found in the Oxford English Dictionary even though others besides Harrington have used it, sometimes as a different word from "phoneme." (See, e.g. Fuhrken 1932, where "phonem" is defined as "one sound or a series of sounds forming a connected whole", whereas "phoneme" is "a sound and its varieties in one and the same language.")

I was one of the sceptics in the Department as far as the "upstairs" phoneme and its objectives were concerned. Conversation downstairs in the laboratory was apt to make fun of the "joneme", which was not very difficult to do. I have now come rather to admire it, and to think it has applications beyond applied phonetics. I have come to think, after experimenting in various ways, that it provides, in teaching general phonetics to beginners the best foundation on which to base consideration of phonology in general.

A remarkable expansion of linguistics in British universities took place

---

[1] John Peabody Harrington (1884–1961) spent most of his career working for the Bureau of American Ethnology at the Smithsonian Institution, specialising in the Indian languages of California.

after the War, and phoneticians trained in the Jones tradition played an important part in the foundation and development of many new departments. This success story may now be coming to an end. The whole academic world is under threat, I know; but it may be that linguistics and phonetics are among the more vulnerable subjects. The rapid growth in recent years of linguistics and phonetics has meant that there are a large number of departments in Britain—too many, some may think; and it is likely that in some quarters it will be felt that some departments are expendable. Already in Scotland, we hear, the departments at St. Andrews and at Glasgow are to be closed shortly. Chairs and vacant lectureships are not being filled—as, indeed, in other departments. A short list of applicants was established for my Chair, when I retired, but it did not get as far as an appointment being made. I am sad to finish on such a despondent note, but I feel sure there will be a considerable shrinkage of linguistics in the academic world in the near future. Let us hope that the invaluable tradition consolidated and transmitted by Daniel Jones will nevertheless be preserved.

REFERENCES

Abercrombie, D. (1980). *Work in Progress* (No. 13). Department of Linguistics, Edinburgh University. Reprinted in *Forum Linguisticum*, 1980 *5*, 169–178.

Bloomfield, L. (1914). *An introduction to the study of language*. New York: Holt.

Bloomfield, L. (1935). *Language* (British edition). London: Allen & Unwin.

Fuhrken, G. E. (1932). Standard English. Cambridge: Cambridge University Press.

Haldeman, S. S. (1860). Analytic orthography. *Transactions of American Philosophical Society*. Philadephia: Philosophical Society.

Harrington, J. P. (1912). Notes on certain usages. *American Anthropologist, 14*, 190.

Jones, D. (1909). *Pronunciation of English* 4th ed., Cambridge: Cambridge University Press.

Jones, D. (1931). On phonemes. *Travaux du Cercle linguistique de Prague, 4*, 74–79.

Jones, D. (1917). *English pronouncing dictionary* London: Dent.

Jones, D. (1950). *The phoneme, its nature and use* 2nd ed., Cambridge, England: Heffer.

Jones, D., & Passy, P. (1907). Alphabet organique. *Maître Phonétique*. November/December, supplement.

Ladefoged, P. (1960). The value of phonetic statements. *Language, 36*, 387–396. (Also in P. Ladefoged (ed.), 1967, *Three areas of experimental phonetics* (pp. 50–142). London: Oxford Univesity Press.

Laver, J. D. M. H. (1965). Variability in vowel perception. *Language and Speech, 8*, 95–121.

Lyons, J. (1968). *Introduction to theoretical linguistics*. Cambridge: Cambridge University Press.

McClure, J. D. (1972). A suggested revision for the Cardinal Vowel System. *Journal of the International Phonetic Association, 2*, 20–25.

Michaelis, H., & Jones, D. (1913). *English phonetic dictionary*. Hanover: Carl Meyer.

O'Connor, J. D. (1973). *Phonetics*. London: Pelican.

Swadesh, M. (1934). The phonemic principle. *Language, 10*, 117–129.

Tax, S. (Ed.). (1966). *An appraisal of anthropology today*. Chicago: University of Chicago Press.

Trager, G. L. (1943). Review of *Phonetics* by K. L. Pike. *Studies in Linguistics, 2*, 16.

Uldall, H. J., & W. Shipley (1966). *Nisenan texts and dictionary*. Berkeley: University of California Press.

3

Relative Power of Cues: F_O Shift Versus Voice Timing*

Arthur S. Abramson
Leigh Lisker

1. BACKGROUND

The acoustic features that provide information on the identify of phonetic segments are commonly called "cues to speech perception." These cues do not typically have one-to-one relationships with phonetic distinctions. Indeed, research usually shows more than one cue to be pertinent to a distinction, although all such cues may not be equally important. Thus, if two cues, x and y, are relevant for a distinction, it may turn out that for any value x, a variation of y will effect a significant shift in listeners' phonetic judgments but that there will be some values of y for which varying x will have negligible effect on phonetic judgments. We say, then, that y is the more powerful cue.

A good deal of evidence now exists to show that the timing of the valvular action of the larynx relative to supraglottal articulation is widely used in languages to distinguish homorganic consonants. The detailed properties of the distinctions thus produced depend on glottal shape and concomitant laryngeal impedance or stoppage of airflow, as well as on the phonatory state of the vocal folds. Such acoustic consequences as the presence or absence of audible glottal pulsing during consonant closures or constrictions, the turbulence called aspiration between consonant release and onset or resumption of pulsing, and damping of energy in the region of the first formant have all been subsumed (Lisker & Abramson 1964,

* This work was supported by Grant HD-01994 from the National Institute of Child Health and Human Development to Haskins Laboratories. An oral version of this chapter was presented at the Tenth International Congress of Phonetic Sciences, Utrecht, 1–6 August, 1983.

25

1971) under a general mechanism of voice timing. In utterance-initial position, the phonetic environment in which consonantal distinctions based on differences in the relative timing of laryngeal and supraglottal action have been most often studied, this phonetic dimension has commonly been referred to as voice onset time (VOT).

Although the acoustic features just mentioned, and perhaps some others, may be said to vary under the control of the single mechanism of voice timing, it is of course possible, by means of speech synthesis, to vary them one at a time to learn which of them are perceptually more important. We must not forget, however, that such experimentation involves pitting against one another acoustic features that are not independently controlled by the human speaker.

A relevant feature not yet mentioned is the fundamental frequency (F_O) of the voice. If we assume a certain F_O contour as shaped by the intonation or tone of the moment, there is a good correlation between the voicing state of an initial consonant and the F_O height and movement at the beginning of that contour (House & Fairbanks 1953; but see also O'Shaughnessy 1979 for complications). After a voiced stop, F_O is likely to be lower and shift upward, while after a voiceless stop it will be higher and shift downward (Lehiste & Peterson 1961). Although the phenomenon has not been fully explained, it is at least apparent that it is a function of physiological and aerodynamic factors associated with the voicing difference.

The data derived from the acoustic analysis of natural speech can be matched by experiments with synthetic speech that demonstrate that F_O shifts can influence listeners' judgments of consonant voicing (Fujimura 1971; Haggard, Ambler, & Callow 1970; Haggard, Summerfield, & Roberts 1981). Of further interest in this connection is the claim that phonemic tones have developed in certain language families through increased awareness of these voicing-induced F_O shifts and their consequent promotion to distinctive pitch features under independent control in production (Hombert, Ohala, & Ewan 1979; Maspero 1911).

Our motivation for the present study was to put F_O into proper perspective as one of a set of potential cues to consonant voicing coordinated by laryngeal timing. After all, our own earlier synthesis (Abramson & Lisker 1965; Lisker & Abramson 1970) yielded quite satisfactory voicing distinctions without F_O as a variable. In addition, Haggard et al. (1970) may have exaggerated its importance in the perception of natural speech by their use of a frequency range of 163 Hz, one very much greater than, for example, the range of less than 40 Hz found for English stop productions by Hombert (1975). We set out to test the hypothesis that the separate perceptual effect of F_O is small and dependent upon voice timing, while the dependence of the voice timing effect on F_O is virtually nil. We used native speakers of English as test subjects.

2. PROCEDURE

Making use of the Haskins Laboratories formant synthesizer, we prepared a pattern appropriate to an initial labial stop followed by a vowel [ɑ]. Variants of this pattern were then synthesized with VOT values of 5, 20, 35, and 50 msec after the simulated stop release.

These values were chosen because of earlier work (Figure 3.1) that determined English voicing judgments for a VOT continuum ranging from 150 msec before release to 150 msec after release. This range of VOT values was sampled at 10 msec intervals, except for the span from 10 msec before release to 50 msec after release, which was sampled at 5 msec intervals. Those stimuli for which voice onset followed release, that is, to the right of 0 msec on the abscissa, had noise-excited upper formants during the interval between the burst at VOT = 0 and the onset of voice. In the labial data at the top of the figure, the perceptual crossover point between /b/ and /p/ falls just after 20 msec of voicing lag. Thus, we expected that the extreme values of our more limited range would be heard as unambiguous /b/ and /p/, given an unchanging F_O, while the category boundary, lying somewhere between, might be shifted one way or the other as the F_O was varied. In addition to a set of VOT variants having an F_O fixed at 114 Hz, we imposed onset frequencies of 98, 108, 120, and 130 Hz, values commensurate with ranges reported for natural speech (Hombert 1975; House & Fairbanks 1953; Lea 1973; Lehiste & Peterson 1961). That is, the F_O at voicing onset for each variant began at one of those frequencies and shifted upward or downward to a level of 114 Hz, where it stayed for the rest of the syllable. These F_O shifts were of three durations, 50, 100, and 150 msec. These fitted with our own cursory observations and bracketed the value of 100 msec found by Hombert (1975). We recorded the resulting 52 stimuli—two tokens of each—in three randomizations and played the tapes to 11 native speakers of English for labeling as /b/ or /p/. The subjects, three women and eight men, represented a wide variety of regional dialects, 10 in the United States and one in Britain.

3. RESULTS

The overall results are shown in Figure 3.2. The three panels are for the durations of F_O shift. The abscissa of each panel shows the four

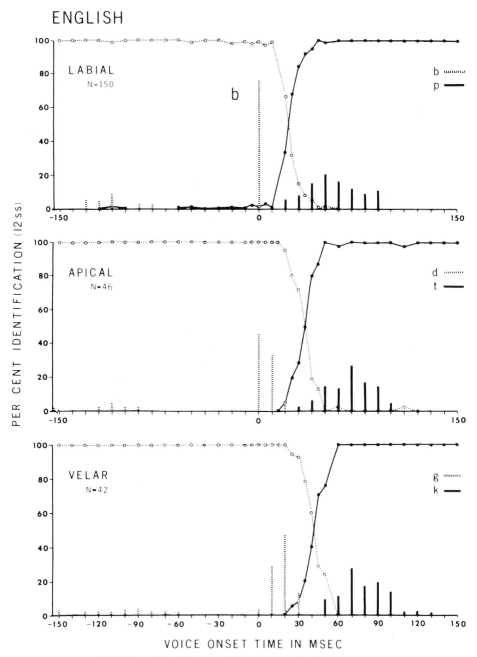

Figure 3.1 English voicing judgments for stops varying in VOT. Below each pair of curves is a histogram (from Lisker & Abramson 1964) of frequency distributions of VOT in speech. Reproduced from Lisker and Abramson (1970).

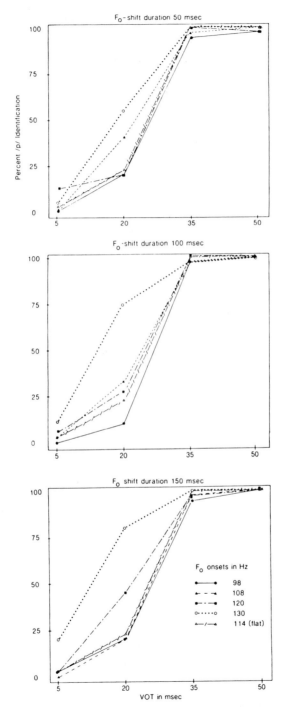

Figure 3.2 Effects of F_O shifts on identification of VOT variants as English labial stops.

VOT values, while the ordinate gives the percentage identified as /p/ for each VOT. The coded line standing for the variants with a flat F_O of 114 Hz is, of course, a plot of the same data in all three panels. The 50% perceptual crossover point for the flat F_O falls at about 25 msec of VOT. This is consistent with the results for the more finely graded series of stimuli in Figure 3.1. Indeed, for all conditions in Figure 3.2, it is VOT that is the main causative factor, regardless of F_O, with perceptual cross-overs in the region of the VOT of 20 msec. With hindsight we can say that additional stimuli with VOTs of 15 and 25 msec would have given more precision. At the same time, we do note effects of the fundamental frequency shifts: In each panel there is much spread of data points for 20 msec and virtually none for 35 and 50 msec.

In Figure 3.3 we focus on the results for the stimuli with a VOT of 20 msec, the one that shows the major effect of F_O shifts. For each of the four F_O onsets we see the percentage of /p/ responses. The coded lines stand for the three durations of F_O shift. A rather general upward trend in /p/ responses is evident as F_O onset rises. A two-way analysis of variance yielded a significant main effect for F_O onset (F[3,30] = 36.45, $p < 0.001$) and a strong interaction between shift duration and F_O onset for each duration (F[6,60] = 6.00, $p < 0.01$).

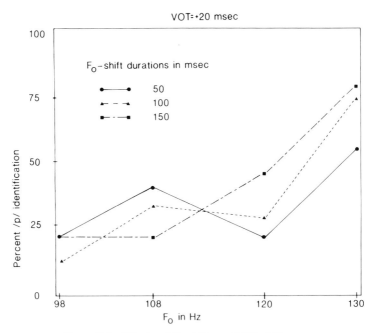

Figure 3.3 Effects of F_O shifts on VOT of 20 msec.

Figure 3.4 focuses on the F_O onset of 130 Hz, the one that had the highest number of /p/ identifications. The /p/ responses for this F_O onset at all four VOT values are shown. Coded lines stand for the three shift durations; the flat F_O plot, marked "no shift," is repeated from Figure 3.2. It is once again obvious that the major effect is at the VOT of 20 msec, with the deviation from "no shift" increasing with greater shift duration.

The spread of points at the VOT of 5 msec in Figure 3.4, although much smaller than that at 20 msec, made us look for significant effects in individual cells of the confusion matrix underlying all our plots. That is, wherever we found apparent effects of fundamental frequency at VOT values other than 20, the locus of the main effect, we did a one-tailed t-test for significant deviations from 100%. All such suspicious clusters of responses were at VOT values of 5 msec and 35 msec; for the former, we expected 100% /b/ identifications and for the latter, 100% /p/ identifications. We found three such significant deviations, all of them at the VOT of 5 msec: (1) 120 Hz onset and 50 msec duration ($t[10] = 2.70$, $p < 0.01$), (2) 130 Hz onset and 100 msec duration ($t[10] = -2.51$, $p < 0.025$), (3) 130 Hz onset and 150 msec duration ($t[10] = 2.799$,

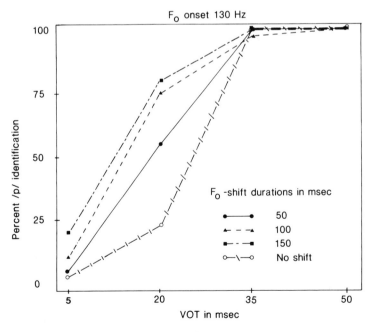

Figure 3.4 Effects of VOT and shift durations on onset of 130 Hz.

$p < 0.01$). No such significant deviations were found at the VOT values of 35 msec and 50 msec.

4. CONCLUSION

We conclude that there is a modest effect of fundamental frequency shifts on judgments of consonant voicing even within more natural ranges of F_O perturbation[1] than those in Haggard et al. (1970). This is much like the results obtained in the investigation of Thai in an attempt at determining the plausibility of arguments on the rise of distinctive tones (Abramson 1975; Abramson & Erickson 1978).

Although they too used a more natural F_O range, Haggard et al. (1981) used an experimental design and stimuli that were somewhat different from ours; their aims were also rather different. To the extent that their data and ours are comparable, they support each other.

If, for the sake of considering the question of relative power of acoustic cues in the perception of a phonetic distinction, we separate fundamental-frequency shifts from the other cues linked to the dimension of voice timing, voice onset time is clearly the dominant cue. Only VOT values that are ambiguous with a flat F_O are likely to be pushed into one labeling category or the other by F_O shifts in a forced-choice test. Finally, there are values of VOT that are firmly categorical; they cannot be affected by F_O. There are, however, no values of fundamental frequency that cannot be affected by voice onset time.

NOTES

1. The normal ranges of F_O variation linked to consonant voicing, not only in citation forms but especially in running speech (Lea 1973; O'Shaughnessy 1979), have still not been well described. We have begun a study of this matter with different sentence intonations as a variable (Abramson and Lisker 1984) and hope to present a full report soon.

REFERENCES

Abramson, A. S., & Lisker, L. (1984). Stop voicing, intonation, and the F_O contour. *Journal of the Acoustical Society of America, 75,* S40 (Abstract).

Abramson, A. S. (1975). Pitch in the perception of voicing states in Thai: Diachronic implications. *Haskins Laboratories Status Report on Speech Research, SR-41,* 165–174.

Abramson, A. S., & Erickson, D. M. (1978). Diachronic tone splits and voicing shifts in Thai: Some perceptual data. *Haskins Laboratories Status Report on Speech Research, SR-53*(2), 85–96.

Abramson, A. S., & Lisker, L. (1965). Voice onset time in stop consonants: Acoustic analysis and synthesis. *Proceedings of the 5th International Congress of Acoustics,* Liege.

Fujimura, O. (1971). Remarks on stop consonants: Synthesis experiments and acoustic cues. In L. L. Hammerich, R. Jakobson, & E. Zwirner (Eds.), *Form and substance: Phonetic and linguistic papers presented to Eli Fischer-Jørgensen.* Copenhagen: Akademisk Forlag.

Haggard, M. P., Ambler, S., & Callow, M. (1970). Pitch as a voicing cue. *Journal of the Acoustical Society of America, 47,* 613–617.

Haggard, M., Summerfield, Q., & Roberts, M. (1981). Psychoacoustical and cultural determinants of phoneme boundaries: Evidence from trading F$_O$ cues in the voiced–voiceless distinction. *Journal of Phonetics, 9,* 49–62.

Hombert, J. M. (1975). *Towards a theory of tonogenesis: An empirical, physiologically and perceptually-based account of the development of tonal contrasts in language.* Unpublished doctoral dissertation, University of California, Berkeley.

Hombert, J. M., Ohala, J., & Ewan, W. (1979). Phonetic explanation for the development of tones. *Language, 55,* 37–58.

House, A. S., & Fairbanks, G. (1953). The influence of consonant environment upon the secondary acoustical characteristics of vowels. *Journal of the Acoustical Society of America, 25,* 105–113.

Lea, W. (1973). Segmental and suprasegmental influences on fundamental frequency contours. In L. Hyman (Ed.), *Consonant types and tone. Southern California Papers in Linguistics* (Los Angeles), *1.*

Lehiste, I., & Peterson, G. E. (1961). Some basic considerations in the analysis of intonation. *Journal of the Acoustical Society of America, 33,* 419–423.

Lisker, L., & Abramson, A. (1964). A cross-language study of voicing in initial stops: Acoustical measurements. *Word, 20,* 384–422.

Lisker, L., & Abramson, A. S. (1970). The voicing dimension: Some experiments in comparative phonetics. *Proceedings of the 6th International Congress of Phonetic Sciences.* Prague: Academia.

Lisker, L., & Abramson, A. S. (1971). Distinctive features and laryngeal control. *Language, 47,* 767–785.

Maspero, H. (1911). Contribution a l'étude du système phonétique des langues thai. *Bulletin de l'Ecole Française d'Extrême-Orient, 19,* 152–169.

O'Shaughnessy, D. (1979). Linguistic features in fundamental frequency patterns. *Journal of Phonetics, 7,* 119–145.

4

Dynamic Modeling of Phonetic Structure*

Catherine P. Browman
Louis M. Goldstein

1. INTRODUCTION

Much linguistic phonetic research has attempted to characterize phonetic units in terms of measurable physical parameters or features (Fant 1973; Halle & Stevens 1979; Jakobson, Fant, & Halle 1969; Ladefoged 1971). Basic to these approaches is the view that a phonetic description consists of a linear sequence of static physical measures, either articulatory configurations or acoustic parameters. The course of movement from one such configuration to another has been viewed as secondary. We have proposed (Browman & Goldstein 1984) an alternative approach, one that characterizes phonetic structure as patterns of articulatory movement, or gestures, rather than static configurations. While the traditional approaches have viewed the continuous movement of vocal-tract articulators over time as "noise" that tends to obscure the segment-like structure of speech, we have argued that setting out to characterize articulator movement directly leads not to noise but to organized spatiotemporal structures that can be used as the basis for phonological generalizations as well as accurate physical description. In our view, then, a phonetic representation is a characterization of how a physical system (e.g., a vocal tract) changes over time. In this chapter, we begin to explore the form that such a characterization could take by attempting to explicitly model some observed articulatory trajectories.

Although we want to account for how articulators move over time,

* This research was supported by Grant No. NS-13617 from the National Institute of Neurological and Communicative Disorders and Stroke and Grant No. HD-01994 from the National Institute of Child Health and Human Development.

PHONETIC LINGUISTICS

this does not mean that time per se must appear as a dimension of the description. In fact, a dimension of time would be quite problematic because of temporal variations introduced by changes in speaking rate and stress. For example, suppose our phonetic description were to specify the positions of articulators at successive points in time. As speaking rate changes, the values at successive time points are all likely to change in rather complex ways. Such a representation would not, therefore, be very satisfactory. It would be preferable to describe phonetic structure as a system that produces behavior that is organized in time but which does not require time as a control parameter (as has been suggested, e.g., by Fowler 1977, 1980). Like conventional phonetic representations, such a system does not explicitly refer to time. Unlike these representations, however, it explicitly generates patterns of articulator movement in time and space.

The dynamical approach to action currently being developed, for example, by Kelso and Tuller (1984) and Saltzman and Kelso (1983) provides the kind of time-free structure that can characterize articulatory movement. The approach has been applied to certain aspects of speech production (Fowler, Rubin, Remez, & Turvey 1980; Kelso, Tuller, & Harris 1983; Kelso, Tuller, & Harris in press), as well as to more general aspects of motor coordination in biological systems (e.g., Kelso, Holt, Rubin, & Kugler 1981; Kugler, Kelso, & Turvey 1980). Previous approaches to motor coordination have emphasized the importance of a time-varying trajectory plan for the muscles and joints to follow in the performance of a coordinated activity and require an intelligent executive to ensure that the plan is followed. In the dynamical approach taken by these investigators, actions are characterized by underlying dynamic systems, which, once set into place, can autonomously regulate the activities of sets of muscles and joints over time.

A physical example of a dynamic system is a mass–spring system, that is, a movable object (mass) connected by a spring to some rigid support. If the mass is pulled and the spring stretched beyond its equilibrium length, the mass will begin to oscillate. In the absence of friction, the equation characterizing motion is seen in Eq. (1), and the trajectory of the object attached to the spring can be seen in Figure 4.1.

(1) $m\ddot{x} + k(x - x_0) = 0$

where m = mass of the object

k = stiffness of the spring

x_0 = rest length of the spring

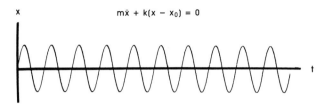

Figure 4.1 Output of undamped mass–spring system. Time (t) is on the abscissa and displacement (x) is on the ordinate.

x = instantaneous displacement of the object

$\ddot{x}$ = instantaneous acceleration of the object

Notice that an invariant organization, that in Equation (1), gives rise to the time-varying trajectory in Figure 4.1. No point-by-point plan is required to describe this pattern of movement, and time is not referred to explicitly. Only the parameter values and the initial conditions need be specified. This undamped mass–spring equation is a very simple example of a dynamic system. It is important to note that this system can give rise to a whole family of trajectories, not just the one portrayed in Figure 4.1. Different trajectories can be generated by changing values of the system's parameters. For example, changing the stiffness of the spring will change the observed frequency of oscillation. Changes in the rest length of the spring and the initial displacement of the mass will affect the amplitude of the oscillations.

This simple mass–spring equation (generally with a linear or nonlinear damping term added), exemplifies the dynamical approach to coordination and control of movement in biological systems in general and of speech articulators in particular. The appeal of this approach lies both in its potentially simple description of articulatory movements (i.e., only a few underlying parameters serve to characterize a whole range of movements) and in its physical and biological generality. In order to be useful for phonetics and linguistics, however, such a dynamic system must be related to phonetic structure. In one early attempt to specify this relationship, Lindblom (1967) proposed that a dynamic description could be used to account for speech-duration data. More recently, Kelso, Vatikiotis-Bateson, Saltzman, and Kay (1985) and Ostry, Keller, and Parush (1983) have analyzed stress and speaking rate variation in terms of the parameters of a dynamic model. In this chapter, we explore a basic linguistic issue that arises in the attempt to couch phonetic representations in the language of dynamics, namely, the definition of the articulatory gesture.

To begin to relate phonetic description to a dynamic system, let us consider a very simple example. Figure 4.2b shows the vertical position of a light-emitting diode (LED) on the lower lip of a speaker of American English as she produces the utterance ['babəbab] in the frame *Say _____ again*. The acoustic closures and releases marked on the articulatory trajectory are determined from the acoustic waveform, shown in Figure 4.2a. Note that the lower lip is raised (toward the upper lip) for the closures and lowered for the vowels. How can this observed lower-lip trajectory be described in terms of a dynamic system? Clearly the lower lip is showing an oscillatory pattern, that is, it goes up and down in a fairly regular way, but it does not show the absolute regularity of our mass–spring system in Figure 4.1. For example, the lip is lower in the full vowels than in the schwa. Thus, a mass–spring organization with constant parameter values will not generate this lower-lip trajectory.

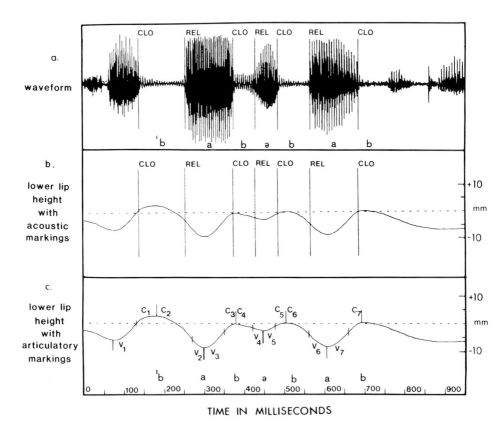

Figure 4.2 Lower-lip height and waveform for single token of ['babəbab].

However, it might be possible to generate this kind of trajectory if the parameter values were changed in the course of the utterance. The underlying dynamic organization, together with the particular changes of the parameters, would then serve to characterize the phonetic structure of the utterance.

It is, of course, obvious that a characterization of lower-lip position over time is not a complete phonetic representation. Nonetheless, in very simple utterances containing only bilabials and a single vowel, it comes quite close to being an adequate phonetic description. Browman, Goldstein, Kelso, Rubin, and Saltzman (1984) have shown that an alternating stress ['mama'mama . . .] sequence can be adequately synthesized using a vocal-tract simulation controlled by only two mass–spring systems— one for lip aperture (the distance between the two lips) and one for lip protrusion. Clearly, however, more complex utterances will require additional dynamic systems and relations among these systems; such interrelations and their implications for phonology are discussed in Browman and Goldstein (1984). Even for the restricted utterances considered here, we simplify the phonetic characterization by considering only the vertical position of the lower lip. We ignore horizontal lip displacement, the upper lip, and the fact that the movements of the lower lip can be decomposed into movements of the jaw and movements of the lower lip with respect to the jaw. The general framework we are operating within (the task dynamics of Saltzman & Kelso 1983) allows us to describe the coordination of multi-articulator gestures, but this is irrelevant to the present chapter, in which we consider only how to describe a particular articulator trajectory as the output of a dynamic system.

The undamped mass–spring system with constant parameter values generates sinusoidal trajectories with constant frequency and amplitude. We show that observed trajectories can be directly modeled as sinusoids whose frequency and amplitude vary at particular points during the utterance. Of particular interest is how to define these points at which the values are changed. Since time is not a parameter of the system, they are defined not with respect to some reference clock but in terms of the inherent cyclic properties of the dynamic system.

One set of inherently definable points at which parameter values can be modulated are the points of minimum and maximum articulator displacement. Modulation at these points is suggested by studies of articulator movement that characterize trajectories in terms of opening and closing gestures (e.g., Kuehn & Moll 1976; Parush, Ostry, & Munhall 1983; Sussman, MacNeilage, & Hanson 1973). Alternatively, points of peak velocity (both positive and negative) can also serve as dynamically definable markers for modulation. In a simple mass–spring system, velocity peaks occur at the resting, or equilibrium, position. These different points of change imply different phonetic organizations, as can be seen with the help of Figure 4.2c. Here we see the same articulatory trajectory as in Figure 4.2b, with the addition of tick marks that indicate the displacement and velocity extrema. These points divide the utterance into intervals, each of which has been labeled with either a C (for consonant) or a V (for vowel). The consonant intervals are those on either side of a displacement peak, and the vowel intervals are those on either side of a displacement valley. Points of peak velocity, indicated by the smaller tick marks on the slopes, separate consonant intervals from vowel intervals. For example, V_1 is the interval from the minimum position of the lower lip in the frame vowel [ey] to the point of peak velocity as the lip starts to raise for the initial [b]. C_1 is the interval from this latter peak velocity point to the center of maximum lower-lip height during the [b]. C_2 is the interval from this displacement peak to the peak velocity as the lower lip lowers for the following vowel [a].

If we change our model parameters only at displacement peaks and valleys, then successive VC or CV intervals (e.g., V_1C_1, C_2V_2) will be characterized with the same set of parameters. This constitutes a phonetic hypothesis that the articulatory trajectories can be modeled as successive CV and VC transition gestures, each with its characteristic values for the dynamic parameters. The parameters for these opening and closing gestures must take into account both the particular consonant and the particular vowel. Thus, this hypothesis provides a phonetic structure rather different from that commonly assumed in linguistics, in that it does not provide a physical characterization of individual consonants or vowels.

An alternative division of the articulatory trajectories is clearly possible if we change parameters at velocity extrema rather than displacement extrema. In this way, successive C intervals will have a single characterization, as will successive V intervals (e.g., C_1C_2, V_2V_3). These new intervals, then, correspond roughly to consonant and vowel gestures, rather than to CV and VC transition gestures. Under this hypothesis, the relationship between the dynamic characterization and more conventional phonetic representations is somewhat more transparent than it is under the transition hypothesis. Note, however, that even under this hypothesis, consonants and vowels are defined in terms of dynamic structures rather than as spatial targets.

In this chapter, then, we present the results of some preliminary modeling of articulatory trajectories with sinusoids (the output of an undamped mass–spring system) under the C–V and transition hypotheses outlined above. In particular, the two hypotheses are contrasted with respect to how the frequency parameter of the sinusoidal model is modulated. The frequency parameter (proportional to the square root of the stiffness of the underlying mass–spring system, assuming a unit mass) is of particular interest, because it controls the duration of a given gesture and thus holds the key to how temporal (durational) regularities can be accommodated in a descriptive system that does not include time as a variable. Therefore, we examine how the frequency of an articulatory gesture varies as a function of stress, position within the item, and vowel quality.

2. METHOD

2.1. Articulatory Trajectories

The trisyllabic nonsense items shown in Table 4.1 were chosen for analysis. Stress is either initial or final, with the second syllable always reduced, and the vowels are either [i] or [a]. The items were recorded by a female speaker of American English in the carrier sentence *Say* _____ *again*. Table 4.1 indicates the number of tokens of each of the items that were analyzed.

Movements of the talker's lips and jaw were tracked using a Selspot system that recorded displacements, in the midsagittal plane, of LEDs placed on the nose, upper lip, lower lip, and chin. The Selspot output was recorded on an FM tape recorder and was later digitally sampled at 200 Hz for computer analysis. To correct the articulator displacements for possible movements of the head, the Selspot signal for the nose LED was subtracted from each of the articulator signals. Each resulting articulator trajectory was then smoothed, using a 25 ms triangular window. For the present purpose, only the vertical displacement of the lower lip was analyzed.

Displacement maxima and minima were determined automatically using a peak-finding algorithm. Instantaneous velocities were computed by

Table 4.1
NONSENSE ITEMS USED IN ANALYSIS

Utterance	Number of tokens
bibə'bib	11
'bibəbib	14
babə'bab	10
'babəbab	11

taking the difference of successive displacement samples. The maxima and minima of the resulting velocity curves were determined using the same program as for the displacements. Displacement and velocity extrema were used to divide each token into seven C and seven V intervals, as shown in Figure 4.2c.

2.2 Modeling

Each successive interval of each token was modeled as the output of a simple mass–spring system by fitting sinusoids to the articulatory trajectories. We generated the model trajectories using a sine-wave equation directly, Equation (2), in order to emphasize the inherent cyclic properties of dynamic systems. Recall that frequency is related to stiffness and amplitude to rest length and maximum displacement. Thus, we controlled frequency, amplitude, and equilibrium position (rest length). (Phase is discussed below.) The individual model points, $x'(i)$, for an interval were generated according to Equation (2) for the ith point in the interval (one point every 5 ms):

(2) $x'(i) = x_0 + A \sin (wi + \phi)$

  where x_0 = equilibrium position

     A = amplitude

     w = frequency (in degrees per sample point)

     ϕ = phase

Frequency varied every two-interval gesture, where the gestures were defined according to the two hypotheses outlined in the previous section. For the C–V hypothesis, a gesture included the two intervals between successive velocity extrema (e.g., C_1C_2, V_2V_3). For the transition hypothesis, a gesture included the two intervals between successive displacement extrema (e.g., V_1C_1, C_2V_2). We posit that a gesture constitutes a half cycle. Therefore, the frequency was computed as the reciprocal of twice the combined duration of the two intervals comprising a gesture. For example, the frequency used to model intervals C_1 and C_2 under the C–V hypothesis was $1 / (2 * (\text{duration of } C_1 + \text{duration of } C_2))$. Similarly, the frequency for intervals C_2 and V_2 under the transition hypothesis was computed as $1 / (2 * (\text{duration of } C_2 + \text{duration of } V_2))$.

Since our primary interest in this study was in the frequency parameter, we allowed the values of the equilibrium position and amplitude to change every interval. The values were determined from the initial and final displacement of the interval, adjusted for phase. The phase angle for a sine wave is 90 degrees at maximum displacement (the peaks) and 270 degrees at minimum displacement (the valleys). Amplitude and equilibrium position values were determined by the constraint that model and data agree exactly at these points, both in phase and in displacement. That is, the observed peaks and valleys were assumed to be the displacement extrema generated by the underlying model. The analogous assumption was not possible for the velocity extrema, however, since often the velocity extrema were not midway between the displacement extrema, as they would be if the parameter values were not changing (see Figure 4.1). Thus, the observed velocity extrema did not correspond to 0 and 180 degrees in the modeled trajectories. Rather, the phases for these points in the model were permitted to vary according to the constraint that model and data agree exactly here as well as at the displacement extrema.

3. RESULTS

Sinusoidal models are strikingly successful in fitting the articulatory data. Figure 4.3a shows the model trajectory generated for the C–V hypothesis superimposed on the real trajectory for our sample token of ['babəbab]. The curves lie almost completely on top of one another, diverging substantially only during the C_1, C_2, and C_6 intervals. This particular token is the best modeled of all ['babəbab] tokens, as measured by the mean square error of the modeled points. The token with the worst fit, not only for this utterance but for all the utterances, is shown in Figure 4.3b. Again the curves lie almost completely on top of one another, diverging substantially only in the same places as in Figure 4.3a.

In general, the modeled trajectories for both hypotheses and for all utterances fit comparably to the trajectories shown in Figure 4.3a. Table 4.2 gives the mean square error averaged across all tokens for each of the four utterances under the C–V and transition hypotheses. The two hypotheses differ by only a small amount, but the C–V hypothesis appears to be consistently better. Comparison of individual tokens supports this slight superiority of dividing the trajectory into consonant and vowel gestures.

The contribution of different intervals of the trajectories to the error can be seen in Figure 4.4. The four curves show the model and data superimposed for the best tokens of each of the utterance types under the C–V hypothesis. Utterances with [i] are shown on the left (a and b), and utterances with [a] are shown on the right (d and e). The graphs at the bottom of the figure show the mean square error for the individual

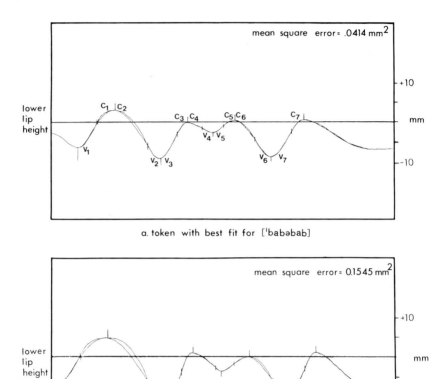

a. token with best fit for [ˈbabəbab]

b. token with worst fit : [ˈbababab]

Figure 4.3 Sample comparisons of superimposed model (C–V hypothesis) and data trajectories.

Table 4.2
MEAN SQUARE ERROR AVERAGED ACROSS TOKENS

Utterance	Mean square error (mm²)	
	C–V hypothesis	Transition hypothesis
bibə'bib	.0154	.0171
'bibəbib	.0466	.0615
babə'bab	.0358	.0471
'bababab	.0907	.1220

intervals from V_1 to C_7. These are averages across all tokens of a given utterance. Again, results for utterances with [i] are shown at the left and with [a] at the right. Intervals occurring in stressed and unstressed syllables are shown separately.

The error distributions show that the worst fit is found for item-initial stressed consonants, for both [a] and [i] utterances. In particular, interval C_2, the release of this initial stressed consonant, is poorly modeled relative to the other intervals. The release of the stressed consonant is also relatively poorly modeled in final syllables containing [a]. Examining the trajectories in the poorly modeled regions of ['babəbab] in Figure 4.4d, we can see that the actual consonant trajectory (indicated by arrows) shows a flatter top than that predicted by sinusoidal trajectories. This can, perhaps, be explained by noting that it tends to occur in regions in which the lower lip is raised quite high against the upper lip. The flattening may be the result of some limit on the compressibility of the lips. Alternatively, it may be that there is some tendency for initial stressed consonants to be held, suggesting a somewhat different kind of dynamic system (e.g., a damped mass–spring).

The error distributions also show a clear tendency for the reduced syllables to have the smallest error. This may partly be due to the fact that the actual displacement differences between the beginning and end of such intervals tend to be very small, and, given that the ends are perfectly modeled, there simply is not much room for error. Similarly, there is some tendency for utterances with [i] to show less error than utterances with [a]. Again, the lower lip shows less movement with [i] than [a], leaving less room for error. However, the smaller amplitude of movement does not completely account for the better fit. Correlations between amplitude of movement and error are not high, for example, .242 for [babə'bab]. Thus, the straightforward mass–spring model we have chosen to investigate appears to be adequate for the unstressed and reduced syllables but needs to be modified for stressed, item-initial consonants.

In addition to goodness-of-fit considerations, a dynamic phonetic structure can also be evaluated with respect to how well it can elucidate systematic variation. For example, we can examine how the values of the model parameters vary as a function of context. Given the preliminary nature of our modeling, we simply show some easily observable trends, rather than present a detailed statistical analysis.

The bars with solid lines in Figure 4.5a show the mean value of the frequency parameter for the consonant gesture under the C–V hypothesis, as a function of the consonant's stress and position within the item for the two vowel contexts. Only the three consonants preceding vowels

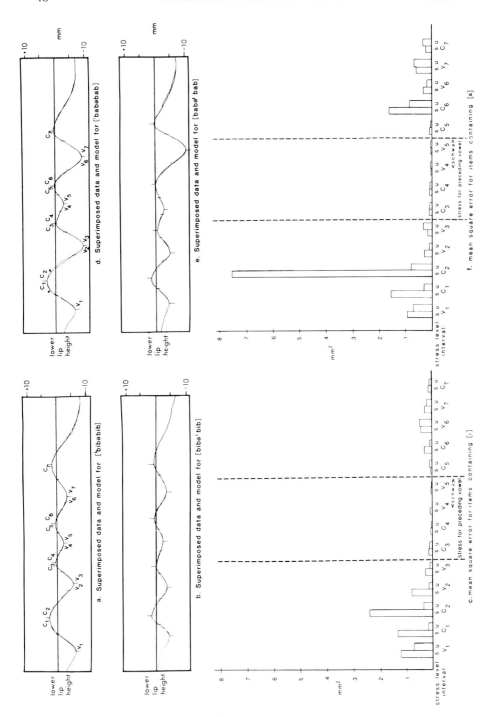

are shown. The first thing to note about the data is that the nature of the vowel in the item ([i] or [a]) has little effect on the consonant frequency, (although unstressed [b] has a lower frequency before [a] than before [i]). That is, consonant frequency is relatively independent of vowel. Stress, however, clearly shows a systematic influence on the frequency of the [b] gesture. The consonant has a higher frequency in unstressed syllables than in stressed syllables for both the initial and final syllables in the item. In the medial reduced syllable, the consonant has the highest frequency of all. Kelso et al. (1985) also found unstressed gestures to be stiffer than stressed gestures, which is equivalent to an increase in frequency. This pattern of variation is completely consistent with the lengthening effect of stress as measured acoustically (e.g., Klatt 1976; Oller 1973). Additionally, there is variation according to position. Item-initial stressed consonants are lower in frequency than consonants in the final syllable of the item. Again, this is consistent with observed acoustic word-initial consonant lengthening (Oller 1973).

The vowel gestures are analyzed in a similar way in Figure 4.5b. Reduced vowels have higher frequencies than full vowels, as expected from the consonant data. Full vowels, however, do not behave quite as systematically as the consonants. For unstressed full vowels, there is little or no difference between [i] and [a] in frequency. Stressed full vowels, however, show a slight difference depending on whether the item contains [i] or [a]. Stressed [i] has a slightly higher frequency than stressed [a], which corresponds to the measured acoustic duration difference noted, for example, by Umeda (1975). (Reduced vowels show a possible compensatory effect, in that reduced vowels in items containing [i] have a lower frequency than those in items with [a].) The effect of stress for the full vowels is also not completely regular but rather depends upon position. Only vowels in initial syllables show lower frequencies when stressed. Note, however, that vowels in final syllables are lower in frequency than those in initial syllables, which is in agreement with the acoustic effect of final lengthening (Klatt 1975). It may be, then, that the final-lengthening effect washes out temporal differences between stressed and unstressed vowels in the final syllable. (At least one of Oller's 1973 subjects shows this kind of pattern). Looked at in another way, when the initial vowel is stressed, it has about the same frequency as the unstressed final vowel in the same item. That is, the final lengthening effect is similar in magnitude to the stress effect. This is consistent with

---

Figure 4.4 Best fit and error distributions by intervals for comparison of model (C–V hypothesis) and data trajectories; s = stressed interval, u = unstressed interval; for reduced intervals C_3–V_5, s = preceding vowel stressed, u = preceding vowel unstressed. Arrows indicate data.

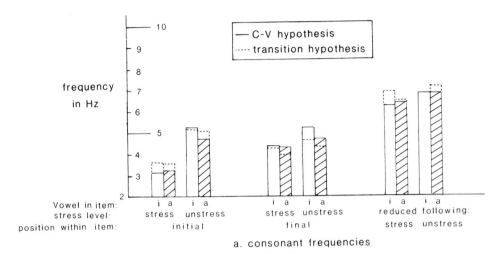

a. consonant frequencies

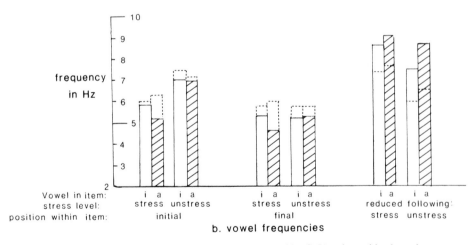

b. vowel frequencies

Figure 4.5   Consonant and vowel frequencies generated by C–V and transition hypotheses, according to vowel in item, stress level, and position within item. For reduced consonants and vowels, always in medial position, stress or unstress refers to the preceding syllable.

acoustic and perceptual investigations of stress patterns (Fry 1958; Lea, 1977).

The bars with dotted lines superimposed on the solid-line bars in Figure 4.5 show the mean frequencies obtained under the transition hypothesis. For reasons to be discussed in the next section, the CV transitional gestures have been superimposed on the corresponding C gestures, and the VC transitions on the corresponding V gestures. For example, the consonant in initial position, which represents the consonant closing and release (C_1C_2) under the C–V hypothesis, represents, under the transition hypothesis, the consonant release and movement to the following vowel (C_2V_2). Similarly, the initial vowel represents V_2V_3 under the C–V hypothesis and V_3C_3 under the transition hypothesis. Comparison of the dotted lines and solid bars shows substantial similarity. The only important differences are in the frequencies of the reduced vowels, which in the transition hypothesis are not higher than the full vowels. This is perhaps not surprising, given that the VCs that constitute the reduced syllables (V_5C_5) include the initial consonant interval (C_5) of the following unreduced syllable.

To summarize, both the C–V hypothesis and the transition hypothesis fit the data quite well (except for stressed item-initial consonants) and generate very similar frequencies. The two hypotheses differ slightly in that the C–V hypothesis provides marginally better fit and they predict differing patterns of frequencies for reduced vowels. Only stressed and reduced vowels show a difference in the frequencies generated for items containing [a] and items containing [i]. Stress level, however, has a generally consistent effect, with stressed syllables having the lowest frequency, unstressed syllables somewhat higher, and syllables containing reduced vowels having the highest frequency. This stress effect fails only for full vowels in final syllables, which in addition display lowered frequencies relative to initial syllables. Consonants, in contrast, have lower frequencies in initial syllables than in final. These stress and position effects are consistent with acoustic duration effects noted in the literature. Thus, well-known aspects of the temporal organization of speech can be accounted for in a model that does not explicitly refer to time.

4. IMPLICATIONS AND PROSPECTS

The success of a very simple dynamic system in modeling the observed trajectories of individual gestures gives important empirical support to the dynamic approach to phonetic structure. The approach is theoretically appealing because it provides a way of explicitly generating articulator trajectories from a time-free sequence of parameter specifications for consonants and vowels. This is made possible by recognizing, as suggested by Fowler (1977, 1980) and Fowler et al. (1980), that a phonetic structure is not just a linear sequence of parameter, or feature, values but also must be described as some particular dynamic organization that the parameter values serve to modulate. The successive changes in parameter values can be linked to particular points in the underlying dynamic organization. This differs from conventional phonetic representations that do not provide any explicit way of generating articulatory trajectories from a sequence of parameter specifications.

The present model is only a preliminary validation of the general approach. A number of improvements need to be made before it can be claimed to have predictive power. In particular, the interval-by-interval specification of amplitude, with endpoints exactly matched, needs to be replaced with a procedure that allows amplitude to be specified over longer stretches. The determination of frequency should be made in a way that is less vulnerable to experimental (and theoretical) error in determining the endpoints of the gestures. Both frequency and amplitude should ultimately be determined by general linguistic parameters, for example, stress level and position, rather than by item-specific trajectory matching. These improvements can be carried out using the present simple undamped mass–spring dynamic model. In addition, alternative dynamic models need to be explored in order to account for the poorly matched item-initial stressed consonants as well as the interarticulator compensation effects discussed in Saltzman & Kelso (1983).

Another area to be investigated further is the organization of the underlying phonetic structure. This chapter compared two organizational hypotheses: consonant–vowel gestures and transitional gestures. While both hypotheses fit the data quite well in this preliminary test, there is some indication that additional organizational hypotheses should be explored in future modeling attempts.

In the comparison of the two hypotheses, the CV transition was equated with the C, and the VC transition with the V. This was a post hoc decision, based on the similarity of frequencies when the two hypotheses were so equated. In fact, the frequencies would not appear similar at all if the CV transitions were equated with Vs, rather than with Cs, and the VC transitions were likewise switched. Why the frequencies should line up this way is not clear. It may simply be the case that the intervals immediately following the displacement extrema, which are the intervals common to the C (or V) gestures and their equated transition gestures, are those in which frequency is crucially controlled. This interpretation is supported by results from an additional analysis in which frequency was determined interval by interval rather than by using two contiguous intervals. In this analysis, exactly those intervals following the displacement extrema displayed the stress and position patterns discussed in the preceding section, while the alternate intervals showed no clear relationship to the linguistic variables. However, there is also a more interesting account. This involves positing a structure in which frequency is fixed over a larger span of at least three intervals, for example, $C_1C_2V_2$ and $V_2V_3C_3$.

These longer gestures constitute a kind of overlapping organization (V_2 appears in both above) that is independently motivated by the kinds of coarticulatory phenomena typically observed in speech (see the overlapping segment analysis of coarticulation presented by Fowler 1983).

Some such concept of overlapping gestures is also suggested by another regularity observable in the frequency patterns. The frequency of a consonant gesture under the C–V hypothesis is lower than the frequency of the vowel that follows it. This is counter to the common assumption that consonants involve short, rapid movements, while full vowels correspond to longer movements. It might, of course, be a startling new result. Or it may simply be that the choice of endpoints needs to be improved. But such a counterintuitive result may also be indicative of a basic flaw in the hypothesis generating the result. One obvious candidate is the assumption, in both hypotheses investigated, of independent, sequential gestures. Such an assumption was useful as a starting point, but is unlikely to be accurate. Rather, some form of overlap of the gestures— coarticulation—would likely give a better picture and will be permitted in future modeling attempts. A possible overlapping structure is one in which consonantal gestures are phased relative to ongoing vowel gestures (Tuller, Kelso, & Harris 1982).

Finally, the comparison of the C–V hypothesis with the transitional hypothesis carries certain implications, not only for future research into phonetic organization, but also for the interpretation of past studies. Investigations into the nature of speech articulator movements have tacitly assumed the transition hypothesis (e.g., Kuehn & Moll 1976; Parush et al. 1983; Sussman et al. 1973) and have consequently couched the description of their results in terms of opening and closing gestures. The present study, however, shows that the C–V hypothesis provides an organization that captures all of the same generalizations in the data as the transitional hypothesis; one that fits the data as well as or better than the transitional hypothesis; and moreover, one that is more immediately relatable to traditional linguistic units. In addition, while the two hypotheses generally produce equivalent frequency analyses, in at least one case—that of reduced vowels—they appear to differ substantively. The present study does not constitute evidence for one hypothesis over the other, given the overall similarity in fit. However, it does constitute evidence that the C–V organization, or some variant thereof, warrants serious consideration in the interpretation of speech articulator-movement data. In general, we think that bringing dynamic principles to bear on problems of linguistic organization will lead to more linguistically relevant accounts of speech production as well as to a much richer, yet simple, conception of phonetic structure. The structure comprises an underlying dynamic system with associated parameter values. Together, the system and its parameters explicitly generate patterns of articulator movement. In addition, as we have demonstrated, such structures can retain the useful descriptive properties of more conventional phonetic representations.

REFERENCES

Browman, C. P., Goldstein, L., Kelso, J. A. S., Rubin, P., & Saltzman, E. (1984). Articulatory synthesis from underlying dynamics. *Journal of the Acoustical Society of America, 75,* S22–23. (abstract).

Browman, C. P., & Goldstein, L. (1984). *Towards an articulatory phonology.* Unpublished manuscript.

Fant, G. (1973). Distinctive features and phonetic dimensions. In G. Fant, *Speech sounds and features* (pp. 171–191). Cambridge, MA: MIT Press. (Originally published 1969)

Fowler, C. A. (1977). *Timing control in speech production.* Bloomington, IN: Indiana University Linguistics Club.

Fowler, C. A. (1980). Coarticulation and theories of extrinsic timing control. *Journal of Phonetics, 8,* 113–133.

Fowler, C. A. (1983). Converging sources of evidence on spoken and perceived rhythms of speech: Cyclic production of vowels in monosyllabic stress feet. *Journal of Experimental Psychology: General, 112,* 386–412.

Fowler, C. A., Rubin, P., Remez, R. E., & Turvey, M. T. (1980). Implications for speech production of a general theory of action. In B. Butterworth (Ed.), *Language production* (pp. 373–420). New York: Academic Press.

Fry, D. B. (1958). Experiments in the perception of stress. *Language and Speech, 1,* 126–152.

Halle, M., & Stevens, K. N. (1979). Some Reflections on the theoretical bases of phonetics. In B. Lindblom & S. Ohman (Eds.), *Frontiers of speech communication research* (pp. 335–353). New York: Academic Press.

Jakobson, R., Fant, C. G. M., & Halle, M. (1969). *Preliminaries to speech analysis: The distinctive features and their correlates.* Cambridge, MA: MIT Press.

Kelso, J. A. S., Holt, K. G., Rubin, P., & Kugler, P. N. (1981). Patterns of human interlimb coordination emerge from the properties on nonlinear limit cycle oscillatory processes: Theory and data. *Journal of Motor Behavior, 13,* 226–261.

Kelso, J. A. S., & Tuller, B. (1984). A dynamical basis for action systems. In M. S. Gazzaniga (Ed.), *Handbook of neuroscience* (pp. 321–356). New York: Plenum.

Kelso, J. A. S., Tuller, B., & Harris, K. S. (1983). A 'dynamic pattern' perspective on the control and coordination of movement. In P. MacNeilage (Ed.), *The production of speech* (pp. 137–173). New York: Springer-Verlag.

Kelso, J. A. S., Tuller, B., & Harris, K. S. (in press). A theoretical note on speech timing. In J. S. Perkell & D. Klatt (Eds.), *Invariance and variation in speech processes,* Hillsdale, N.J.: Erlbaum.

Kelso, J. A. S., Vatikiotis-Bateson, E., Saltzman, E. L., & Kay B. (1985). A qualitative dynamic analysis of reiterant speech production: Phase portraits, kinematics, and dynamic modeling. *Journal of the Acoustical Society of America, 77,* 266–280.

Klatt, D. H. (1975). Vowel lengthening is syntactically determined in a connected discourse. *Journal of Phonetics, 3,* 129–140.

Klatt, D. H. (1976). Linguistic uses of segmental duration in English: Acoustic and perceptual evidence. *Journal of the Acoustical Society of America, 59,* 1208–1221.

Kuehn, D. R., & Moll, K. L. (1976). A cineradiographic study of VC and CV articulatory velocities. *Journal of Phonetics, 4,* 303–320.

Kugler, P. N., Kelso, J. A. S., & Turvey, M. T. (1980). On the concept of coordinative structures as dissipative structures: I. Theoretical lines of convergence. In G. E. Stelmach & J. Requin (Eds.), *Tutorials in motor behavior* (pp. 3–47). New York: North-Holland.

Ladefoged, P. (1971). *Preliminaries to linguistic phonetics.* Chicago: University of Chicago Press.

Lea, W. A. (1977). Acoustic correlates of stress and juncture. In L. M. Hyman (Ed.), *Studies in stress and accent.* Los Angeles: University of Southern California.

Lindblom, B. (1967). Vowel duration and a model of lip mandible coordination. *Speech Transmission Laboratory Quarterly Progress Report, STL-QPSR-4,* 1–29.

Oller, D. (1973). The effects of position in utterance on speech segment duration. *Journal of the Acoustical Society of America, 54,* 1235–1246.

Ostry, D. J., Keller, E., & Parush, A. (1983). Similarities in the control of speech articulators and limbs: Kinematics of tongue dorsum movement in speech. *Journal of Experimental Psychology: Human Perception and Performance, 9,* 622–636.

Parush, A., Ostry, D. J., & Munhall, K. G. (1983). A kinematic study of lingual coarticulation in VCV sequences. *Journal of the Acoustical Society of America, 74,* 1115–1125.

Saltzman, E. L., & Kelso, J. A. S. (1983). Skilled actions: A task dynamic approach. *Haskins Laboratories Status Report on Speech Research, SR-76,* 3–50.

Sussman, H. M., MacNeilage, P. F., & Hanson, R. J. (1973). Labial and mandibular dynamics during the production of labial consonants: Preliminary observations. *Journal of Speech and Hearing Research, 16,* 397–420.

Tuller, B., Kelso, J. A. S., & Harris, K. S. (1982). Interarticulator phasing as an index of temporal regularity in speech. *Journal of Experimental Psychology: Human Perception and Performance, 8,* 460–472.

Umeda, N. (1975). Vowel duration in American English. *Journal of the Acoustical Society of America, 58,* 434–455.

5

The Vocal Tract in Your Pocket Calculator

Gunnar Fant

1. INTRODUCTION

At home, without proper computing facilities and programming experience, I am frequently faced with calculating a vocal tract response function, for example, determining transfer functions or resonance frequencies or assessing the relative salience of an element within the model. Formerly, I made a note of the problem and waited until the day when an overbooked laboratory computer and already fully occupied associates were free. However, impatience and curiosity fed a second impulse. Could the problem not be solved immediately with paper and pencil and pocket calculator?

Over the last few years, a number of situations of this type have led me from the frustration of having to wait to the satisfaction of doing it myself. This has been a process of learning elementary programming strategy by finding solutions that fit the limited capacity of a programmable calculator. The real breakthrough came when I started using a Casio 602P with its pocket-sized printer capable of handling 328 program steps if 46 memories are reserved.

A limited handling capacity also demands maximal efficiency, which, of course, is of principal merit when expanding the scope of programs to optimize laboratory routines or for the design of special hardware systems.

The presentation in this chapter is mainly directed towards loss-free conditions, but I also demonstrate how log-magnitude transfer functions may be compiled directly from the loss-free transfer function supplemented by a faked lossy part inferred from bandwidth versus frequency functions. A more detailed presentation of vocal tract network analysis including relevant boundary conditions and losses, superposition, glottal interaction,

PHONETIC LINGUISTICS

and consonantal transfer functions is found in Badin and Fant (1984).

2. THE VOCAL TRACT NETWORK

We shall pursue a frequency domain modeling of the vocal tract with
an overall supraglottal configuration, as in Figure 5.1. The system is a
combination of T-network analogs of homogeneous arbitrary length,
transmission lines, and lumped-element representation of shunting cavities
within the nasal system and of vocal cavity wall impedances. The ter-
minations R_O, L_O, and R_{ON}, L_{ON} are the radiation impedances at the
lips and at the nostrils. The wall impedances are also equipped with
radiation resistances to represent the radiation from the neck and cheeks
during voiced occlusives. Fant (1960) and Wakita and Fant (1978) provide
relevant data on radiation load, wall-impedance effects, and loss elements.

3. NETWORK ELEMENTS

There are basically two different approaches to vocal tract network
modeling. One is to divide the tract into a relatively large number of
equal-length elementary sections. The other is to operate with modules
of specified length and area, in which case a complete representation of
one-dimensional wave propagation is needed. The latter module can also
be applied to the unit-length modeling to increase the accuracy. In general,
however, the unit-length approach assumes sufficiently short sections of

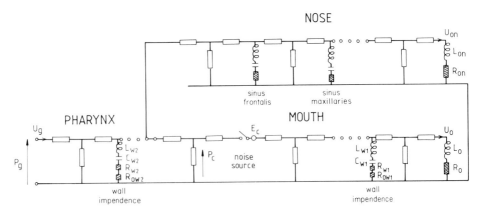

Figure 5.1 Basic vocal tract network with T-network modules and shunting branches
for nasal sinuses and lumped wall impedance.

the order of 0.5 cm that the lumped-element representation, Figure 5.2, is a good approximation. The finite-length model in Fig. 5.2 is the classical T-network uniquely defined by its series and shunt elements:

(1) $a = Z \tgh \theta/2$

    $b = Z/\sinh \theta$

Under loss-less conditions the characteristic impedance is $Z = \rho c/A$, where $\rho = 1.14 \times 10^{-3}$ is the density of air and $c = 35300$ cm/sec, the velocity of sound under normal speaking conditions. A tube of length l has the propagation constant

(2) $\theta = \dfrac{j\omega l}{c} + \alpha l = j\phi + \alpha l$

Under loss-less conditions with $\alpha = 0$, we note that $\sinh \theta = j\sin \phi$, $\tgh \theta/2 = j\tg \phi/2$ and $\cosh \theta = \cos \phi$. With a sufficiently short length the T-network, Eq. (1), reduces to

(3) $a = j\omega L/2$

    $b = \dfrac{1}{j\omega C}$

where $L = \Delta l \rho/A$ and $C = \Delta l A/\rho c^2$.

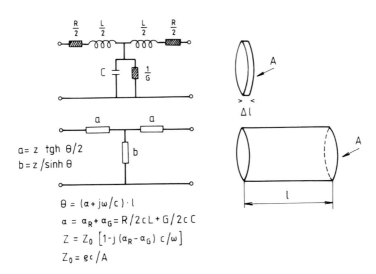

    $a = z \tgh \theta/2$
    $b = z /\sinh \theta$

    $\theta = (a + j\omega/c)\cdot l$
    $\alpha = \alpha_R + \alpha_G = R/2cL + G/2cC$
    $Z = Z_0 \left[1 - j(\alpha_R - \alpha_G) c/\omega\right]$
    $Z_0 = \rho c /A$

Figure 5.2   T-network module of a very short tube.

The general finite length equivalent in Figure 5.3, Eq. (1), satisfies the basic input–output equations for pressure P and flow U at the terminals of a transmission line

(4) a. $P_i = U_i Z_i \coth \theta_i - U_{i-1} Z_i / \sinh \theta_i$

    b. $P_{i-1} = U_i Z_i / \sinh \theta_i - U_{i-1} Z_i \coth \theta_i$

The loss-less $Z_i = \rho c / A_i$ is also a reasonable approximation for small losses. It holds exactly if frictional and heat conducting losses are of equal magnitude; this, however, is not the case. In a more exact treatment, the complex form of Z_i (see Figure 5.3 and Fant 1960: 29, Eq. 1.21-3), should be used. The index i refers to the left terminal of section i and $i-1$ to the right terminal (downstream).

The input impedance of a tube with the right end short circuited (acoustically terminated by open space), $Z_B = 0$ is

(5) $Z_{i,i} = a + \dfrac{ab}{a+b} = Z_i \operatorname{tgh} \theta_i$

with the right end open circuited (acoustically terminated by a hard wall) $Z_B = \infty$

(6) $Z_{i,i} = a + b = Z_i \coth \theta_i$

The next step is to study an arbitrary loading condition. After some manipulation of hyperbolic functions, we derive

(7) $Z_{i,i} = Z_i \dfrac{\operatorname{tgh} \theta_i + Z_B/Z_i}{1 + \operatorname{tgh} \theta_i (Z_B/Z_i)} = Z_i \operatorname{tgh}\left(\theta_i + \operatorname{artgh}\dfrac{Z_B}{Z_i}\right)$

The input impedance to section i from the left side may thus be written

(8) $Z_{i,i} \dfrac{P_i}{U_i} = Z_i \operatorname{tgh}\left[\theta_i + \operatorname{arctgh}\dfrac{Z_{i-1}}{Z_i} \operatorname{tgh}(\theta_{i-1} + \cdots\right]$

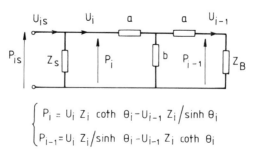

$\begin{cases} P_i = U_i Z_i \coth \theta_i - U_{i-1} Z_i/\sinh \theta_i \\ P_{i-1} = U_i Z_i/\sinh \theta_i - U_{i-1} Z_i \coth \theta_i \end{cases}$

Figure 5.3 T-network module of an arbitrary length tube. The calculation proceeds upstream from Z_B to U_i/U_{i-1} to U_{is}/U_i.

This is a simple recursive algorithm for calculation of any vocal tract input impedance (Fant 1960; Liljencrants & Fant 1975). The starting point is at the radiation load

(9) $Z_B = R_0 + j\omega L_0$

An alternative approach is to derive a volume velocity transfer function factorized by successive steps along the network. The transfer from one section $i - 1$ to the upstream section i in Figure 5.3 is most readily derived from Eq. (4b), noting that $Z_B = P_{i-1}/U_{i-1}$

(10) $\dfrac{U_i}{U_{i-1}} = \cosh \theta_i + \dfrac{Z_B}{Z_i} \sinh \theta_i$

The input impedance $Z_{i,i}$ seen downstream from the left-hand terminal of section i is derived from Eq. (4a):

(11) $Z_{i,i} = \dfrac{P_i}{U_i} = Z_i \left(\cosh \theta_i - \dfrac{U_{i-1}}{U_i} \right) \dfrac{1}{\sinh \theta_i}$

At the left of the input shunt Z_s, we note a flow

(12) $U_{i,s} = U_i(1 + Z_{i,i}/Z_s)$

and a correspondingly modified input impedance:

(13) $Z_{i,s} = P_{is}/U_{is} = Z_{i,i}(1 + Z_{i,i}/Z_s)^{-1}$

The recursive routine for handling a unit section is thus the following:

1. Specify the right-hand side loading impedance as initial conditions.
2. Apply Eq. (10) for calculating the flow transfer to the left terminal.
3. Apply Eq. (11) for the input impedance (downstreams) at the left terminal and store it.
4. If the input is shunted, correct for flow and impedance by Eqs. (12) and (13) to carry the calculation to the left side of the shunt.

The radiation inductance may be expressed as

(14) $L_0 = \rho l_0 / A_0$

where A_0 is the radiating terminal area and l_0 is an equivalent length that is approximately

(15) $l_0 = 0.8(A/\pi)^{0.5}$

We now have the choice of either short-circuiting boundary conditions and adding l_0 to the length of section $i = 1$ or to adopting the more precise lumped-element termination that leads to step 2 above, that is,

(16) $\quad \dfrac{U_1}{U_0} = \cosh \theta_1 + \left(\dfrac{R_0 A_0}{\rho c} + j\omega \dfrac{l_0}{c} \right) \sinh \theta_1$

This is the starting equation for the general lossy case.

For the loss-less case with $\sinh \theta_i = j\sin \phi_i$, we find

(17) $\quad \dfrac{U_1}{U_0} = \cos \phi_1 - \dfrac{\omega l_0}{c} \sin \phi_1$

(18) $\quad Z_{i,1} = \dfrac{\rho c}{A_1} \left(\cos \phi_1 - \dfrac{U_0}{U_1} \right) \dfrac{1}{j\sin \phi_1}$

Next step is to determine U_2/U_1 from Eq. (10) in which now $Z_B = Z_{i,i-1}$ and $Z_i = Z_2 = \rho c / A_2$ followed by updating $U_i/U_0 = (U_2/U_1)(U_1/U_0)$. In general, for the loss-less case, substituting Eq. (11) into Eq. (10)

(19) $\quad U_i/U_{i-1} = \cos \phi_i + jA_i \sin \phi_i, Z_{i,i-1}/\rho c$
$\qquad = \cos \phi_i + A_i \sin \phi_i (A_{i-1} \sin \phi_{i-1})^{-1}(\cos \phi_{i-1} - U_{i-2}/U_{i-1})$

For calculations with all sections of the same length Δl, we find

(20) $\quad \phi_i = \phi_{i-1} = \omega \Delta l / c = \Delta \phi$

(21) $\quad U_i/U_{i-1} = \cos \Delta \phi + (\cos \Delta \phi - U_{i-2}/U_{i-1})A_i/A_{i-1}$

Equation (21) is applied in program A, Eq. (19) in program B, and the impedance method of Eq. (8) in program C (see section 4).

A nasal sinus cavity or a part of the wall impedance both have the general form of a series $R_s L_s C_s$ branch shunting the line:

(22) $\quad Z_s = j\omega L_s \left(1 - \dfrac{1}{\omega^2 L_s C_s} \right) + R_s$

It is convenient to express Z_s with $R_s = 0$ as

(23) $\quad Z_s = j \dfrac{\omega}{c} \cdot \dfrac{\rho c}{A_s} \cdot l_s \left(1 - \dfrac{F_s^2}{f^2} \right)$

where l_s and A_s are the length and cross-sectional area of the inlet to the sinuses, $L_s = \rho l_s / A_s$, and F_s is the resonance frequency of the sinus as a Helmholtz resonator. The factor ρc cancels out in the ratio $Z_{i,i}/Z_s$ and need not be enumerated in any vocal tract transfer calculation.

The wall impedance may be treated in an analogous form and can be included as a subroutine in any section or be lumped into two branches, for example, one 4 cm above the glottis and one 2 cm behind the lips. The design criteria is to achieve an overall closed-tract resonance frequency of the order of $F_w = 190$ Hz and a bandwidth of $B_w = 75$ Hz (see Wakita & Fant 1978; Fant, Nord, & Branderud 1976). A reasonable approximation is to omit any wall impedance in the vocal tract network and perform a final correction of formant frequencies by

(24) $\quad F_n^2 = F_{ni}^2 + F_w^2$

where F_{ni} is the hardwall estimate of F_n. Alternatively, this correction may be introduced already in the transfer function as a frequency trans-formation of the velocity of sound.

(25) $\quad c_e = c[1 - F_w^2/f^2]^{-\frac{1}{2}}$

A corresponding bandwidth increment of

(26) $\quad \Delta B_w = B_w \left(\dfrac{F_w}{F_n}\right)^2$

is well established. Incidentally, the approximation Eqs. (24) and (25) applies exactly if it is conjectured that the thickness of the walls is proportional to $A(x)^{-0.5}$, that is, increases inversely with the tube radius (Fant 1972).

Estimates of wall thickness, or more generally, of the area dependency of L_w thus range from L_w being independent of area to being inversely proportional to area. The corresponding difference in calculated format frequencies is small. The major effect is that F_1 of open back vowels is increased by an additional 50–75 Hz in the case of a constant L_w. More research is needed to clarify true vocal tract conditions.

A few words should be said about log-magnitude calculations of transfer functions. The log-magnitude envelope may be synthesized from formant frequencies and bandwidths. With five formats,

(27) $\quad L(f) = -10 \log_{10} \prod_1^5 [(1 - x_n^2)^2 + x_n^2/Q_n^2] + K_{rs}$

where $x_n = f/F_n$, $Q_n = F_n/B_n$, and K_{rs} is the correction for poles above F_5:

(28) $\quad K_{rs} = 0.433x_0^2 + 0.00071x_0^4 (dB)$

(29) $\quad x_0 = 4l_{tot}f/c$

and l_{tot} is the total length of the vocal tract. A novel alternative is to estimate the loss factor N_a in the direct expression of the transfer function to arrive at

(30) $\quad L(f) = -10 \log_{10}[N_b^2 + N_a^2]$

By equating the complex form $H = (N_b + jN_a)^{-1}$ with the complex factorized products of elementary conjugate poles (Fant 1960), one arrives at

(31) $\quad N_a(f) = \dfrac{-B_n(f) \times N_b'(f)}{2}$

where N_b' is the frequency derivative of the loss-less transfer denominator.

To determine N_b' is part of the standard prediction procedure to calculate the poles, that is, the zeros of N_b, by means of a linear approximation. Given the value $N_b(i)$ at frequency F_i and the derivative estimate

(32) $\quad N_b' = \dfrac{N_b(i) - N_b(i-1)}{F_i - F_{i-1}}$

we arrive at a next better estimate of

(33) $\quad F_{i+1} = F_i - N_b/N_b'(i)$

Average bandwidth versus frequency may be estimated by some simple approximation, for example,

(34) $\quad B(f) = 15\left(\dfrac{500}{f}\right)^2 + 20\left(\dfrac{f}{500}\right)^{\frac{1}{2}} + 3\left(\dfrac{f}{500}\right)^2$

or if formant frequencies have been determined beforehand

(35) $\quad B(f) = 15\left(\dfrac{500}{f}\right)^2 + 20\left(\dfrac{f}{500}\right)^{\frac{1}{2}} + \dfrac{F_2}{2000}\left[1 + \dfrac{(F_3 - F_2)}{(F_4 - F_3)} \times 2\right]\dfrac{f^2}{500^2}$

A more exact procedure is to use the formula of Fant (1972) for arriving at each of B_1 B_2 B_3 B_4 B_5 and then to interpolate linearly with stepwise changes at formant frequencies. Those who have some experience in dealing with vocal tract losses and bandwidths will recognize the f^2 dependency of radiation losses, the f^{-2} dependency of the wall vibration component, and the $f^{\frac{1}{2}}$ dependency of surface losses. Specific deviations from the average rule of Eq. (34) are found, especially in $B3$ with some possible improvements if Eq. (35) is used. Glottal damping adds bandwidth components of highly varying and nonlinear amounts depending on vocal tract shape, formant number, and the specific phonatory mode, generally of the order of 0–100 Hz when translated into an equivalent reduction of formant levels.

To calculate the log magnitude of the transfer function from formant synthesis Eq. (27) is computationally much faster than the direct approach, Eq. (30), while the latter has the advantage that it is merely an extension of the basic vocal tract program and that no correction for higher poles is needed. The complete program incorporating specific vocal tract losses will require a substantially greater computation time.

4. PROGRAMS

A few programs written for the Casio 602P are shown in Figs. 5.4–5.7. Notations are, on the whole, self-explanatory. SAVE invEXE means print out, PAUSE is a short display of operating memory content, HLT is stop and display, GOTO refers to LBL flags, and GSBP to subprograms, DSZ is a countdown of memory 00 by one and skip the next command at zero. A useful feature is indirect addressing by commands IND Min and IND MR. $+/-$ means change of sign and $x = 0$ or $x \geqslant 0$ is a conditional jump, that is, the next command is executed only if the condition is satisfied.

4.1. Program A

Program A, Fig. 5.4, calculates the loss-less volume velocity transfer with the area function quantized in 0.5 cm steps as in Eq. (21). Resonance frequencies are automatically calculated and stored and may be optionally printed out if a printing command instruction is added to PO, program part 1. Program part 2 contains initial settings of branching routes in the program and the starting positions of the indirect addressing of area data and calculated resonance frequencies. Each new run through the vocal tract model at a new frequency starts at LBL1. The recurrent main loop for any vocal tract section is located in 4.

Load impedances, Eq. (18), M53, and the radiation reactance in part 3 are normalized by division by ρc and multiplication by $\sin \Delta\phi$ to simplify the main loop.

Part 5 directs the program to the test of change of sign in 6 when a minimum of two runs through the tract has been performed and directs the program to continue interpolation if it is already in the interpolation mode. The recurrent interpolation subroutine, Eq. (33), is contained in part 7. It is terminated when the current frequency value differs less than one Hz from the previous value. The residual error will then be an order of magnitude smaller. Part 8 updates frequency and function values for ongoing interpolation and part 9 executes the storage of final values of resonance frequencies in the reserved memory allocation. The short display in PAUSE may be extended to a printout command (as exemplified in program B).

The memory listing shows the state after the execution of calculations

```
PROGRAM LIST                              LBL3
M00-55,F-4F  224steps                     MR43 x MR 44 = +/-
                                    6     x≥0 GOT04
1                                         GSPB2
   *** P0                                 GOT07
   PAUSE
              •••002steps                 LBL4
                                          ( MR44 - MR43 ) ÷ (
   *** P1                           7     MR1F - MR3F ) = ÷
   RAD                                    MR44 = 1/x +/-Min40
   1 Min42 Min41                          ABS - 1 = x≥0 GOT05
2  0 Min55                                GOT06
   48 Min4F
   LBL1                                   LBL5
   1 Min47 Min44 M+55             8       0 Min41
   MRF Min00                              GSPB2
                                          MR40 M+1F GOT01
   MR1F
   PAUSE ÷ 11236 =                        LBL6
3  Min45 x 1,6 x ( MR01                   MR40 + MR1F = IND
   ÷ π ) √ = ÷ MR01 x            9        Min4F
   MR45 sin = +/- Min53                   PAUSE
   MR45 cos Min46                         1 M+4F Min41 Min42
                                          MR4F - 53 = x=0
   LBL2                                   HLT
   MR46 + IND MR47 x
   MR53 = Min54 x MR44                    LBL7
4  = Min44                        10      MR2F M+1F GOT01
   MR46 - MR54 1/x = ÷                              •••198steps
   IND MR47 = Min53
   1 M+47                                 *** P2
   DSZ GOT02                      11      MR44 Min43
                                          MR1F Min3F
   MR44                                             •••008steps
   PAUSE
   MR41 x=0 GOT04
5  MR42 x=0 GOT03
   0 Min42
   GSBP2
   GOT07
```

Figure 5.4 Program A for Casio 602P. Formant frequencies are calculated within 0.1 Hz from the loss-less vocal tract volume velocity transfer function. Area function quantized in 0.5 cm steps is inserted in M01–M39. Calculated formant frequencies are stored in M48–M52.

```
MEMORY LIST
M00-55,F-4F 224steps

M00=           0,
M01=           4,        A₁ = A₀
M02=           3,2        |
M03=           1,6        |
M04=           1,3        |
M05=           1,            [i]
M06=           0,65        |
M07=           0,65        |
M08=           0,65        |
M09=           0,65       A₉
M0F=          33,       nr of sections

M10=           0,65      A₁₀
M11=           0,65        |
M12=           0,65        |
M13=           1,3        |
M14=           2,6        |
M15=           4,          |
M16=           6,5        |
M17=           8,          |
M18=           8,          |
M19=          10,5       A₁₉
M1F= 4649,288858         F

M20=          10,5       A₂₀
M21=          10,5        |
M22=          10,5        |
M23=          10,5        |
M24=          10,5        |
M25=          10,5        |
M26=          10,5        |
M27=          10,5        |
M28=           8,          |
M29=           8,         A₂₉
M2F=         400,         ΔF
```

```
M30=           2,        A₃₀
M31=           2,          |
M32=           2,6        |
M33=           3,2        A₃₃
─────────────────────
M34=           3,2
M35=           3,2
M36=           3,2
M37=           3,2
M38=           2,6        A₃₉
M39=           2,6
M3F=    4640,35183

M40= -0,06159202
M41=           1,
M42=           1,
M43= 0,020302038
M44= -1,40888141ε-04
M45= 0,413785053
M46= 0,915605499
M47=          34,        Ind Aₙ
M48=     226,9139        F₁
M49=  2274,91927        F₂
M4F=          53,        Ind Fₙ

M50= 3070,368999        F₃
M51= 3721,682663        F₄
M52= 4649,227266        F₅
M53= 580,5893395
M54=  -5,3851158ε-04
M55=          30,        nr of runs
```

Figure 5.4 (*continued*)

on the Russian [i] vowel. Input area allocations are reserved in M01–M39 and calculated resonance frequencies in M48–M52. As evidenced by M55, the [i] vowel needed 30 runs through the tract, that is, 30 pairs of frequency and function values, to calculate five formants with the prescribed accuracy of much better than 1 Hz. This is more than three times fewer than the algorithm of Liljencrants and Fant (1975), which was based on a stepdown in frequency increment and reversal of its sign after each observed change-of-function sign. The interpolation algorithm is an order of magnitude faster and still provides a superior accuracy over the direct approach of scanning the function at small intervals, for example, 20 Hz and performing one interpolation only.

The gross-step frequency increment ΔF must be chosen smaller than the anticipated distance between any two formants. A reduction of the size of ΔF from 400 Hz to 200 Hz demands 37 runs instead of 30 and $\Delta F = 100$ demands 57 runs. The relatively modest increase relates to the increased accuracy of the first interpolation in a formant region. I would recommend the choice of $\Delta F = 200$ Hz as a general routine. If accuracy demands are extreme, one could select a smaller threshold for the last frequency step, for example, 0.1 Hz instead of 1 Hz in part 7. The cost is, on the average, three extra runs only for the total of five formants, which indicates a high degree of convergence. The probable error becomes an order of magnitude smaller than the threshold for terminating the interpolation.

It is important to ensure that the tabulation of the area functions of Fant (1960:115) is correctly interpreted. The first row at $x = 0$ does not pertain to an elementary section and should be discarded to ensure a correct length representation. It simply specifies the area at the assumed radiating plane, while the first section is that of $x = 0.5$ cm. A prolongation with an $x = 0$ section would cause F_3 of [i] to decrease by about 200 Hz. Table 5.1 is a tabulation of the five first-formant frequencies of the Russian vowels derived from the loss-less model.

Table 5.1

FORMANT FREQUENCIES OF RUSSIAN VOWELS DERIVED FROM LOSS-LESS MODEL

	u	o	a	e	i	ɨ
F_1	237	504	640	419	227	289
F_2	600	866	1082	1967	2275	1518
F_3	2383	2389	2464	2790	3070	2412
F_4	3710	3457	3597	3563	3722	3465
F_5	4056	4018	4132	4246	4649	4192

Table 5.2
FORMANT FREQUENCIES OF RUSSIAN VOWELS CORRECTED FOR WALL
EFFECTS

	u	o	a	e	i	ɨ
F_1	304	539	668	460	296	346
F_2	629	887	1099	1976	2282	1530
F_3	2391	2397	2471	2796	3076	2419
F_4	3715	3462	3602	3568	3726	3470
F_5	4060	4022	4136	4250	4652	4196

After correction with the standard formula for wall effects, Eq. (24), we arrive at the modified values shown in Table 5.2.

4.2. Program B

Program B, shown in Figure 5.5, pertains to a 10-section vocal tract model, each section specified by its length and area. These are stored in M01–M10 and M11–M20. The number of sections incorporated is input in M36. The program has two alternative modes. One is initiated by presetting M41 = 1, which opens the route for determination, storage, and printout of the five first formants. The other mode selected by M41 = 2 provides a printout of the log-magnitude transfer function at intervals set by M2F. The imaginary, that is, lossy, part of the transfer function Eq. (31) has been inferred by a bandwidth versus frequency function, Eq. (34), located in part 11 of the program. Bandwidths could be displayed by a printout command, GSBPO, after Min 32 in part 11. The starting point for frequency MIF should not be set to zero but to a small value, for example, 0.01 Hz.

When reducing the tabular data of 0.5 cm interval quantized area functions to a smaller number of sections with in general a greater length, the averaging should be based on $1/A_x$ rather than on A_x values. The procedure will ensure a correct low-frequency behavior. A strength of the model is that there exist no constraints in the choice of the length of a section. This is important for accurately modeling the larynx tube and, thus, preserving a reasonable accuracy in F_4. Length properties at the lip end are also crucial, and a narrow slit between the teeth cannot easily be modeled by a 0.5 cm unit.

One option available in Program B is to include the radiation inductance as a lengthening of tube 1. This is done by setting the radiating area $A_0 = 0$ in MOF and then adding 0.8 times the radius to the length of tube 1. The latter end-correction algorithm changes F_1 and F_2 of the

```
        PROGRAM LIST
        M00-43,F-3F  320steps

1       *** P0
        SAVE invEXE
        FIX9
                    ...005steps

        *** P1
        RAD
        1 Min42
        21 Min38
2       0 Min37
        LBL1
        11 Min29
        1 Min39 Min35
        1 M+37
        MR36 Min00

        MR1F
        PAUSE ÷ 5618 = Min31
3       X 0.8 X ( MRF ÷ π )
        √ = ÷ MR11 = +/-
        Min43

        LBL2
        MR31 X IND MR39 =
        Min28 cos Min26 +
        MR28 sin Min27 X IND
        MR29 X MR43 = Min34
4       X MR35 = Min35
        MR26 - MR34 1/x = ÷
        IND MR29 ÷ MR27 =
        Min43
        1 M+29 M+39
        DSZ GOTO2
```

```
        MR41 - 2 = x=0 GOTO0
        MR41 x=0 GOTO4
        MR42 x=0 GOTO3
5       LBL0
        MR42 x=0 GOTO4
        0 Min42
        GSBP2
        GOTO8

        LBL3
        MR33 X MR35 = +/-
6       x≥0 GOTO4
        GBSP2
        GOTO8

        LBL4
        ( MR35 - MR33 ) ÷ (
        MR1F - MR3F ) =
        Min30
7       MR41 - 2 = x=0 GOTO9
        MR30 ÷ MR35 =1/x
        +/- Min40 ABS - 1 =
        x≥0 GOTO5
        GOTO6

        LBL5
        0 Min41
8       GSBP2
        MR40 M+1F GOTO1

        LBL6
        MR40 + MR1F = IND
        Min38
        PAUSE
9       PAUSE FIX1
        GSBP0
        1 M+38 Min41 Min42
        MR38 - 26 = x=0
        HLT
```

Figure 5.5 Program B. Ten-tube representation of the vocal tract. Preselect M41 = 1 for calculation of formant frequencies and M42 = 2 for calculation of log magnitude of transfer function with losses introduced from bandwidth versus frequency subroutine in 11.

```
        LBL8
10      MR2F M+1F GOTO1
        LBL9

        MR1F FIX0
        GSBP0
11      ÷ 500 = Min32 x² × 2
        + MR32 √ × 20 + MR32
        1/x x² × 15 = Min32

        × MR30 ÷ 2 = x² +
        MR35 x² = log × 10
12      +/- =
        PAUSE FIX1
        GSBP0

        MR1F - 4500 = x≥0
        HLT
13      GSBP2
        GOTO8
                    •••303steps

        *** P2
        MR35 Min33
        MR1F Min3F
14                  •••008steps

        *** P3
                    •••001steps


MEMORY LIST
M00-43,F-3F 320steps

    M00=        0,
    M01=        1,          1₁
    M02=        0,5
    M03=        1,
    M04=        3,5
    M05=        0,5
    M06=        0,5
    M07=        1,
    M08=        6,5
    M09=        1,          1₉
    M0F=        4,          A₀
```

M10=	1,	l_{10}
M11=	3,6	A_1
M12=	1,6	
M13=	1,15	
M14=	0,65	
M15=	1,3	
M16=	2,6	
M17=	5,	
M18=	10,	
M19=	2,	A_9
M1F=	4591,191376	F
M20=	2,9	A_{10}
M21=	224,8625227	
M22=	2201,27574	
M23=	3022,009159	F_n
M24=	3778,099883	
M25=	4591,186979	
M26=	0,684244739	
M27=	0,72925245	
M28=	0,817228796	
M29=	21,	Ind A
M2F=	400,	ΔF

```
M30= -2,23582837E-03
M31= 0,817228796
M32= 35,20550033
M33= 0,014651214
M34=  -2,0454446E-05
M35= -9,82985052E-06
M36=        10,          nr sections
M37=        29,          runs
M38=        26,
M39=        11,          Ind 1
M3F= 4584,634055

M40=  -4,3965139E-03
M41=        1,
M42=        1,
M43= 23117,58493
```

F_n	
224,9	F_1
2201,3	F_2
3022,0	F_3
3778,1	F_4
4591,2	F_5

Figure 5.5 *(continued)*

vowels [a] and [i] by less than 1 Hz, while F_3 and F_4 are lowered by less than 27 Hz. In case of the neutral single tube resonator of effective length 17.65 cm and 6 cm² cross-sectional area, the difference is 0 Hz in F_1, -2 Hz in F_2, -11 Hz in F_3, -28 Hz in F_4, and -44 in F_5. The correct handling of the radiation impedance as a lumped-element termination becomes important when incorporating losses. In the frequency range above 4000 Hz one should also include a frequency-dependent modification of the radiation inductance.

4.3. Program C

We now proceed to a test of the algorithm for calculating five formant frequencies from the input impedance of the vocal tract as seen from the glottis, as in Eq. (35). The program is shown in Figure 5.6. This is achieved in P1 after which we may call P2 to calculate formant bandwidths in part 9 and then to calculate the log magnitude of the volume velocity transfer function in 12 by means of the standard frequency domain synthesis including the correction for higher poles, 13. By consistent use of indirect addressing, the program becomes compact. The central core of the recursive operation is contained in 3.

Because of limited memory space, the maximum number of tube sections, M03, has been set to five. Length and area are stored in M11–M15 and M21–M25. Observe that l_1 should be the effective length, end correction included. Calculated formant frequencies are stored in M31–M35 and bandwidths in M25–M30.

The interpolation procedure for finding formant frequencies now becomes more tricky. The linear estimation in part 6 is performed on the inverse of the impedance to find its zero points. When a pole comes close to a zero, there is a risk that the pole will be skipped or that the interpolation never converges. The situation may be improved somewhat by the following strategy. Pursue the gross steps set by M2F until the current value of the impedance is found to be smaller than the previous value. With sufficiently small steps this should be a sufficient criterion for finding the poles, that is, the infinity points of the impedance. Next test for an additional criterion, the change of sign. If this is not met with, there is apparently both a pole and a zero within the previous frequency step. In that case, 5 avoids faulty function by ordering a half step back in frequency. In spite of this precaution it was found that the gross steps for the vowel [i] should be 200 Hz or smaller. With more critical vocal tract configurations, one might need much smaller gross steps or a more sophisticated search procedure.

This program is about twice as fast as the transfer function Program

B, if the same number of vocal tract sections is employed and if the same number of formants and the same gross step are selected. With a five-section vocal tract and gross frequency steps of 100 Hz, it takes Program C 60 rounds in 3.5 minutes to calculate and to store five formants, while Program B performs the same task in the same time with 400 Hz steps and 29 rounds only. Needless to say, the result is exactly the same within 0.1 Hz, providing Program A is run with end correction instead of lumped radiation inductance. Program A with 33 sections of 0.5 cm performs the same task in eight minutes. Our Eclipse laboratory computer is of the order of 1000 times faster.

The effect of reducing the number of vocal tract sections from ten, as in program A, to five, as in program B, can be seen by inspecting the memory printouts. For the vowel [i], the major difference lies in F_3, which comes out 250 Hz too low in the 5-tube case. This is due to the lack of definition of the curvature in the palatal region. A more effective approach retaining a small number of sections would be to adopt the network analog for horn-shaped structures (Fant 1960: 30). The procedure is similar to that of dealing with the shunting wall impedance. Other vowels, for example, [a], are less sensitive to a reduction of the number of sections.

4.4. Program D

This program is intended for finding the poles of a volume-velocity transfer function when the vocal tract network contains shunting elements such as nasal sinuses or wall impedance branches. In both instances a shunt takes the form of a serial resonance RLC branch. The specific version, documented in Fig. 5.7, takes in ten vocal tract tube sections of which the first six in M01–M06 for length and M11–M16 for area are modeled close to the Fant (1960) nasal-area function and the remainder M07–M10 and M17–M20 are reserved for the pharynx. The combination could represent a velar or palatal nasal consonant. The first nasal shunt is located between sections 3 and 4 and is tuned to 399 Hz. The second one is inserted between sections 4 and 5 and is tuned to 1399 Hz. Each of these, presumably the sinus maxillaries and the sinus frontalis, are in the loss-free case specified by resonance frequencies and cross-sectional entrance area in the connection between the main nasal channel and the sinus with the length of this connection normalized to 1 cm. The length, or rather the length-over-area ratio, can be selected in P2 and P3, part 7.

Part 1 contains initial settings for indirect addressing, 2 the propagation constant and radiation inductance, and 3 the main recurrent updating of

PROGRAM LIST
M00-39,F-3F   352steps

*** P0
          ···001steps

1

*** P1
RAD
6 10^x +/- Min04
0 Min06
1 Min07
31 Min37

LBL1
1 M+16
11 Min36
21 Min01
20 Min02
2

MR1F
PAUSE ÷ MR38 = Min3F
X MR11 = Min05
MR03 - 1 = Min00 x=0
GOTO3

LBL2
1 M+36 M+01 M+02
MR05 tan X IND MR01
3   ÷ IND MR02 = tan^{-1} +
IND MR36 X MR3F =
Min05
DSZ GOTO2

LBL3
MR05 tan Min05
MR07 x=0 GOTO5
4   MR05 - MR04 = x≥0
GOTO6
MR05 X MR04 = x≥0
GOTO4
GOTO5

LBL4
5   MR2F ÷ 2 = M-1F
GOTO1

LBL5
MR1F - MR06 = ÷ (1
- MR05 ÷ MR04) =
Min08
6   0 Min07
MR05 Min04
MR1F Min06
MR08 M-1F ABS - 1 =
x≥0 GOTO1

MR1F IND Min37
GSBP3
MR37 - 35 = x=0
7   HLT
1 M+37
1 Min07
9 10^x +/- Min04
GOTO7

LBL6
MR05 Min04
LBL7
8   MR1F Min06 + MR2F =
Min1F GOTO1
          ···165steps

*** P2
31 Min37
26 MinF
LBL1
IND MR37 ÷ 500 =
9   Min09 1/x x2 X 15 +
MR09 √ X 20 + (2 +
(MR33 - MR32) ÷ (
MR34 - MR33)) X
MR32 ÷ 2000 X MR09
x2 = IND MinF

GSBP3
1 M+37 M+F
10   MR37 - 36 = x=0
GOTO2
GOTO1

Figure 5.6 Program C. Five-section representation of the vocal tract. Select P1 for calculation of formant frequencies from the input impedance (part 3), then select P2 for calculation of log magnitude transfer function from a factorized five-pole synthesis with higher pole correction. Before calling P2, input total vocal tract length in M16. In P1, M16 stores the number of runs.

```
      LBL2                          LBL4
      1 Min05                       MR05 1/x log × 10 =
      MR1F                          Min20
11    GSBP3                         MR1F ÷ 8825 × MR16
      26 MinF                       x² Min36 × MR18 +
      31 Min37                 13   MR19 × MR36 x² = +
                                    MR20 =
      LBL3                          GSBP3
      MR1F ÷ IND MR37 = x²          MR1F - MR39 = x≥0
      Min10                         HLT
      IND MRF x² ÷ IND              MR2F M+1F GOTO2
      MR37 x² = × MR10 + (
12    1 - MR10 ) x² = ×                          •••180steps
      MR05 = Min05
      1 M+F M+37                    *** P3
      MR37 - 36 = x=0          14   FIX2
      GOTO4                         PAUSE
      GOTO3                         SAVE invEXE
                                                 •••006steps
```

MEMORY LIST
M00-39,F-3F 352steps

M00=	0,		M20=	8,040871375	
M01=	25,	Ind A₁	M21=	3,6	A₁
M02=	24,	Ind Aᵢ₋₁	M22=	1,27		
M03=	5,	nr of	M23=	0,75		
M04=	-3759,07054	sections	M24=	8,8		
M05=	1,		M25=	2,4	A₅
M06=	4430,885036		M26=	83,0145024	B₁
M07=	0,		M27=	90,55183075		
M08=	0,04794479		M28=	131,8370644	B₄
M09=	8,861674182		M29=	223,5983271	
M0F=	28,		M2F=	100,	ΔF
M10=	0,		M30=	274,0250136	B₅
M11=	1,9	l₁	M31=	233,549364	F₁
M12=	1,5		M32=	2110,49605	F₂
M13=	4,5		M33=	2777,573517	F₃
M14=	7,5		M34=	3915,916975	F₄
M15=	2,	l₅	M35=	4430,837091	F₅
M16=	60,		M36=	15,	Ind 1
M17=	0,		M37=	32,	runs
M18=	0,433		M38=	5618,17	
M19=	7,1ε-04		M39=	5000,	
M1F=	0,	F	M3F=	0,788670516	

Figure 5.6 (*continued*)

```
PROGRAM LIST
M00-44,F-3F  312steps

*** P0
                ···001steps

*** P1
RAD
1 Min41
21 Min26
LBL1
11 Min29
1 Min39 Min35
MR36 Min00

MR1F
PAUSE ÷ 5618 = Min31
× 0.8 × ( MR11 ÷ π )
√ = ÷ MR11 = +/-
Min40

LBL2
MR31 × IND MR39 =
Min28 cos Min43 +
MR28 sin Min44 × IND
MR29 × MR40 = Min34
× MR35 = Min35
MR43 - MR34 1/x = ÷
IND MR29 ÷ MR44 =
Min40
MR39 - 4 = x=0
GSBP2
MR39 - 3 = x=0
GSBP3
1 M+29 M+39
DSZ GOTO2

MR1F - 4100 = x≥0
HLT
MR35 × ( 1 MR1F x²
÷ MR27 x² ) × ( 1 -
MR1F x₂ ÷ MR30 x² )
= Min35
MR41 x=0 GOTO3
GSBP5
0 Min41 GOTO1
```

```
LBL3
MR35 × MR33 = +/-
x≥0 GOTO4
GSBP5
GOTO1
LBL4
MR35 - MR33 = ÷ (
MR1F - MR3F ) = ÷
MR35 = 1/x +/- M+1F
MR1F FIX0 IND Min26
SAVE invEXE

MR26 - 25 = x=0
HLT
1 M+26
MR2F M+1F
1 Min41 GOTO1
                ···228steps

*** P2
0.2 Min37
MR27 Min42
GSBP4
                ···011steps

*** P3
0.2 Min37
MR30 Min42
GSBP4
                ···011steps

*** P4
MR31 ÷ MR37 × ( 1 -
MR42 x² ÷ MR1F x² )
= 1/x × MR40 +/- + 1
= Min38 × MR35 =
Min35
MR40 ÷ MR38 = Min40
                ···042steps

*** P5
MR35 Min33
MR1F Min3F + MR2F =
Min1F
                ···013steps
```

Left margin numbers: 1, 2, 3, 4, 5, 6, 7, 8, 9

```
MEMORY LIST
M00-44,F-3F 312steps

     M00=          0,
     M01=          2,        lengths:
     M02=          2,
     M03=          2,
     M04=          2,        nose
     M05=          2,5
     M06=          2,
     M07=          7,
     M08=          2,
     M09=          0,        pharynx
     M0F= 8,685889638

     M10=          0,
     M11=          1,5       areas:
     M12=          3,
     M13=          6,
     M14=          6,        nose
     M15=          5,
     M16=          4,
     M17=          4,
     M18=          2,        pharynx
     M19=          0,
     M1F= 318,4653678
```

```
     M20=          0,
     M21=        268,        P₁
     M22=        478,
     M23=       1077,               poles
     M24=       1463,
     M25=       2098,        P₅
     M26=         25,
     M27=       1399,        zero
     M28= 0,113373217
     M29=         11,
     M2F=         50,

     M30=        399,        zero
     M31= 0,056686608
     M32=  0,37299246
     M33= 0,077964437
     M34=  0,9900351
     M35=  0,9900351
     M36=          8,
     M37=        0,2
     M38= 0,709529364
     M39=          1,
     M3F=        250,

     M40= -0,02089055
     M41=          1,
     M42=       1399,
     M43= 0,993580137
     M44= 0,113130499
```

Figure 5.7 (*continued*)

flow and impedance along a section including a shunt if specified by address to P2 and P3 and, finally, to P4 in 8, which contains the subroutine for flow and impedance change across a shunt. The only zeros that can exist in the nasal output under the prescribed conditions are the short-circuiting resonance frequencies of the nasal sinuses. In 4 these are removed by frequency domain division (inverse filtering).

The interpolation procedure in 5, LBL4, is for simplicity limited to a single estimate once a reversal of sign is found. For a reasonable accuracy of the order of 1–2 Hz, this implies a rather small size recurrent frequency step of the order of M2F = 20–50 Hz. The memory space reserved for five pole frequencies, M21–M25, is no limitation for calculating higher poles, which can be printed out or stored in a second round of the

Figure 5.7 Program D. Six-section representation of the nasal tract including two sinuses coupled to a pharynx of max four sections. Resonance frequencies estimated by one interpolation only.

Table 5.3

RESONANCE FREQUENCIES OF VELAR–PALATAL NASALS. A. $A_{S1} = A_{S2} =$ 0.2 cm^2; B. $A_{S1} = A_{S2} = 0.1$ cm^2; C. Same as A but the locations of shunts are reversed; D. Same as A but both shunts are inserted at x = 6 cm; E. Velo-pharyngeal port A_6 narrowed to 0.1 cm^2, otherwise as A; F. Same as C, but $A_7 = 6$ cm^2; G. Pharynx constricted in the middle, otherwise as A: $l_7 = l_9 = l_{10} = 2$ cm, $l_8 =$ 3 cm, $A_7 = A_9 = 4$ cm^2, $A_8 = A_{10} = 2$ cm^2; H. Fujimura–Lindqvist subject for comparison; I. Nasal system alone, $A_6 = 0$.

pole	A	B	C	D	E	F	G	H	I
1	268	294	260	269	197	257	273	250	297
2	478	451	497	479	310	453	490	520	672
3	1077	1077	1052	1066	697	1086	1023	1100	1449
4	1462	1431	1476	1472	1451	1469	1448	1500	2496
5	2098	2094	2106	2114	2175	2159	1931	1900	4064
6	2954	2944	2950	2975	2505	2965	3004	2700	
7	3740	3733	3740	3741	4015	3818	3877	3700	
							3955		

complete program. In general, because of the high density of poles in nasal sounds, one needs at least seven.

The model has been quantified for a maximal fit with the Fujimura–Lindqvist sweep frequency analysis of nasal consonants (Lindqvist & Sundberg 1972). The first four poles generated by our model depart less than 50 Hz from the life data.

In Table 5.3 some results obtained with the pocket calculator are shown.

A tentative evaluation suggests that the poles 2, 3, and 4 may be described as nasal, while poles 1, 5, and 6 are more associated with the entire system. It remains to study the nasal model as a shunt inserted in the oral system and vice versa and to add the nasal and oral branches to arrive at a complete model. The logical procedure is to isolate the all-pole function and then determine each of the nasal and oral output zero functions and, finally, inverse filter the mixed output with the all-pole function to arrive at the zero function of the mixture.

REFERENCES

Badin, P. & Fant, G. (1984). Notes on vocal tract computation. *Speech Transmission Laboratory Quarterly Progress and Status Report, 2–3,* 53–108.

Fant, G. (1960). *Acoustic theory of speech production.* The Hague: Mouton.

Fant, G. (1972). Vocal tract wall effects, losses, and resonance bandwidths. *Speech Transmission Laboratory Quarterly Progress and Status Report, 2–3,* 28–52.

Fant, G., Nord, L., & Branderud, P. (1976). A note on the vocal tract wall impedance. *Speech Transmission Laboratory Quarterly Progress and Status Report, 4,* 13–20.

Fujimura, O., & Lindqvist, J. (1971). Sweep-tone measurements of the vocal tract characteristics. *Journal of the Acoustical Society of America, 49*, 541–558.

Liljencrants, J., Fant, G. (1975). Computer program for VT-resonance frequency calculations. *Speech Transmission Laboratory Quarterly Progress and Status Report, 4*, 15–20.

Lindqvist, J., & Sundberg, J. (1972). Acoustic properties of the nasal tract. *Speech Transmission Laboratory Quarterly Progress and Status Report, 1*, 13–17.

Wakita, H., & Fant, G. (1978). Toward a better vocal tract model. *Speech Transmission Laboratory Quarterly Progress and Status Report, 1*, 9–29.

6

Some Basic Vowel Features, Their Articulatory Correlates, and Their Explanatory Power in Phonology*

Eli Fischer-Jørgensen

1. INTRODUCTION

For the description and explanation of universal constraints and tendencies in phonological patterns and phonological change, one needs detailed models of speech production and speech perception. It is also necessary to have a general frame of reference in the form of a system of more abstract phonetic dimensions according to which the speech sounds of a language can be grouped into classes. These dimensions, which, according to a now generally accepted but not quite unambiguous terminology, are also called features and which can be considered potentially distinctive, must not only have correlation to speech production and speech perception, but also be adequate for the description of phonological patterns and rules.

In this chapter I consider only vowel features, and only some basic articulatory features that have been the subject of debate in recent years, that is, vowel height (or degree of openness), position from front to back, and tenseness.

2. CRITICISM OF THE TRADITIONAL SYSTEM

Since the days of Bell and Sweet it has been the tradition to describe vowel systems by means of the basic features high–low, front–back,

* This paper is a revised and enlarged version of my contribution to the Phonetic Explanation in Phonology symposium at the Tenth Congress of Phonetic Sciences, Utrecht, 1983. The phonetic discussion, in particular, is more detailed in this chapter.

PHONETIC LINGUISTICS

rounded–unrounded, and, for some languages, tense–lax. This system, which was defined in articulatory terms, has been severely criticized for not covering the articulatory facts.

As early as 1910 E. A. Meyer found that lax [ɪ] may have a lower tongue position than generally assumed; for example, North German [ɪ] is often lower than [e:]. G. O. Russell (1928, 1936) attacked the traditional system of classical phonetics on the basis of a large number of x-ray photos, particularly of American English but also of German and French. He found that often the tongue position was not as one should expect: [ɪ] might, for example, be lower than [e], and for the back vowels there were great discrepancies. For [ɒ], [ɔ] and [ɑ] the point of articulation was rather in the pharynx, whereas [u] might almost be a front vowel. On the whole, the importance of the pharynx cavity for vowel sounds had not been realized. He did not have much influence, though, perhaps because of his very aggressive tone. He called listening to speakers' sounds and then recording them in terms of their physiological character "a wildly unscientific absurdity," and he characterized the traditional physiological dimensions (particularly high–low) as purely imaginary.

The criticism was renewed by Peter Ladefoged (1962, 1971, 1975, 1976). Like Russell, he maintained that Bell, Sweet, and their followers had described their auditory impressions but translated them into physiological terms and that these did not correspond to physiological reality. He showed, among other things, that in the x-ray photos of Stephen Jones' cardinal vowels [o] and [ɔ] were lower than front [a], whereas [ɑ] was still lower, as far as the highest point of the tongue is concerned. On the whole, high vowels do not all have the same height ([u] often being lower than [i]), and [u] is often advanced compared to [o]. Ladefoged, DeClerk, Lindau, and Papçun (1972) also found a rather large individual variation in the articulation of front tense and lax vowels in American English. Ladefoged finds a much closer agreement between traditional vowel descriptions and acoustic facts. As an example he compares H. J. Uldall's placement of the Danish vowels in Jones' cardinal vowel chart and a plot of the formant frequencies of Danish vowels, height corresponding to the frequency of F_1, and front–back to the difference between the first and second formant (Ladefoged 1976). Joos (1948) made a similar observation, comparing Jones' cardinal vowel chart with both Holbrook and Carmody's x-ray vowel quadrilateral and an acoustic chart of French vowels and finding a greater similarity in the latter case. But this is not so astonishing, since Jones' cardinal vowels (apart from [i] and [ɑ]) were based on auditory impressions of equal distances.

Nearey (1978), who has analyzed the vowels of three American English speakers, also emphasizes that individual variation is more pronounced in articulation than in the acoustic pattern and that the traditional vowel features are more closely related to the acoustic aspect.

The most severe attack on the classical vowel system has been made by Sidney Wood (1975b, 1982), based on an analysis of 38 sets of x-ray photos of 15 different languages. He found that [ɪ] and [ʊ] are often lower than [e] and [o] and that the height relations between [o, ɔ] and [a, ɑ] are random. He also emphasizes that the classical system neglects the pharynx cavity completely and thus cannot account adequately for the relations between vowel production and vowel acoustics and that there is no clear relation between the dimensions front–back and high–low and the function of the muscles. He concludes that the model is not only inaccurate but irrelevant to the processes of speech production, that it is a complete illusion and must be rejected and replaced by a new model.

3. A LESS CRITICAL VIEW OF THE CLASSICAL SYSTEM

I agree with Catford (1981) that the criticism of the classical system is exaggerated. In the first place, even when accepting the premises of the critics, for example, that the classical system describes the position of the highest point of the tongue, many x-ray photos show a quite good agreement with the traditional description, as shown for instance by Lindau (1978) for five American English speakers. Ladefoged's own vowels, which he quotes (1976) as an example of bad agreement, are not too bad either. Nobody has ever claimed that all high vowels should have the same height or that front or back vowels of different height should lie on one vertical line. For front vowels it is evident that the lower vowels are normally gradually retracted, and the fact that many languages have a somewhat advanced [u] does not invalidate the general classification. Further, Ladefoged's worst example (Stephen Jones' cardinal vowels) (Ladefoged 1971) should not be given too much weight. The x-ray photos were taken in 1929, at a time when the technique was much less advanced than today, the subject had a chain lying along the surface of his tongue and another chain through his nose hanging down behind the uvula (Catford 1981), and, moreover, I have been told that he had all the teeth on one side of his mouth extracted in order to get nice pictures! It is, of course, laudable that he suffered so much for science, but his discomfort hardly contributed to the naturalness of his pronunciation.

In the second place, some of the more serious criticisms raised by

Ladefoged and Wood lose their force when it is realized that they are mainly objections against Daniel Jones' cardinal vowel chart, which was meant as a practical device for fieldwork and not as a theoretical vowel system and which differs from the classical system at various points. As mentioned above, it was in the first place an auditory chart, but both Jones himself and his pupils also tended to interpret it physiologically in the sense that it indicated the position of the highest point of the tongue. Ladefoged (1971: 67) says that for the past hundred years vowels have been described in terms of the highest point of the tongue. But I do not think this is correct. Catford (1977, 1981) states that neither Bell nor Sweet used the term. He is not sure about their followers, since Jespersen mentions it as a current term in 1889. But Jespersen does not use the phrase "highest point of the tongue." He talks about the highest "part of the tongue." What he discusses is whether one should talk about tongue height or (as he and many others preferred) about the distance from the palate. As far as I can see, none of the founders of classical phonetics mentions the highest point of the tongue, neither Jespersen, nor Sievers, nor Viëtor, nor Passy, nor Storm. They therefore often use the terms "degree of openness" or "distance" instead of "height." The same is true of their followers on the European continent with the exception of some more recent works influenced by Jones. It seems to be a particular British tradition introduced by Jones in *The Pronunciation of English* in 1909 (not in his *Outline of English Phonetics* in 1918, as I have stated previously [Fischer-Jørgensen 1983]). It is an attempt at a more precise description, but the highest point of the tongue is rather variable and a much too precise concept to be used in a general vowel system. What is implied in the classical system is the distinction between an advanced and a retracted tongue body (sometimes including a central position) and the overall distance between the articulating part (front or back or central) and the palate.

Similarly, the fact that for example, English [ɪ] and [ʊ] are often lower than [e] and [o] is primarily an argument against Jones' placement of the former vowels above [e] and [o] in the vowel chart. It is true that nothing in the system prevents placement of a relatively low American English [ɪ] below [e] as Catford (1981) remarks. What is disturbing is that they are placed sometimes above and sometimes below [e] and [o] for different speakers. The cause of the trouble is that Jones did not like to recognize tenseness as a separate vowel dimension but preferred to describe [ɪ] as a lowered and retracted [i] and [ʊ] as a lowered and less rounded [u]. If tenseness is recognized as a separate dimension, then [ɪ] and [ʊ] are simply the highest lax vowels and their exact relation to [e] and [o] is not relevant. This is the position taken by various phoneticians within the classical tradition. The height of [ɪ] and [ʊ] thus cannot be used to criticize the traditional vowel system as such.

The attitude to this dimension has, however, also been somewhat hesitating within classical phonetics. One reason is probably that Bell's description was evidently wrong. He used the terminology "primary versus wide" and thought that the wide (e.g., lax) vowels have a retracted soft palate and an expansion of the pharynx. Sweet, who used the terminology narrow–wide, explained the difference as depending on the shape of the tongue, which is more convex in narrow (tense) vowels and more flattened and relaxed in wide (lax) vowels. The narrowing is thus not the result of raising the whole body of the tongue with the help of the jaw as in [i] versus [e] but of bunching up the part with which the sound is formed. Thus, in passing from [i] to [e], one does not go via [ɪ]. This description is much more to the point, but it was not generally accepted. Jespersen (e.g., 1897–1899, 1914) gave a somewhat different formulation: He described the difference as a thinner versus broader channel between the articulating part of the tongue and the palate, which did not necessarily involve a generally lower tongue position. Others emphasized muscle tension as the decisive difference (e.g., Sievers 1901), and the difference is now generally called tense–lax. Almost all British phoneticians have followed Jones in not recognizing tense–lax as an independent dimension, whereas a good number of Scandinavian, German, and Dutch phoneticians have accepted the distinction. The difference is also clearer in German and Dutch than in English, where all vowels are relatively lax but where the difference is at least clear for high vowels. But it is true that many phoneticians found E. A. Meyer's (1910) and Russell's (1928) findings that [ɪ y ʊ] often had a lower tongue position than [e ø o] disturbing because they are generally perceived as auditorily closer to [i y u]. This auditory impression may be caused partly by the fact that [ɪ y ʊ] in German, for example, are the highest lax vowels and thus systematically high and partly by orthography; Danish listeners described German [ɪ y ʊ] cut out of words and presented in isolation as close to Danish [ɛː œ ɔː] (Fischer-Jørgensen 1973).

The tense–lax distinction has been widely accepted in modern phonology. The definitions given by Jakobson and Halle (1956) and by Chomsky and Halle (1968) are based on the idea of a difference of muscular tension leading to a greater deviation from the neutral position of the vocal tract. The terms tense–lax have also been applied to the difference that is at the basis of vowel harmony in a number of West African languages. Ladefoged (1964) uses this terminology (though only as a tentative label), but at the same time he shows that the decisive difference, at least in Igbo, lies in an advancement or retraction of the tongue root. Halle and

Stevens (1969) think that this is also the main characteristic of the tense–lax difference found in, for example, the Germanic languages, and they therefore propose to use the term "advanced tongue root" in both cases. However, Stewart (1967), Ladefoged *et al.* (1972), and Lindau, Jacobson, and Ladefoged (1972) showed that these features should not be confounded (see also Lindau 1978, who proposes to call the African feature "expansion"). Whereas the tongue root movement is really an independent feature in various African languages, it is not consistent and is closely related to tongue-height differences in English. The two features are also different acoustically (see the acoustic graphs of African languages in Lindau *et al.* 1972 and the graphs of German in Jørgensen 1969). Finally, expansion does not have the close relation to length generally found for tense–lax. Since the articulatory correlates of the tense–lax difference in English seem to vary according to speakers (Ladefoged *et al.* 1972), Ladefoged (1975) proposes to define the difference in purely distributional terms (lax vowels being those that do not occur in open syllables), whereas Lindau (1978) gives an acoustic definition (peripheral vs. central).

More recently Wood (1975a, 1982) has undertaken an extensive investigation of the articulatory characteristics of tense and lax vowels in a number of languages. He finds that in various languages [i] and [ɪ] have approximately the same jaw opening, whereas for [e] and [ɛ] it is lower; conversely [i] and [e] have approximately the same tongue bunching, whereas [ɪ] and [ɛ] have a flattened tongue. There are exceptions; the six informants investigated by Ladefoged *et al.* (1972) all have the distinction in jaw opening described by Wood, but only three have a clear difference in tongue lift. On the whole, however, the tendency is very clear (see also Fischer-Jørgensen 1973). The same tendencies also appear from the measurements of jaw opening for Dutch vowels by Zwaardemaker and Eijkman (1928) and Kaiser (1941) and, for example, in x-ray photos of Telugu taken by Nagamana Reddy, which I had occasion to see. Thus, whether [ɪ] is lower or higher than [e] is a more accidental consequence of the relative extent of the two movements involved (tongue flattening and jaw opening), but at any rate [ɪ] has less constriction than [i] at the place of articulation. Wood states that this is true of all other lax vowels compared to their tense counterparts, with the exception of [o/ɔ]. At the same time lax vowels have a narrower pharynx cavity (except for tense [ɑ] versus lax [a]) and less pronounced lip activity. Wood (1975a) has shown through synthesis that these different factors may be of different acoustical importance. It is clear, however, that they can all be regarded as consequences of one single difference: tense versus lax articulation, the latter involving a flattening of the tongue, which is closely connected with less space in the pharynx as well as less jaw opening and less pronounced lip activity. There exist few EMG recordings of the muscular tension, and only American English has been investigated. There seems to be a clear difference in the tension of the genioglossus (Smith & Hirano 1968; Raphael & Bell-Berti 1975; Alfonso & Baer 1981; Alfonso, Honda, Baer, & Harris 1982) and of the inferior longitudinal (Raphael & Bell-Berti 1975), whereas there are contradicting results for the styloglossus for [u/ʊ]. (EMG recordings of German and Dutch vowels would be an obvious task for the future.)

It thus seems clear that tenseness (which is often, but not always, combined with length) is an independent vowel dimension. Height should therefore be indicated separately for tense and lax vowels.

The most serious objection to the traditional height dimension seems to be the irregular height relations between back vowels, as described by Wood (1975b). However, as in the preceding cases, this is primarily disturbing for Jones' cardinal vowel system, where the unrounded back vowel [ɑ] is placed in the same column as the rounded vowels [u o ɔ] because, in many languages, [ɑ] is the only low back vowel, whereas the higher back vowels are generally rounded. But from the point of view of a general system of vowel features, [ɑ] does not belong in this series but in the series of unrounded back vowels [ɯ ɤ ʌ ɑ]. Thus the fact that [o] and [ɔ] may be lower is only crucial if height is taken to be an absolute property, not if it is taken to be a relative property within each series of rounded and unrounded, front and back vowels, a view that would be in accordance with Jakobson's conception of distinctive features.

Thus, if tenseness is considered a separate dimension and height is taken to mean the relative distance between the articulating part of the tongue and the palate within each of the series of rounded or unrounded, tense or lax, front or back vowels, most of the inconsistencies between these traditional labels and the articulatory facts disappear.

What remains of the criticism is that the pharynx cavity, which could not be observed when the classical system was set up, has been neglected. The description does not take account of the fact that the most narrow constriction for [a] and [ɑ] and generally for [o ɔ] is in the pharynx, and as degree and place of constriction in the total vocal tract are essential for the calculation of the acoustic output, the classical system is not the most adequate starting point for such calculations. It is true that, since there are strong constraints on the possible positions of the tongue body (e.g., a low back vowel necessarily has a narrow pharynx and a high front vowel a wide pharynx), it has been possible to set up correlations between the features of the classical system and formant frequencies, but the causal relations are not clear if the pharynx is not taken into account.

Wood also argues that the connection between vowel articulation and muscle activity becomes much clearer in a model based on constriction place than in the traditional model. This is not quite convincing. The relations are complicated in either case (for the relation between muscle activity and the traditional dimensions, see Catford 1977:186; Halle 1982).

4. NEW FEATURE SYSTEMS

It is evident that models of vowel production must be based on these later insights, that is, they must take account of constrictions in the total vocal tract. And it is possible to construct new feature systems that are connected more closely to these new models.

However, phoneticians do not agree on the number of constriction places. Catford (1977) tentatively sets up six places, but he does not find this very useful for the description of vowel systems. Lindblom and Sundberg's model of vowel production (1969, 1971) is based on place and degree of constriction, jaw position, width and height of lip opening, and larynx height. They set up three places of constriction: palatal [i e ɛ], velar [u], and pharyngeal [o a ɑ]. Tongue height is a derived parameter, controlled by means of both jaw position and tongue raising relative to the jaw. In optimal articulation jaw and tongue go together, but there may be compensations. In the 1969 paper, a system of binary features is based on this model and applied to the Swedish vowels. It contains the features ± palatal, velar, pharyngeal, close, open, and labial. It is not, however, mentioned in later publications, and I therefore do not discuss it in detail.

Wood operates with four places of constriction: the hard palate, the soft palate, the upper pharynx, and the lower pharynx. There are thus four categories of vowels: palatals (all front vowels except [æ]), velars ([u] and [ʊ]), velopharyngeals ([o] and [ɔ]), and low pharyngeals ([æ a ɑ]). Wood stipulates four separate places of constriction, not a continuum, thus denying the existence of central vowels. His arguments are partly empirical (the analysis of x-ray photos from many languages), partly theoretical: These are the places where the spectrum is relatively insensitive to moderate displacement according to Stevens' quantal theory and Fant's nomograms. He also adduces sound typology (Wood 1982:72), pointing to the fact that languages with only three vowel phonemes generally use the three places mentioned by Stevens (/i a u/), and if there are five phonemes the normal type is /i ɛ a ɔ u/. But he does not mention that in languages with four vowel phonemes it is extremely rare to find his four basic vowel types /i u o a/, the most common types being /i u a/ plus /ɛ/ or /ɨ/ (see e.g., Crothers 1978). The typological argument is thus very weak.

In Wood's system the tense vowels [i u o ɑ] may have lax counterparts with less constriction [ɪ ʊ ɔ a]. Moreover, the jaw may be close or open. This adds a distinction to palatal vowels, [e] and [ɛ] being the open counterparts to [i] and [ɪ]. The palatovelar vowels are considered to be (redundantly) close, the pharyngeal vowels (redundantly) open. Finally, vowels may be rounded or unrounded.

On this basis he sets up a binary feature system (Wood 1982:168):

constriction	palatal	palatovelar	pharyngovelar	low pharyngeal
vowel	i ɪ e ɛ	u ʊ	o ɔ	ɑ a
palatal	+ + + +	+ +	− −	− −
velar	− − − −	+ +	+ +	− −
pharyngeal	− − − −	− −	+ +	+ +
open	− − + +	− −	+ +	+ +
round	− − − −	+ +	+ +	(−) −
tense	+ − + −	+ −	+ −	+ −

He does not comment on this table. Evidently it has been a problem to translate a place dimension with four places into a binary feature system. This has the consequence that he has had to call his velar place palatovelar, and his upper pharyngeal place velopharyngeal, which conceals the quantal point of view. It would have been more in keeping with his own description to set up a multivalued dimension with four steps.

It may also be argued that the place of constriction is just as variable as the highest point of the tongue. Front vowels may have their maximal constriction at the alveolar ridge (Straka 1978 even calls the French palatals alveopalatals, or simply alveolars). An [o] may have its maximum constriction at the velum, at the uvula, or in the pharynx, depending on such factors as the shape of the individual palate and the position of the velum. But Wood (1982:142) is aware of this, saying that ''place of maximal constriction'' is ambiguous in natural speech. What matters is the direction of the tongue-body movement. Even with this precaution one may sometimes doubt. In Danish [o:] and [ɔ:] the main direction of the movement seems to be towards the soft palate, although they have at the same time a narrower pharynx compared to [u] (see Figure 6.1). Danish [o:] is very close, and it might perhaps be described as an *u*-like vowel. This would require a step ''open'' for velar vowels.

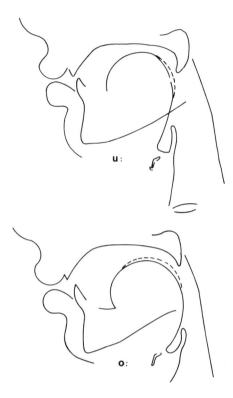

Figure 6.1   Tracings of X-ray photos of Danish [u:] and [o:], said in isolation.

5. THE USEFULNESS OF THE TRADITIONAL FEATURE SYSTEM AND WOOD'S SYSTEM IN PHONOLOGICAL DESCRIPTIONS

A feature system based on constriction place may come closer to a model for vowel production (but it seems rather difficult to translate it into a two- or three-dimensional figure resembling the formant chart); but as stated in the introduction, a feature system should also be usable in phonological descriptions, and Wood expressly emphasizes that his model has more explanatory power in this respect than the traditional system. For this purpose, however, I find the classical system clearly superior.

Wood only allows for two steps in vowel height (or openness), and for the back vowels the traditional height differences are partly reinterpreted as difference of place. But there are many languages with three degrees of openness, and Danish even has four (/i e ɛ æ/). Wood considers [æ] a pharyngeal vowel, and it therefore must be distinguished by a different feature from /ɑ/, which is probably a separate phoneme in Advanced Standard Copenhagen (Basbøll 1972). According to his practice for English, Wood must then describe Danish /æ/ as lax. The same must be done for /ɛ œ ɔ/, both in Danish and in languages with similar systems. But there is no justification for describing Danish /ɛ œ ɔ æ/ as lax (apart from the fact that a certain laxing is normally combined with lowering). Danish has both long and short vowels with, in most cases, almost the same quality. In the series /i e ɛ æ/ there is a gradual lowering of the tongue height (as can be seen in x-ray photos and palatograms) and generally a gradual lowering of the jaw, which appeared in a recording of jaw opening for three Danish informants. With the exception of e/ɛ for one of the informants, all differences were significant (the data will be published later). This speaks against considering any of the vowels as lax. As for Swedish, Lindau (1978) quotes a case of diphthongization in the Swedish Skåne dialect that can only be formulated in a simple way on the basis of four degrees of openness. The English vowel shift also requires more degrees of openness to describe the diphthongization of /i: u:/, the development of /e: o:/ to /i: u:/, of /ɛ: ɔ:/ to /e: o:/, and of /a:/ via /æ:/ to /e:/.

Now this might be partly remedied by adding more steps to the close–open dimension without changing the rest of the system, but in phonological rules /a/ does not go with /e ø o/ as it should according to Wood's feature system, where it has the same degree of openness. It behaves like a lower vowel. There are, for example, languages where /e: ø: o:/ are diphthongized to /iə yə uə/, whereas /a:/ is not diphthongized, as in Old High German.

There are also a number of well-known universal phonetic tendencies connected with vowel height. Low vowels are longer than high vowels; they are pronounced on a lower pitch and have more intensity. These differences are gradual: [a] is longer than [ɛ], [ɛ] than [e], [e] than [i]. Similar tendencies exist for pitch and intensity. It is not a difference between two categories: high and low. These differences are generally not perceived, but when Danish speakers are asked to adjust synthetic vowels to an appropriate length and to find the boundary between short and long vowels, they make [ɛ] longer than [i], and they place the boundary at a lower value for [i–i:] than for [ɛ–ɛ:] (Petersen 1974). These are phonetic differences, but they may turn up in historical developments, so that long high vowels become short vowels (e.g., in Dutch), or short low vowels are lengthened (e.g., English /æ/).

However, it is possible to quote one example where [ɑ o ø e] go together and behave as one class. In French there are common rules of lengthening and distribution for [ɑ o ø] and (partly) /e/ versus /a ɔ œ ɛ/. This induced Thorsen (Thorsen, Jensen, & Landschultz 1971) to describe /a ɑ/ not as low vowels but as pharyngeal vowels. The common property for /ɑ o ø e/ versus /a ɔ œ ɛ/ was then described as a more close timbre versus a more open timbre, later called tense versus lax. I wonder, however, whether it is correct phonetically to call French /a ɔ œ ɛ/ lax vowels. They do not sound lax to me. Wood (1982: 139) found the tongue to be lower relative to the mandible in French /ɛ/ than in [e] in three sets, but the jaw is also more open, and in Straka's x-ray pictures (1950) /ɛ œ ɔ/ have a larger jaw opening than /e ø o/, whereas /a/ has a slightly smaller opening than /ɑ/. In the case of the low pharyngeal vowels it is difficult to judge tenseness on the basis of the constriction, because two conflicting tendencies are at work: (1) a narrower constriction at the point of articulation (i.e., the pharynx) in tense vowels, and (2) a narrower pharynx in the lax vowels. Wood considers [ɑ] as generally tense. This is probably true of German, where it is long as are other tense vowels, but in Dutch it is the front [a] that is long.

The French example can be considered to support Wood. But in all the other cases mentioned we need the traditional height dimension where [a ɑ] are the lowest vowels.

As for the use of four places of constriction, it makes the formulation of various phonological rules and developments rather complicated. In Germanic umlaut, back vowels are changed to front vowels before an /i/ in the following syllable (and /ɑ/ is also raised). In Finnish and Turkish vowel harmony, back vowels are changed to front vowels after front vowels. These rules can only be formulated very clumsily in terms of four places of articulation. The same is true of the allophonic fronting of back vowels in palatal surroundings in Russian.

There are, however, a few cases where the feature pharyngeal for vowels might perhaps give a simpler and more explanatory formulation, for example, in the cases of assimilation of vowels to pharyngeal or uvular consonants, as found in Greenlandic before /ʁ/ and /q/, where /i u a/ ([i u æ]) become [æ ɒ ɑ] (as mentioned by Wood). However, as [æ], which becomes [ɑ] in this position, is considered to be pharyngeal beforehand, but not [i] and [u], the formulation will not be simple. The same reasoning is valid for the ʁ-coloring of Danish vowels (described by Basbøll 1972 and by Basbøll & Kristensen 1975). Perhaps it is just as acceptable to say that vowels may be retracted and lowered before pharyngeal consonants (see also the discussion of front–back and high–

low in relation to Danish [æ–ɑ] in Basbøll 1984 and Fischer-Jørgensen 1984).

This raises the more general problem of the utility of having common features for vowels and consonants whereby assimilations between vowels and consonants could be formulated in a more explanatory way. Jakobson's features grave–acute and compact–diffuse were not satisfactory in this respect. But instead of using traditional consonantal features for the vowels, the goal may also be reached by using the traditional vocalic features for consonants, as was done by Chomsky and Halle (1968) (see the discussion in Fischer-Jørgensen 1975:230ff) and Halle (1982). Ladefoged (1971) proposes to specify both consonants and vowels as high–low, front–back and in terms of place of articulation (palatal, velar, pharyngeal). This seems somewhat complicated. But it might be possible to call the vowel front–back dimension palatal–nonpalatal, and use non-palatal as a cover term for velar, upper pharyngeal (or uvular), and lower pharyngeal. One might then use the specification in the (rather few) cases where it seems adequate.

The general conclusion of this discussion is that we cannot do without the traditional classical dimensions front–back and high–low.

6. THE AUDITORY INTERPRETATION OF THE DIMENSIONS HIGH–LOW AND FRONT–BACK

Russell, Ladefoged, and Wood agree in the assumption that the dimensions high–low and front–back as used by Bell and Sweet were in reality a translation of their auditory impressions into physiological terms and thus an illusion. Catford (1977, 1981) rejects this assumption. He says that there is ample internal evidence in the works of Bell and Sweet to show that they were really observing tongue positions. Sweet in particular was very explicit on this point. He criticized the German phoneticians for basing their vowel systems on auditory similarity instead of on production. He also recommended whispering the vowels in order to better feel the muscular sensations and said that training of the vocal organs is a better way of learning sounds than doing it by ear. If Bell and Sweet had built on auditory impressions they would also, as Catford remarks, have placed [ʏ] and [ɯ] between [i] and [u] and not set up rounding as a separate dimension. I think it is true that these old phoneticians (and also Jespersen), who did not have the possibiity of looking at x-ray photos, worked much harder than we currently do to train their muscular sensations. Catford concludes that the classifications of Bell and Sweet

were primarily based upon their "highly trained perception of proprioceptive and tactile sensations, not upon the misinterpretation of auditory
sensations" (1981:30).

Ladefoged, however, does not draw the same conclusion from his
criticism of the traditional system as Wood. It is true that he also wants
to set up a new model of speech production (Harshman, Ladefoged, &
Goldstein 1977). The model is based on a factor analysis of 18 cross
sections of the vocal tract for 10 English vowels, resulting in two factors:
(1) a forward movement of the root of the tongue together with raising
of the front part, approximately from [o] to [i], and (2) a raising of the
back of the tongue, approximately from [ɑ] to [u]. But he does not want
to set up a new feature system on this basis. He finds that the traditional
features have proved to be useful for the description of phonological
sound patterns (in Ladefoged 1975 he only gives the supplementary terms
"palatal" and "velar" for front and back), whereas he thinks that we
need a larger number of physiological and acoustic parameters for the
purpose of describing the differences among languages. It must be possible
to map the phonological features onto basic phonetic parameters, either
physiological or acoustic, but this is not necessarily a one-to-one relation
(Ladefoged 1980). As for the traditional dimensions, he finds that rounding
can be described simply in physiological terms, whereas the physiological
correlates of front–back and high–low cannot be used in language description. They have, however, clear auditory and acoustic correlates,
height corresponding to the frequency of F_1, and front–back to $F_2 - F_1$
(e.g., Ladefoged 1976). I find it difficult to accept this exclusively acoustic–
auditory interpretation.

As for the height dimension, it is probably true that it has a somewhat
simpler connection with its physical than with its physiological correlates,
but, as argued above, when height is taken to be a relative dimension
within each category of vowels, the correlation to the physiological facts
is quite good. It is striking that in experiments intended to bring out the
auditory dimensions it has not proved easy to get at the height dimension.
Many years ago I tried in various ways (Fischer-Jørgensen 1967). Phonetically naive subjects were, for example, asked to group vowels according
to auditory similarity, with the result that very often front vowels [i e
ɛ æ] were put into one group, separated from back vowels, whereas high
and low vowels were never sorted out, not even if only six vowels [i y
u] and [ɛ œ ɔ] were presented. When asked directly if they did not find
that [i y u] belonged together, most declared that [u] does not belong
with [i] and [y]. When subjects were asked to group vowels into bright
and dark, thin and thick, small and large, and so on, or, for example,
to place them on a scale from dark to bright, the same dominating

dimension from dark to bright came out in almost all cases, irrespective of the pairs of adjective used. Only when they were asked about tight–loose and compact–diffuse did something that looked more like the vertical dimension appear, but [i y u] were designated as compact, and [ɛ œ ɔ] as diffuse, in contradistinction to Roman Jakobson's terminology. I think this indicates that the subjects were guided mainly by tactile sensations in this case. When, in some cases, subjects were asked to pay more attention to their articulation, [u] got somewhat closer to [i] and [y]. In more recent experiments (see, e.g., Terbeek 1977), based on more refined methods, when, for instance, subjects are asked to judge the similarity among sounds presented in triads and the results are factor analysed, vowel height also turns up. But, altogether, the evidence for height as an exclusively auditory dimension is not very strong.

Moreover, a number of phonetic and phonological rules and developments involving height are better understood when described in articulatory terms. The relatively longer duration of lower vowels can hardly be explained from an auditory point of view, whereas it may be assumed that a more extensive jaw movement takes longer time. Preliminary measurements of jaw opening have shown that the maximum aperture is reached later in low vowels. It may not be economical to accelerate the movement so much that full compensation is achieved. As for intrinsic F_0, there have been different explanations, but there are at least some plausible articulatory explanations. In the case of palatalization of velars before front vowels (which Ladefoged 1972 also describes as an articulatory development) the difference in palatalizing power between [i e ɛ a] must also be explained on the basis of articulation.

However, the regularity of F_1-correspondences point to an auditory adjustment. I therefore think that height should be considered to have clear physiological as well as auditory correlates, both of which play a role in phonological systems and developments.

The dimension front–back is more complicated. Here two articulatory dimensions, front–back and rounded–unrounded, combine to form one auditory dimension: the dark–bright dimension, which was often used in pre-Bell vowel systems. This is, certainly, a dominating auditory dimension, which shows up in experiments dealing with auditory similarity and in phonetic symbolism; it is also prevalent in the patterning of vowel systems, where /u/ and /i/ are extremely common because they are maximally different on the horizontal dimension (Trubetzkoy's "Helligkeit") of a two-dimensional auditory vowel space, whereas /ɯ/ and /y/, which are closer together on this dimension, are rare (Crothers 1978; Lindblom 1980), although both /i–u/ and /ɯ–y/ are distinguished by two articulatory features. As shown by Ladefoged (1962), even trained phoneticians have difficulties in distinguishing between front rounded and back unrounded vowels. It is also very difficult to elicit rounding as a separate feature in experiments with auditory similarity (Terbeek 1977).

However, in many phonological rules and developments the articulatory dimensions front–back and rounded–unrounded are kept apart. For instance, in Russian there is an allophonic contextually conditioned variation between front [i] and mid [ɨ] and between back [u] and fronted [ü] with preservation of the rounding distinction. Further, in Finnish vowel harmony only the front–back dimension is at work, and in Turkish the front–back harmony and the rounded–unrounded harmony function separately according to different rules. Similarly, in i-Umlaut back vowels become front vowels but the rounding difference is preserved; conversely, rounding of vowels in a labial environment does not involve a change in place of articulation. It is possible that perception may play a role at the last stage of the i-Umlaut, where the [i] of the ending may have become so weak that the listener did not hear it and therefore perceived the front feature of the stem vowel as an independent feature (Ohala 1981), but in its start it must have been a mainly articulatory process. On the whole, it seems more plausible to explain such processes of assimilation in motor terms as an anticipation of an articulatory position.

Thus, I do not think we can do without a front–back dimension defined in articulatory terms. It is probably necessary to operate with two articulatorily defined dimensions, front–back and rounded–unrounded, and with an auditorily defined dimension of brightness, which has a causal relation to a combination of the two articulatory dimensions. They all seem to operate in phonology and thus to be in some sense psychologically real. The articulatory features seem to be at work in assimilatory rules and developments, whereas the auditory feature evidently plays a role in the structure of vowel systems. This is in good agreement with Lindblom's assumption that the necessity for sufficient auditory distance between phonemes is the most important determining factor in the structure of vowel systems.

However, the relative importance of the horizontal and the vertical dimension has given some problems. In Liljencrants and Lindblom (1972), the possible acoustic vowel space was calculated on the basis of the speech production model set up by Lindblom and Sundberg (1969, 1971). The calculation was made in terms of formant frequencies. In order to get a two-dimensional space, the frequency of F_2 corrected with respect to F_3 was chosen as one dimension, and the other dimension was the frequency of F_1. By transformation into mel scale, an approximation to an auditory space was obtained. By means of a computer program it was calculated where the vowels had to be placed in this space if maximal distance between all vowels should be obtained for different numbers of vowel phonemes (from 3 to 12). The result was compared with known data on actual vowel systems. The prediction turned out to be quite good for vowel systems with from three to six vowels, but above that limit the model generated too many high vowels, that is, the horizontal dimension was utilized more than the vertical dimension, in contradistinction to the case in natural vowel systems.

In order to bring the model in better agreement with actual vowel systems, it was modified so that the function of the peripheral auditory system was taken more directly into consideration; a filter analysis based on critical bands was used instead of formant analysis, and masking and nonlinear frequency response were taken into account. Moreover, the idea of "maximal" auditory distance was replaced by "sufficient" distance. This model is compared with the older model in Lindblom (1980). It produces a smaller number of high vowels. There are two different versions of the new model. In one of them, which should be closest to the auditory system, phons are changed into sones, but this version gives less good results for vowel systems with a low number of vowel phonemes. The other version operating on phon/Bark gives a better result for systems with few vowels but somewhat less reduction of high vowels in systems with many vowels. Neither of the two versions generates the common seven-vowel system [i e ɛ a ɔ o u]. Lindblom suggests that the vertical dimension may play a greater role in actual systems because F_1 has high intensity and thus is more resistant to noise.

I should like to suggest a different explanation. Perhaps the auditory distance between [i] and [u] really is felt as relatively long compared to the vertical distance between [i] and [a]. The experiments with Danish subjects mentioned above seem to support this, as does the dominant use of the dark–bright opposition in sound symbolism. It may be objected that Danish [i e ɛ æ] are closer together than in most other languages. But why then do we keep them apart phonologically even though we feel them as auditorily related? I suppose production plays a role in this connection. As demonstrated by Lindblom and Sundberg, the simplest way to produce differences in vowel height is by raising and lowering the mandible, and it may be relatively easy to control this movement. First, the proprioceptive sensitivity seems to be more developed for jaw movements than for advancing or retracting the tongue. This may have something to do with the fact that jaw opening and closing is used for other biological purposes, for example, eating. Second, jaw movement is visible. (It may happen that a student starting a phonetics course believes that he produces an [e] by retracting his tongue, but he will not maintain that he produces an [a] by closing his mouth.) Finally, steps in jaw movement have a simple one-to-one correlation with steps in F_1 and thus with steps in auditory impressions of the series [i e ɛ a], whereas the series [i y ɯ u] requires a complicated interplay of tongue and lip movements. Vowel height is a simpler dimension and therefore utilized more extensively.

7. CONCLUDING REMARKS ON EXPLANATION IN PHONOLOGY

Finally, I should like to admit that I have used the terms explanation and explanatory in a somewhat slipshod way. But there are many kinds and steps of explanation. When I argue that front–back is more explanatory than four places of articulation in *i*-Umlaut and vowel harmony rules, the point is that back comprises more cases in one rule, and generalization is a first step in explanation. Distinguishing more than two heights also allows more generalizations, for example, saying that mid vowels [e ø o] have diphthongized, which is not possible if [ɑ] is considered to have the same height.

But when I argue for an articulatory interpretation of front–back in assimilatory developments, it is because the development can then be described by plausible production mechanisms. Those who, like Lass (1980), require that explanations be deductive cause–effect explanations that permit prediction would call the explanations mentioned above understanding and not explanation. But that depends on how the word "explanation" is defined. Here it is used in a wider sense. One can never predict a concrete sound change, but it can sometimes be explained afterwards, and one may assume with high probability that if there is a change it will go in a definite direction. There are very strong phonetic constraints on phonological systems and on sound change, and I agree with John Ohala (e.g., 1983) that it is an important task for phonetics to find these constraints.

But I do not think Ohala is right when he states that the ability of the linguist to predict the future is on a par with the physicist's ability to predict the future (Ohala 1984). It is not only a question of complexity. Language is different from physics. On this point I agree with Ladefoged (1984).

REFERENCES

Alfonso, P. J., & Baer, T. (1981). *An electromyographic–cinefluorographic–acoustic study of dynamic vowel production.* Status Report on Speech Research, Haskins Laboratories, *65*, 109–124.

Alfonso, P. J., Honda, K., Baer, T., & Harris, K. S. (1982). *Multichannel study of tongue EMG during vowel production.* Paper presented at the 103rd meeting of the Acoustical Society of America, Chicago, IL.

Basbøll, H. (1972). Some conditioning phonological factors for the pronunciation of short vowels in Danish with special reference to syllabification. *Annual report of the Institute of Phonetics, University of Copenhagen, 6,* 185–210.

Basbøll, H. (1984). On the relation between vowel height and front–back: A comment on Eli Fischer-Jørgensen's paper "Some basic vowel features, their articulatory correlates and their explanatory power in phonology." *Annual report of the Institute of Phonetics, University of Copenhagen, 18,* 277–284.

Basbøll, H., & Kristensen, K. (1975). Further work on computer testing of a generative phonology of Danish. *Annual report of the Institute of Phonetics, University of Copenhagen, 9,* 265–291.

Catford, I. (1977). *Fundamental problems in phonetics.* Edinburgh: Edinburgh University Press.

Catford, I. (1981). Observations on the recent history of vowel classification. In R. E. Asher & E. J. T. Henderson (Eds.), *Towards a history of phonetics,* papers contributed in honour of David Abercrombie (pp. 19–32). Edinburgh: Edinburgh University Press.

Chomsky, N., & Halle, M. (1968). *The sound pattern of English.* New York: Harper & Row.

Crothers, J. (1978). Typology and universals of vowel systems. In Greenberg, Ferguson, & Moravcsik (Eds.), *Universals of human language* (pp. 93–152). Stanford: Stanford University Press.

Fischer-Jørgensen, E. (1967). Perceptual dimensions of vowels. In *To honor Roman Jakobson* (Vol. 1). (pp. 667–671). The Hague: Mouton.

Fischer-Jørgensen, E. (1973). Perception of German and Danish vowels with special reference to the German lax vowels /I Y U/. *Annual report of the Institute of Phonetics, University of Copenhagen, 7,* 143–194. A shorter version in G. Fant & M. A. A. Tatham (Eds.), 1975, *Auditory analysis and perception of speech* (pp. 153–176). London: Academic Press.

Fischer-Jørgensen, E. (1975). *Trends in phonological theory.* Copenhagen: Akademisk Forlag.

Fischer-Jørgensen, E. (1983). Vowel features and their explanatory power in phonology. In A. Cohen & M. P. R. van den Broecke (Eds.), *Abstracts of the Xth International Congress of Phonetic Sciences* (pp. 259–265). Dordrecht: Foris.

Fischer-Jørgensen, E. (1984). A note on vowel triangles and quadrangles: an answer to Hans Basbøll. *Annual Report of the Institute of Phonetics, University of Copenhagen, 18,* 285–291.

Halle, M. (1982). On distinctive features and their articulatory implementation. To be published in *Natural language and linguistic theory,* 1983.

Halle, M., & Stevens, K. N. (1969). On the feature "advanced tongue root." *MIT Quarterly Progress Report, 94,* 209–215.

Harshman, R., Ladefoged, P., & Goldstein, L. (1977). Factor analysis of tongue shape. *Journal of the Acoustical Society of America, 62,* 693–707.

Jakobson, R., & Halle, M. (1956). *Fundamentals of language.* The Hague: Mouton.

Jespersen, O. (1889). *The articulation of speech sounds represented by means of analphabetic symbols.* Marburg: Elwert.

Jespersen, O. (1897–1899). *Fonetik.* Copenhagen: Det Schubotheske Forlag.

Jespersen, O. (1914). *Lehrbuch der Phonetik.* Leipzig: Teubner.

Jones, D. (1909). *The pronunciation of English.* Cambridge: Cambridge University Press.

Jones, D. (1918). *An outline of English phonetics* Cambridge: Heffers.

Joos, M. (1948). *Acoustic phonetics* (Language Monographs No. 23., Linguistic Society of America. Baltimore, MD: Waverly Press.

Jørgensen, H. P. (1969). Die gespannten und ungespannten Vokale in der norddeutschen Hochsprache mit einer spezifischen Untersuchung der Struktur ihrer Formantfrequenzen. *Phonetica, 19,* 217–245.

Kaiser, L. (1941). Biological and statistical research concerning the speech of 216 Dutch students III. *Archives néerlandaises de phonétique expérimentale XVII,* 92–118.

Ladefoged, P. (1962). The nature of vowel quality. *Revista do Laboratório de fonética experimental da faculdade de letras da universidade de Coimbra.* Also in Ladefoged, P., 1967, *Three areas of experimental phonetics* (pp. 50–142). London: Oxford University Press.

Ladefoged, P. (1964). *A phonetic study of West African languages* (West African Language Monographs 1). Cambridge: Cambridge University Press.

Ladefoged, P. (1971). *Preliminaries to linguistic phonetics.* Chicago: University of Chicago Press.

Ladefoged, P. (1972). Phonological features and their phonetic correlates. *Journal of the International Phonetic Association, 2,* 2–12.

Ladefoged, P. (1975). *A course in phonetics.* New York: Harcourt Brace Jovanovich.

Ladefoged, P. (1976). The phonetic specification of the languages of the world. *UCLA Working Papers in Phonetics, 31,* 3–21.

Ladefoged, P. (1980). What are linguistic sounds made of? *Language, 55,* 485–502. Also in *UCLA Working Papers in Phonetics* 1979, *45,* 1–24.

Ladefoged, P. (1984). 'Out of chaos comes order'; Physical, biological, and structural patterns in phonetics. In A. Cohen & M. P. R. van den Broecke (Eds.), *Proceedings of the Tenth International Congress of Phonetic Sciences* (pp. 83–95). Dordrecht: Foris.

Ladefoged, P., DeClerk, J., Lindau, M., & Papçun, G. (1972). An auditory–motor theory of speech production. *UCLA Working Papers in Phonetics, 22,* 48–75.

Ladefoged, P., Harshman, R., Goldstein, L., & Rice, L. (1977). Vowel articulations and formant frequencies. *UCLA Working Papers in Phonetics, 38,* 16–40.

Lass, R. (1980). *On explaining language change.* Cambridge: Cambridge University Press.

Liljencrants, J., & Lindblom, B. (1972). Numerical Simulation of vowel quality systems: the role of perceptual contrast. *Language, 48,* 839–862.

Lindau, M. (1978). Vowel features. *Language, 55,* 541–563. Also in *UCLA Working Papers in Phonetics, 38,* 49–81.

Lindau, M., Jacobson, L., & Ladefoged, P. (1972). The feature advanced tongue root. *UCLA Working Papers in Phonetics, 22,* 76–94.

Lindblom, B. (1980). Phonetic universals in vowel systems. In J. Ohala (Ed.), *Experimental Phonology,* New York: Academic Press.

Lindblom, B., & Sundberg, J. (1969). A quantitative model of vowel production and the distinctive features of Swedish vowels. In *Quarterly Progress and Status Report, 1,* 14–32, Speech Transmission Lab. Stockholm: Royal Institute of Technology.

Lindblom, B., & Sundberg, J. (1971). Acoustical consequences of lip, tongue and larynx movement. *Journal of the Acoustical Society of America, 50,* 1166–1179.

Meyer, E. A. (1910). Untersuchungen über Lautbildung. *Die neueren Sprachen, 18* (Festschrift Viëtor), 166–248.

Nearey, T. M. (1978). *Phonetic feature systems of vowels.* Bloomington: Indiana University Linguistics Club.

Ohala, J. J. (1981). The listener as a source of sound change. In C. S. Masek, R. A. Hendrick, and M. F. Miller (Eds.), *Papers from the parasession on language and behavior* (pp. 178–203). Chicago: University of Chicago Press.

Ohala, J. J. (1983). The origin of sound patterns in vocal tract constraints. In P. F. MacNeilage (Ed.), *The production of speech* (pp. 189–216). New York: Springer.

Ohala, J. J. (1984). Chairman's opening remarks. Symposium 5: Phonetic Explanation in Phonology. In A. Cohen and M. P. R. van den Broecke (Eds.), *Proceedings of the Tenth International Congress of Phonetic Sciences* (pp. 175–177). Dordrecht: Foris.

Petersen, N. R. (1974). The influence of tongue height on the perception of vowel duration in Danish. *Annual Report of the Institute of Phonetics, University of Copenhagen, 8,* 1–10.

Raphael, L. J., & Bell-Berti, F. (1975). Tongue musculature and the feature of tension in English vowels. *Phonetica, 32,* 61–63.

Russell, G. O. (1928). *The vowel.* Columbus: Ohio State University Press.

Russell, G. O. (1936). Synchronised X-ray, oscillograph, sound and movie experiments showing the fallacy of the vowel triangle and open-closed theories. In D. Jones & D. B. Fry (Eds.), *Proceedings of the IInd International Congress of Phonetic Sciences* (pp. 198–205). Cambridge: Cambridge University Press.

Sievers, E. (1901). *Grundzüge der Phonetik.* Leipzig: Breitkopf und Härtel.

Smith, T., & Hirano, M. (1968). Experimental investigation of the muscular control of the tongue in speech. *UCLA Working Papers in Phonetics, 10,* 145–155.

Stewart, J. M. (1969). Tongue root position in Akan vowel harmony. *Phonetica, 16,* 185–204.

Straka, G. (1950). Système des voyelles du français moderne. *Bulletin de la faculté des lettres de Strasbourg, 28,* 172–180, 220–233, 275–284, 368–375.

Straka, G. (1978). Apropos du classement articulatoire des voyelles. In O. v. Essen, C. Gutknecht, J. P. Köster, & H.-H. Wängler (Eds.), *Hamburger phonetische Beiträge* (Vol. 25, pp. 432–460). Hamburg: Helmut Buske.

Terbeek, D. (1977). *A cross-language multidimensional scaling study of vowel perception.* (*UCLA Working Papers in Phonetics, 37*). Los Angeles: University of California.

Thorsen, O., Jensen, K., & Landschultz, K. (1971). *Fransk fonetik* (mimeographed).

Wood, S. (1975a). Tense and lax vowels—degree of constriction or pharyngeal volume? *Working papers,* 11, 110–134. Lund: Lund University, *Department of General Linguistics.* Also in Wood, S. (1982), pp. 157–182.

Wood, S. (1975b). The weakness of the tongue arching model of articulation. *Working papers,* 11, 55–108. Lund: Lund University, *Department of General Linguistics.*

Wood, S. (1979). A radiographic analysis of constriction location for vowels. *Journal of Phonetics, 7,* 25–43. Also in Wood, S. (1982), pp. 57–75.

Wood, S. (1982). *X-ray and model studies of vowel articulation. Working papers* 23, Lund: Lund University, Department of Linguistics.

Zwaardemaker, H., & Eijkman, L. P. H. (1928). *Leerboek der Phonetiek.* Haarlem: De Erven F. Bohn.

7

Speculations about the Representation of Words in Memory*

Morris Halle

1. INTRODUCTION

The purpose of this chapter is to explore one aspect of a fluent speaker's knowledge of a language. I present reasons for believing that information about the phonic shape of the words is stored in a fluent speaker's memory in the form of a three-dimensional object that for concreteness one might picture as a spiral-bound notebook. I realize that this is a fairly radical claim and that it is likely to be met with considerable skepticism on the part of working phoneticians who have, of course, never encountered spiral-bound notebooks in any of their studies of the sounds produced and the articulations executed by hundreds of speakers of dozens of languages.

2. WHAT IS MEMORIZED

I begin with the negative assertion that it is unlikely that the information about the phonic shape of words is stored in the memory of speakers in acoustic form resembling, for instance, an oscillogram or a sound spectrogram. One reason that this is improbable is that when we learn a new word we practically never remember most of the salient acoustic properties that must have been present in the signal that struck our ears; for example, we do not remember the voice quality of the person who taught us the word or the rate at which the word was pronounced. Not only voice quality, speed of utterance, and other properties directly

* I am grateful to Sylvain Bromberger for many improvements in the content and form of this paper, to Maggie Carracino for technical assistance, and to Rosamond T. Halle for help with the graphics. Shortcomings remaining in the paper are my responsibility exclusively. This work was supported in part by the Center for Cognitive Science, MIT.

linked to the unique circumstances surrounding every utterance are discarded in the course of learning a new word. The omissions are much more radical. For example, there is reason to believe that English speakers do not store in memory such a salient property as, for example, the stress contour of the word. It is known that for a large class of English words stress is determined by Rule 1:

Rule 1:

    a. Stress the antepenultimate syllable if the penultimate syllable is "light"; that is, ends with a short vowel; otherwise,
    b. stress the penultimate syllable.

Examples of words stressed in accordance with this rule are given in (1):

(1)   límerick   jávelin   América   Cánada
       addéndum   veránda   Augústa   Aláska
       decórum   ultimátum marína   rutabága

Not all English words have stress contours that follow directly from (1). Examples of such deviant stress contours are given in (2).

(2)   statuétte   devélop   órchestra

It should be noted that the exceptions are not random; rather, they are stressed in accordance with rules that differ somewhat from (1). Moreover, the existence of exceptions to (1) does not undermine its status: Rule 1 expresses a true regularity that is manifested in a large class of words of the language.

Having established that Rule 1 is true of a large class of English words, one might next inquire whether regularities such as those expressed in Rule 1 are of any significance for speakers of English. There are two diametrically opposed answers that might be offered here. On the one hand, one might argue that these regularities play no role as far as English speakers are concerned; they are discoveries that have been made by professional linguists, and, like many other such discoveries, they have no bearing on the way ordinary speakers of English produce and understand utterances in their language. For example, linguists have established that English is derived from the same protolanguage as Sanskrit, Armenian, Greek, Latin, and Irish, and that the stems of the English words *brotherly* and *fraternal* derive from the same Indo–European root, but these facts surely have no effect on the ability of an ordinary English speaker, say a bright ten-year-old, to speak and understand her teacher, her classmates, or others about her.

By contrast with the preceding, one might respond to our question by suggesting that, unlike the historical or archeological facts noted above, the regularities in Rule 1 are a crucial component of the knowledge that English speakers must have in order to speak and to understand each other. For example, one might speculate that for various psychobiological reasons speakers find it difficult or impossible to memorize the stress contours of words, but they find it easy to compute the stress contours by means of rules such as 1.

This is obviously a fairly bold speculation that will be rejected out of hand unless evidence in support of it is immediately provided.

Some evidence that speakers do not memorize the stress contours of words directly comes from the treatment of foreign words when these are borrowed into English. It is well known that, when borrowed into English, foreign words are frequently anglicized. Thus, for example, the three words in (3) which are fairly recent borrowings from Russian, are stressed in accordance with Rule 1, whereas their original Russian stress contours are as shown in (4).

(3)   bólshevik   Rómanov   babúshka

(4)   bolshevík   Románov   bábushka

It is commonly said that words are anglicized when they have features that English speakers might find difficult or impossible to pronounce. In the present instance, however, this is hardly a plausible explanation, for, as shown in (2), there are English words that have precisely the same stress contours as our three words have in Russian.

A more plausible explanation for the anglicized stress contours of the borrowed words is that the speakers who introduced these words into English did not memorize their original Russian stress contours, because, as suggested above, they find memorizing stress contours difficult or impossible. They, therefore, remembered the words without their original stress contours and supplied them with stress contours by utilizing Rule 1, the standard stress rule for English nouns. In addition to explaining why words borrowed into English from Russian (and other foreign languages) are stressed as illustrated in (3) and not as in (4), our suggestion also provides a rationale for the existence of the regularities in stress contour that we have illustrated in (1). These regularities exist—as already suggested—because speakers find it difficult to memorize the stress contours of each word separately but find it easy to compute the stress contours by means of rules such as Rule 1. The assertion that speakers do not memorize the stress contour of words implies further that rules such as 1 are part of their knowledge of English, that is, that Rule 1 is of interest not just to linguists but also to speakers of English and that words are represented in memory in an abstract form in which many characteristics found in the physical signal are systematically omitted. This is, of course, not a trivial proposal, for it implies that words are represented in memory in a form that is quite abstract in that it omits many characteristics that can be observed in the acoustic signal and the articulatory gymnastics. Moreover, it implies that the process of speaking involves computations of the type made necessary by rules such as Rule 1. While we are still far from being able to demonstrate all this, the evidence accumulated by generative phonology since the late 1950s suggests that the proposal might not be far off the mark.

For some additional evidence supporting the view that words are represented in memory in a quite abstract form, that is, in a form that is indirectly related to the observable articulatory behavior and acoustic signal by means of special rules, consider the following experiment that can be conducted without elaborate equipment and preparations. One can present a list of nonsense syllables such as the one in (5) to fluent speakers of English and ask them to indicate which syllables in the list might have been taken from an unabridged dictionary of the language and which might not.

(5)   flib slin vlim smid fnit vrig plit trit brid blim tnig bnin

It has been my experience that speakers have very clear intuitions about which of these nonsense words are or are not part of English. And on the basis of this experience I have little doubt that most people would regard *vlim, fnit, vrig, tnig, bnin* as unlikely candidates for words of English, but that they are likely to accept the others.

This fact raises two questions: (1) on what basis do speakers make these judgments? and (2) how do speakers acquire the knowledge that underlies these judgments? Since the nonsense syllables in (5) have never been seen by our experimental subjects, it is not possible that they arrive at their judgments simply by checking the list of all the words they know and by discovering that the non–English items are not in the list. We must rather assume that speakers know some general principle that allows them to determine whether any arbitrary sequence of sounds is or is not a well-formed syllable of English. The principle involved in the judgments under discussion is given in Rule 2.

Rule 2:
    English syllable onsets containing two consonants are composed of
    {p t k b d g f θ} followed by {l r w} or of
    {s} followed by {p t k m n l w}.

It may be somewhat puzzling to some that we should know such complicated principles as those in Rule 2 in addition to those in Rule 1, especially since practically none of us is likely ever to have been consciously aware of their existence. It takes, however, but a moment's reflection to convince oneself that there are many things that people know without being conscious of this fact. For instance, major league ball players must surely have knowledge of parabolic trajectories, for each time they catch a ball they must somehow calculate such a trajectory. But no one is likely to want to conclude that baseball players have explicit knowledge of Newton's Laws of Motion, that they can solve differential equations, or even that they can do simple sums. Like the knowledge of parabolic trajectories possessed by ball players, knowledge of syllable onsets is largely implicit knowledge, but that, of course, does not make it any less real.

If lack of awareness on our part is, thus, no bar to the assumption that our knowledge of English includes knowledge of such abstract principles as those in Rules 1 and 2, there remains the question as to how we could have ever come into possession of this knowledge. It obviously could not have been taught to us by our parents or teachers, for they are as little aware of this information as we are. We must, therefore, assume that we somehow acquired it on our own in the course of learning English. Given the conditions under which young children ordinarily learn their mother tongue, the only plausible assumption is that we are so constructed that when we store the words in our memory we simultaneously abstract the distributional regularities in the phoneme sequences that make up these words and that in the course of this procedure we establish that the words obey principles such as those in Rules 1 and 2.

Like our knowledge of what phonetic attributes should be memorized and what attributes should be discarded, the knowledge that we must establish all sequential regularities in words could not have been plausibly learned and must, therefore, be assumed to be innate. It must be part of the genetic equipment by virtue of which humans, unlike members of other species, are capable of learning natural languages. To motivate this story one may speculate that space in our memory is at a premium and that we must, therefore, store in our memory as little information as possible about the phonetic shape of each word, eliminating as many redundancies as possible and placing maximum reliance on our ability to compute the omitted information. For example, as observed above, if Rule 1 is available, information about stress need not be stored in memory. Similarly, given the redundancies noted in Rule 2 we can omit in the representation of English onset clusters beginning with /s/ information about such phonetic features as voicing and continuancy, for these are toally predictable.[1]

In order to realize these economies in memory storage, however, we must be able to compute the omitted features. Thus, we arrive once again at the conclusion that the process of speaking involves rules and computations and that words are represented in memory in a form that omits many of the characteristics directly observable in the acoustic signal and vocal tract gymnastics.

3. HOW IT IS REPRESENTED

If Rule 2 is an integral part of a speaker's knowledge of English, then it must be the case that English speakers represent words in their memory in a form that is compatible with that rule. Since Rule 2 makes reference to discrete speech sounds and to such features as voicing and continuancy, we are led to infer that speakers represent words in memory as sequences of discrete speech sounds or 'phonemes', that is, in a form that resembles transcriptions of language in familiar alphabetic writing systems. The proposition that words are stored in speakers' memories as sequences of phonemes or phonemelike units has been generally accepted by linguists and phoneticians for a long time. There is a considerable body of facts, however, that cannot be readily dealt with by means of representations composed of a single linear sequence of units. For example, all languages utilize variations in the fundamental pitch of the voice in their utterances. Thus, in English, utterances are pronounced with quite different melodies when they are used as a response to a neutral question and when they are intended to express surprise. In response to the neutral question *What are you studying?* the response might be *linguistics,* with a melody composed of the tones M(id)–H(igh)–L(ow); the response to a comment occasioning great surprise would be *linguistics* with a LHH melody. Since speakers normally produce such melodies in their utterances, they must possess a means for representing melodies.

The problem that arises here is that a given tone sequence may be spread over an arbitrary number of syllables. For example, the same two melodies that we encountered above in our little story would have been produced if, instead of the trisyllabic *linguistics,* the response had been the bisyllabic *Brasil* or the decasyllabic *antidisestablishmentarianism.* What this shows is that the tone sequences are independent of the syllable sequences. It should not come as a great surprise that notations like our normal alphabetic writing system or the standard phonetic or phonological transcriptions, which are modeled on our alphabetic writing system and which represent utterances by means of a single linear sequence of symbols, are in principle incapable of handling signals composed of two independent sequences of elements: tones and syllables. Since there are two independent sequences of elements encoded in the signal, the notation must have two independent sequences of symbols and that is what in fact we find in the various notations, some quite ancient, especially designed to record both the melody and the words of a chant or song. In these notations the words were recorded on one line and the melody was recorded by a system of diacritic marks written above the line of letters on what is in effect a second line. (There is even a technical term for such diacritics *neumes,* which Webster defines as "symbols used in the notation of Gregorian chant.") Various informal adaptations of this idea have been employed in phonetic studies of tonal phenomena. It is only quite recently that these tonal notations have been formally investigated. As a result of work by Goldsmith (1979), Williams (1976), Liberman (1975), Pulleyblank (1983), and others on what has been called "autosegmental phonology," great advances have been made in our understanding of such representations. To convey some idea as to what has been learned we examine below an actual example.

4. AUTOSEGMENTAL PHONOLOGY: SOME EXAMPLES

In many languages, tonal melodies serve to distinguish different words. In such languages, for example, two otherwise identical words are differentiated by the fact that one has the melody LH and the other, the melody HL. The tonal differences function, therefore, exactly like other phonetic distinctions, for example, like differences in the quality of the vowels /i/ and /e/ in the words *bit–bet.* And like information about vowel quality, information about the tonal melodies of the different words must be memorized by the speaker of a tone language. Moreover, there is reason to believe that speakers store this information on a separate autosegmental tier; that is, the words in these languages are stored in the form of two parallel sequences of units: the phonemes and the tones. To see why this might be so, consider the facts in (6), where we reproduce three forms of the Mende words *navo* 'money' and *nyaha* 'woman' (data from Leben 1978). The first of the three forms is the bare word, the second gives the word with a suffix meaning 'on', and the third, with a suffix signaling the indefinite plural.

(6)

The word *navo* has the melody LH; the word *nyaha* has the melody LHL. The suffix *ma* is toneless, whereas the suffix *nga* has a melody consisting of a single L tone. Most of the work linking tones to syllables is accomplished by the universal linking convention (see Pulleyblank 1983), which states that tones are linked to vowels one to one and from left to right. Any deviations from this simple correspondence between tones and vowels must be licensed by language-particular rules.

In the examples in (6), the universal linking convention accounts for the fact that *ma*, though inherently toneless, surfaces with a L tone in *nyahama*. The convention fails to account for the cases where the linking between tones and vowels is other than one to one. These are the domain of the language-particular rules, and Mende has two of these. On the one hand, Mende has a rule that spreads the last tone of one morpheme onto the following toneless syllable. It is by virtue of this rule that *ma* has H tone in *navoma*. A second rule links an unlinked tone to the word-final syllable. In consequence of this rule, we find two tones on the last syllable of the bare stem *nyaha* but not elsewhere. There is a third deviation from one to one correspondence in (6): In *nyahanga*, the second L tone remains unlinked. This fact is accounted for by what has been said above. Since neither the universal linking convention nor the tone rules of Mende provide a way for linking the second L tone in *nyahanga* to a vowel of the word, the tone remains unlinked. Since tones can only be pronounced when they are linked to phonemes, this L tone is not pronounced. It is worth noting that the phenomena we have just discussed are totally opaque if tones are viewed as attributes of the individual vowels rather than as an autosegmental sequence parallel to and separate from the sequences of phonemes.

Since two parallel lines define a plane, we can say that the parallel sequences of tones and phonemes in (6) constitute a plane, the tone plane. One of the major insights gained by linguistic research since the early 1970s is that the tone plane is not the only property of phonological sequences that must be represented on its own separate plane. Other entities requiring such treatment are the two major types of constituents that simultaneously make up each word: syllables and morphemes.[2]

Until the 1970s the only means utilized by linguists for delimiting subsequences in the phonetic string have been boundary markers or junctures that are intercalated among the phonemes of the sequence at appropriate points. The problem with this device is that it introduces into the representation all sorts of symbols that, if taken seriously, tend to make the statement of various phonological regularities all but impenetrable, as shown in (7).

(7) $\# + /o/ri/gi/n + a/l + i/ty\# + /$ $\# + /in + /ter + /ment\# + /$

where $\#$ = word boundary, $+$ = morpheme boundary,
$/$ = syllable boundary

It was suggested by Kahn (1976) that syllables should be represented on a separate autosegmental tier, like the tones in (6), and a similar suggestion was made with respect to morphemes by Rotenberg (1978). We illustrate these suggestions in (8) (N, noun; A, adjective; V, verb; M, morpheme; s, syllable).

(8)

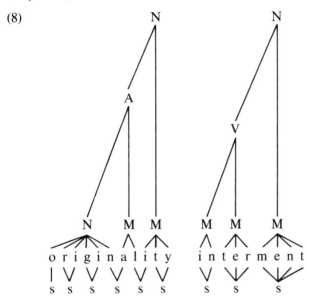

We can say that in (8) there are two planes intersecting in the phoneme sequence or 'skeleton'. We refer to the plane above the phoneme sequence as the morpheme plane and to the plane below the phoneme sequence as the syllable plane.

A noteworthy feature of the plane on which the morphological structure of the word is represented is that the linking lines reflect nested constituent structure of the sort widely encountered in syntax. This kind of constituent structure is not restricted to the morphological plane. In fact, some sort of constituent structure in syllables was tacitly assumed in our discussion of the distributional restrictions on English words. It will be recalled that the restrictions exemplified in (5) apply not just to any subsequence in the syllable but only to what was referred to above as the onset of the syllable. It may have been noticed that in the discussion of the onset above a detailed characterization of the onset itself was not included. This omission may now be repaired. Recent work by Levin (1983), Steriade (1982), and others appears to lead to the conclusion that syllables universally have the constituent structure given in (9). 'Onset' is, therefore, the name given to the phoneme subsequence in the syllable that precedes the rime.

(9)

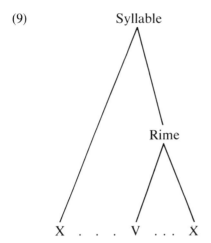

The syllable thus consists of a left-headed constituent, the rime, nested inside of a right-headed constituent. The V(owel), which is the head of the rime, is the only obligatory constituent of the syllable. The presence of any other constituents in the syllable is governed by language-particular rules of the type given in Rule 2 above.[3]

Since English syllable structure is too complex to discuss here, we examine here the syllables of Classical Arabic. Unlike English, which has a very rich syllable repertoire, Classical Arabic permits only the three types of syllable illustrated in (8), with the further limitation that extra-heavy syllables can occur only word finally.

(10)

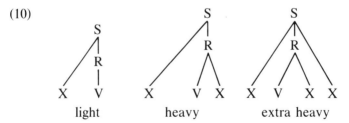

Arabic shares an interesting property with all Semitic languages as well as with a number of non-Semitic languages, such as the African language Hausa and the American Indian language Yokuts. In these languages the syllabification of a word is determined not by the phonemes that compose it, but rather by its morphological structure. To illustrate, I cite in (11) some forms from McCarthy (1984) epitomizing the formation of the so-called broken plurals.

(11)   *jundab*   *janaadib*   'locust'
        sultaan   *salaatiin*   'sultan'

duktar	*dakaatir*	'doctor '
safarjal	*safaarij*	'quince'
maktab	*makaatib*	'office'
miftaaḥ	*mafaatiiḥ*	'key'
nuwwar	*nawaawir*	'white flower'
9andaliib	*9anaadil*	'nightingale'

The first thing to observe about these examples is that while the singular forms may be either bi- or trisyllabic, the plural forms are uniformly trisyllabic. Moreover, the syllable structure in the plural is also fixed. The first syllable is light, the second syllable is heavy, and the third syllable, which always ends with a consonant, has a vowel that is identical in length with that of the second syllable in the singular. This is a typical instance of morphology-driven syllabification, that is, of syllable structure being imposed not by the phonological composition of the word but by the fact that the word belongs to a particular grammatical category, the plural in the case under discussion.

Nor is this all that is determined by the fact that the form is plural. Note that the vowel pattern in all plural forms is the same: /i/ in the last syllable, /a/ in the first and second. The vowel pattern in the plural is, thus, totally unrelated to that of the singular. Only the consonants are not determined by the morphology, by the fact that the word is plural. These convey the lexical meaning of the form. And even their distribution is severely restricted: They occur only in specific positions in the word, and there must be precisely four consonants in every plural form. If the word has more than four consonants in the singular, the extra consonants are omitted, as shown by the words for *quince* and *nightingale* in (11). It would appear, therefore, that the plural form of Arabic nouns consists of the skeleton given in (12) in which the empty slots, represented by X in (12), are filled in by the consonants representing the lexical meaning of the noun.

(12)   X a X aa X i(i) X

It was pointed out by McCarthy (1979) that if the consonants are represented on a separate autosegmental tier, the linking of the consonants to the empty slots in the skeleton (12) is effected by the same left-to-right one-to-one convention that is regularly encountered in tone languages; compare this with our discussion of Mende tones in (6) above. Notice that this convention predicts that if the noun has more than four consonants the extra consonants will remain unlinked and that it will not be any four, but precisely the first four consonants that will be linked to the empty slots. And as we have seen in the last line of (11), this prediction is fully borne out.

We now recall the proposal made above that syllable structure must be represented on a separate autosegmental plane. Formally this means that, instead of as in (12), Arabic noun plurals should be represented as in (13):

(13)

It turns out that skeleta having the syllabic structure given in (13) are found in other parts of Arabic morphology. For instance, in the verb inflection there are several forms with the syllable structure in (13) but differing in the vowels that appear in it. Thus, in the perfective active the vowels are all /a/, whereas in the perfective passive the vowels are /u/ in the first two syllables and /i/ in the third. In the light of these facts, McCarthy suggested that the vowels should also be represented on a separate autosegmental plane and that the skeleton, that is, the line of intersection of the different autosegmental planes, should, therefore, consist exclusively of empty slots. If this is done, then we can further postulate that in the plurals of (11) the vowel melody consists of the sequence /a i/, of which the latter is linked by a morphological rule to the head of the last rime. The universal linking convention will then link /a/ to the head of the first rime, and a language-particular spreading rule will link /a/ to the empty rime slots in the first syllable.

The different autosegmental planes—the vowels, the consonants, the syllabic structure, the morphological constituency, and so on—all intersect in the skeleton core, which can be viewed as being the counterpart of the spine of the spiral-bound notebook referred to at the beginning of this essay. I have tried to present a picture of this type of representation in Figure 7.1.

The three autosegmental planes shown in the figure are, of course, not the only ones encountered. As indicated above, tone must be represented on an autosegmental tier of its own. Hayes (1980) and Halle and Vergnaud (in preparation) have shown that stress should also be represented autosegmentally. Moreover, Poser (1982), Yip (1982), and others have provided telling arguments for representing still other phonological properties of words on separate autosegmental tiers. As noted above, to the best of my knowledge there are no promising alternative notations to the multi-tiered autosegmental representation that has been described here. Since there can be no doubt that speakers must have

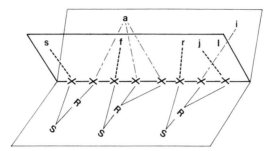

Figure 7.1 A representation of the Arabic word *safaarij* 'quince' (pl.).

knowledge of the complicated and varied facts that autosegmental representations permit us to capture, I conclude that this multi-tiered three-dimensional representation properly reflects an aspect of linguistic reality, in particular the form in which speakers store information about the shape of words in memory.

NOTES

1. The feature of voicing is the cue that distinguishes /p t k/ from /b d g/. The fact that the former but not the latter set can appear after /s/ might be captured by a special rule that redundantly supplies the feature of voicelessness to stops in position after /s/. Given such a rule, the language would not need to specify voicelessness for stops after /s/, since that information would be supplied by the rule.
2. The ordinary commonsense notion of syllable serves adequately for present purposes, so nothing further needs to be said about it at this point. We assume for present purposes that a morpheme is the smallest phoneme subsequence that has independent semantic or grammatical function. As shown in (7), the words *originality* and *interment* are each composed of three morphemes.
3. It is a canard put out, no doubt, by graduate students in Slavic who failed their qualifying examination that Polish has a particularly complicated syllable structure. While Polish syllable structure is far from simple, it is not significantly more complicated than that of English where syllables may end in strings such as [ɪksθs] or [ɛnkθs] as in *sixths, lengths*.

REFERENCES

Goldsmith, J. A. (1979). *Autosegmental phonology*. New York: Garland Press.
Halle, M., & Vergnaud, J.-R. (1980). Three dimensional phonology. *Journal of Linguistic Research, 1*, 83–105.
Halle, M., & Vergnaud, J.-R. (in preparation). *Grids and trees: An essay on stress*.
Hayes, B. (1980). *A metrical theory of stress rules*. Unpublished MIT doctoral dissertation distributed by Indiana University Linguistics Club.
Kahn, D. (1976). *Syllable-based generalizations in English phonology*. Unpublished doctoral dissertation, MIT.

Leben, W. R. (1978). The representation of tone. In V. Fromkin (Ed.), *Tone: a linguistic survey* (pp. 179–219). New York: Academic Press.

Levin, J. (1983). *Reduplication and prosodic structure.* Unpublished manuscript, MIT.

Liberman, M. Y. (1975). *The intonational system of English.* Unpublished doctoral dissertation, MIT.

McCarthy, J. (1979). *Formal problems in Semitic phonology and morphology.* Unpublished doctoral dissertation, MIT.

McCarthy, J. (1984). A prosodic account of Arabic broken plurals. In I. R. Dihoff (Ed.), *Current approaches to African linguistics.* Dordrecht: Foris Publications.

Pierrehumbert, J. B. (1982). *The phonology and phonetics of English intonation.* Unpublished doctoral dissertation, MIT.

Poser, W. J. (1982). Phonological representations and action-at-a-distance. In H. van der Hulst & N. Smith (Eds.), *The structure of phonological representation* II (pp. 121–158). Dordrecht: Foris Publications.

Pulleyblank, D. G. (1983). *Tone in lexical phonology.* Unpublished doctoral dissertation, MIT.

Rotenberg, J. (1978). *The syntax of phonology.* Unpublished doctoral dissertation, MIT.

Steriade, D. (1982). *Greek prosodies and the nature of syllabification.* Unpublished doctoral dissertation, MIT.

Williams, E. (1976). Underlying tone in Margi and Igbo. *Linguistic Inquiry, 7,* 463–484.

Yip, M. (1982). Reduplication and C-V skeleta in Chinese secret languages. *Linguistic Inquiry, 13,* 637–661.

8

Universal Phonetics and the Organization of Grammars*

Patricia A. Keating

1. INTRODUCTION

Phoneticians have long been interested in the relation between phonetics and phonology, especially since the rather explicit proposals of Chomsky and Halle (1968) in *Sound Pattern of English* (SPE). Much of the attention has focused on the nature and substance of the phonetic feature system; Ladefoged (e.g., Ladefoged 1971, 1980) has been a notable participant in this discussion. However, it is of some theoretical interest that, in the SPE model, phenomena that might be called "phonetics" are found in two separate places. On the one hand, the phonetic rules that convert binary into scalar feature values are part of the phonological component of the grammar. On the other hand, the part of phonetics actually called phonetics is not technically in the grammar. It is a largely universal and predictable component that translates a segmental phonetic transcription into continuous physical parameters. Broadly speaking, this extragrammatical physical phonetics is the locus of many of the traditional (as well as current) concerns of phoneticians—articulation, timing, and coarticulation, for example. In this chapter I consider the division of labor between phonology and phonetics in more detail and suggest a direction for revision in the model.

Figure 8.1 gives a schematic view of the relevant parts of the SPE model. First, the phonological component of the grammar contains both phonological rules that operate on binary-valued features and language-

* Earlier versions of this work were presented as talks to helpful groups at the University of British Columbia, the University of California at Irvine, the 1983 International Congress of Phonetic Sciences, and the Phonetics Lab at UCLA. I would especially like to thank Peter Ladefoged, Vicki Fromkin, Marie Huffman, Bruce Hayes, and John Ohala for comments on the manuscript, and John Westbury for our collaborations.

PHONETIC LINGUISTICS

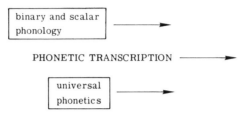

PHYSICAL REPRESENTATION

Figure 8.1 The SPE Model.

specific phonetic-detail rules. The phonetic-detail rules convert binary phonological feature specifications into quantitative phonetic values, called the "phonetic transcription," or systematic phonetic representation. These rules in part depend on universal phonetic constraints concerning possible combinations and contrasts. "Given the surface structure of a sentence, the phonological rules of the language interact with certain universal phonetic constraints to derive all grammatically determined facts about the production and perception of this sentence. These facts are embodied in the 'phonetic transcription' " (Chomsky & Halle 1968:293). According to Chomsky (1964), phonological rules apply until a representation in a universal phonetic alphabet results. The phonetic transcription represents "what the speaker of a language takes to be the phonetic properties of an utterance, given his hypotheses as to its surface structure and his knowledge of the rules of the phonological component"; it is not a direct record of the speech signal and is only one "parameter determining the actual acoustic shape of the tokens of the sentence" (Chomsky & Halle 1968:293, 294). The physical utterance itself is not generated by the grammar; the phonetic transcription is the terminal output of the grammar.

As such, the phonetic transcription must be further interpreted (translated, spelled out, realized) as a physical phonetic representation by a phonetic component that is not technically part of the grammar. The assumption here is that, with the right phonetic representation, any utterance in any language can be interpreted by a set of phonetic conventions. The translation from discrete segments to articulations that exist in time is treated as being automatic; the phonetic component includes, for example, "the different articulatory gestures and various coarticulation effects— the transition between a vowel and an adjacent consonant, the adjustments in the vocal tract shape made in anticipation of subsequent motions, etc." (Chomsky & Halle 1968:295).[1] Chomsky and Halle further suppose that these phonetic conventions are universal rules, that the same phonetic rules can interpret a phonetic transcription in any language. Although not strictly necessary within the general model, this view certainly is an appealing one. The phonology contains the language-specific statements required to produce a detailed enough transcription to allow phonetic interpretation, and the phonetics converts that transcription into a physical utterance in a quite automatic way. This distinction between language-specific rules and automatic low-level phonetic rules is in some ways similar to the distinction between extrinsic and intrinsic allophones (MacNeilage 1970) or between soft and hard coarticulation (Fujimura & Lovins 1978). The phonetic rules are often thought to be directly motivated by, or be identical to, physical constraints on articulation or perception, although Chomsky and Halle apparently do not hold this view.

The SPE model of grammar thus specifies a very constrained relation between phonological and phonetic representations. The use of phonetic features in phonological representations ensures that lexical representations and phonological rules can be evaluated for their phonetic naturalness (the Naturalness Condition, Postal 1968). However, the phonetic representation may, under this theory, be much broader or much narrower than a traditional transcription. Here the phonetic transcription is defined by its position in the model between the phonological and phonetic components. It follows, then, that the fewer universals of phonetic realization posited, the narrower the phonetic transcription will have to be, while the more such phonetic universals there are, the broader the transcription will be. Suppose, for example, that speakers interpreted all phonetic properties as grammatical ones. In that case, the phonetic transcription as defined by the theory and generated by the grammar would be much narrower than the traditional segmental phonetic transcription. Such a view is found in Pierrehumbert's work (1980) on intonation. The language-specific quantitative rules in her system directly output something very close to a physical utterance.

How could a more traditional phonetic transcription be maintained if speakers interpreted phonetic properties as grammatical? Clearly we would have to say that the interpretive rules of the phonetic component are part of the grammar. This move would recast the phonetic component so that it is no longer mainly the domain of universal conventions. Would such a revision be completely arbitrary, just to preserve the phonetic transcription? We might propose that, rather than provide automatic aspects of interpretation, the phonetic component derives any aspect of a representation in which continuous time is involved (Anderson 1974). Then the phonetic component could still do much of the work of deriving the physical phonetic form of an utterance, and the transcription could be a fairly broad one.

Some revision in the SPE model is required in one of these directions simply because in fact there does not appear to be a well-defined body of phonetic universals that operate automatically across languages. Phoneticians are aware that many supposed universal rules of phonetic interpretation have exceptions. What is to be made of these exceptions, of the phonetic rules, and of the phonetic component of the SPE model? Is there any role for a universal phonetic component, in or out of the grammar? And what is the relation of near-universals to physical phonetic constraints?

Questions about the nature of phonetic rules do not disappear if we reject the SPE model of grammar. In fact, the importance of the issue is only increased when we look at alternative theories proposed in the 1970s. Some rejections of the SPE model have been based on phonetic naturalness as a defining property of phonology. In these views, naturalness, in turn, is generally linked to the mechanisms of speech production and to phonetic universals (e.g., natural generative phonology, Hooper 1976). Phonological rules are constrained to be those natural rules that are exceptionless because they are directly physiologically motivated.

In this paper I examine three known phonetic patterns in light of the SPE model and the discussion above. With the first pattern, I discuss the fact that phonetic patterns are not necessarily automatic results of speech physiology. With the second pattern, I illustrate that they need not be universal and that they can operate as abstract phonological rules. With the third, I consider the limitations of physiology in determining phonetic patterns. While none of these types of observations is original, taken together they lead to some tentative proposals about the place of phonetic patterns in grammars.

2. INTRINSIC VOWEL DURATION

In most if not all languages, low vowels such as [a] and [æ] are longer than high vowels such as [i] and [u], all things being equal (Lehiste 1970). Not only can this phonetic pattern be observed across languages, but a physical explanation has been suggested. As Lehiste notes, lower vowels require a greater articulatory movement; if movement velocity is nearly the same across vowels, lower vowels are longer. Furthermore, the observed differences in vowel duration could be accounted for by automatic biomechanical effects rather than by deliberate temporal control. Lindblom (1967) provided an explicit account of such an automatic effect with a mechanical model of jaw activity. Of course, since Lindblom mentioned that compensations in vowel durations could be made, he did not intend the model to account automatically for all aspects of intrinsic vowel duration. However, his work is important because in principle it could provide such an account. Lindblom's model showed that if the force input to jaw lowering muscles had the same duration but different amplitudes for different vowels, biomechanical sluggishness would automatically result in the correct vowel-duration pattern. That is, if the jaw gets a harder, but not longer, send-off for lower vowels, which translates automatically into longer movements, then no explicit timing representation is needed. By hypothesis, all vowel heights have the same representation for duration at every point in their production. Thus no information about intrinsic vowel duration need be included in a grammar, since intrinsic vowel duration patterns can be accounted for automatically in a universal component. Such a view is compatible with what Fowler (1980) called "extrinsic timing" models, in which time is never specifically included in the plan for an utterance but is introduced only in production. That is, here is a case where, apart from any cross-linguistic data, modeling of the speech-production mechanism supports an automatic phonetic universal.

An experiment by Westbury and Keating (1980) investigated this claim about speech production in a physiological study of spoken vowels. Electromyographic (emg) techniques were used to study the force input to a jaw-lowering muscle for vowels, the anterior belly of the digastric (ABD). Three American speakers read items of the form /sVts/ 15 times each, where V = each of ten English vowels. We recorded simultaneously on channels of FM tape the speech signal from a microphone, the mandible displacement from a strain-gauge device attached to a tooth splint, and the emg signal from the ABD as measured with hooked wire electrodes. We then measured the acoustic vowel duration from the speech signal, the extent and timing of jaw displacement from the movement signal, the emg duration from the emg waveform, and the emg maximum amplitude from the rms time envelope.

Our results replicated the earlier finding by others (see Lehiste 1970 for literature review) of intrinsic vowel duration: Lower vowels are longer in acoustic duration than higher vowels, especially (but not crucially) if the English phonological distinction between tense–lax or long–short vowels is taken into account. The measurements also showed (as expected) that lower vowels have a lower jaw position than higher vowels. In addition, the two measures were statistically correlated: The vowels with the lower jaw position had longer acoustic durations. The longer durations were due to longer travel times, not longer steady states. Thus we obtained the data enabling us to address the question of force input. We found that the emg duration and maximum amplitude both showed the same pattern across vowels, with low vowels having longer durations and higher amplitudes of emg activity, correlating with jaw displacement. That is, more extensive and longer movements are made with a force input that is both longer in duration and higher in amplitude: The abd muscle fires longer and more actively; loosely speaking, it pushes both longer and harder to go farther.

We conclude, then, that at the level of neural control tapped by measuring emg activity, vowels are represented as having different durations, since the muscle firing varies in duration, like the acoustic vowel signal. Thus vowel duration differences are not due directly to sluggishness of the jaw; rather, they are controlled as such. This result in itself does not show that vowel-duration differences must be language specific or represented in the grammar. Durations could be provided at a very late stage in production before motor commands are issued, by the phonetic component. However, if vowel duration is a controllable parameter, it is in principle available for language-specific manipulation. Thus we should expect to find languages with different vowel-duration patterns. Such patterns could be seen, for example, when low vowels are considered phonologically short and are produced with short travel times and high velocities.

We may still wonder why so many languages have similar patterns of intrinsic vowel durations. Though the pattern is not a necessary one, it must be convenient in some sense. It may be that some physical patterns and movements are preferred over others because of general principles of economy of effort and motor control (e.g., Nelson 1980). The point here, though, is that such principles must be more subtle than absolute mechanical constraints of the sort that might have been proposed. Physical factors clearly influence vowel duration, but they do not control it.

3. EXTRINSIC VOWEL DURATION

Consider next the general finding that vowels are shorter before voiceless obstruents than before voiced obstruents or sonorants.[2] Chen (1970) surveyed a number of languages, including some described in the literature, and found such vowel duration differences in all of them. Of seven languages studied, all showed at least a 10% difference in vowel duration. This was so whether the vowel and consonant were word final and tautosyllabic or word medial and heterosyllabic. Chen suggested that some contextual durational difference is universal and physiologically determined, although languages may individually exaggerate this difference by rule, for example, English. Although there were problems with Chen's cross-language comparisons,[3] it has generally been accepted that vowel-length differences depending on consonant voicing constitute a phonetic universal, albeit one whose mechanism is not understood. Fromkin (1977) uses this result to argue that the vowel duration effect is given by phonological rule in English (that is, is represented in the phonetic transcription) but is automatically supplied by universal phonetic conventions in other languages without the exaggeration. However, the pattern is not a universal one, and it must be given by rule even in some languages that do not exaggerate the effect.

As part of a study on Polish voicing contrasts (Keating 1979), Polish vowel durations before voiced and voiceless consonants were measured for the pair *rata–rada*. Polish, like other Slavic languages, has a rule of word-final devoicing, so there are no voicing contrasts at the end of isolated words. Thus the durational phenomenon can only be studied in medial position, although based on Chen's survey and on the English studies cited below a robust difference is still to be expected. Twenty-four speakers in Wrocław, Poland, were recorded reading this pair, and durations of the stressed syllabic nuclei were measured from a computer-implemented oscillographic display at the Brown University Phonetics Lab. The mean duration of [a] before [t] was 167.4 msec and of [a] before [d], 169.5 msec. The ratio of these two means is .99. In addition, the ratio of the two vowel durations was computed for each individual speaker. The mean of these 24 ratios is 1.0. These data indicate that Polish vowel duration does not vary systematically according to the voicing of the following consonant.

Comparable data for English vowels before medial stops have been collected by Sharf (1962) and Klatt (1973). The pre-voiceless to pre-voiced ratios they obtained were .75 and .79, respectively. A higher ratio, .89, was obtained by Port (1977), using sentence contexts rather than word lists. (Since English flaps its medial alveolar stops before stressless vowels, these data are for vowels before labials and velars.)

The finding that Polish, unlike English, does not shorten vowels before voiceless consonants was extended by recording speakers of Czech. As both Czech and Polish are West Slavic languages, they are similar in many ways, but Czech has phonemic vowel-length contrasts. Thus it seemed possible that Czech would also fail to differentiate vowel durations according to consonant voicing, so that vowel duration could be reserved for the phonemic length contrast. Three native speakers of Czech read several words of the following form:

$$\begin{Bmatrix} p \\ ml \end{Bmatrix} \begin{Bmatrix} a \\ a: \end{Bmatrix} \begin{Bmatrix} t \\ d \end{Bmatrix} \text{V (C)}$$

The number of phonemic short and long vowels was balanced. The mean duration of vowels before [t] was 193.7 msec, before [d], 204.2 msec. The ratio of these two means is .95, and the mean of the individual ratios is .98. Thus there is a slight tendency for vowels to be shortened before voiceless consonants, but the difference in durations did not reach statistical significance ($t_{30} = -.37$, $p > .20$). In sum, neither Czech nor Polish disyllables show the supposed universal vowel shortening before voiceless consonants.

One line of explanation that has been offered for vowel length differences involves the fact that closure-interval durations also vary with voicing and are inversely related to the vowel durations. That is, voiceless stops have longer closure intervals than do voiced stops. In English and presumably other languages with vowel lengthening, the two ratios, vowel and closure, essentially balance each other, so that the syllable duration is relatively constant. What happens to closure, and syllable, durations in Polish? Closure durations for the same 24 pairs were also measured. The mean duration for [t] was 130.1 msec and for [d], 91.5 msec. The ratio of these means is 1.42, and the difference is statistically significant ($t_{23} = 8.81$, $p < .001$). Comparable data for English labial stops are Lisker's (1957) ratio of 1.60, and Port's (1977) ratio of 1.35 (again, from sentence contexts). Thus Polish, like English, has longer closure durations for voiceless stops. Because Polish shows the closure but not the vowel effect, its syllable durations are not balanced.

This finding indicates that the vowel-shortening effect, in those languages where it occurs, is not physiologically determined by the closure-duration effect. Of course, there could still be some nonphysiological relation between closure and vowel duration that some languages could choose to implement. For example, language-specific prosodic factors like stress or rhythm could make it desirable to balance intrinsic syllable durations. This factor may operate more powerfully in a language like English, with variable stress and vowel reduction, than in a language like Polish, with fixed stress.

Thus the possibility that vowel shortening before voiceless consonants is an (automatic) phonetic universal is not supported by an investigation of Polish and Czech. Further counterevidence from Saudi Arabic is found in Flege (1979). He found that long /a:/ was not significantly longer before word-final /d/ than /t/. Therefore, we know that this rule cannot be placed in a universal phonetic component because it does not occur universally across languages. Rules of phonetic vowel duration as a function of voicing of a following consonant must be language specific.

Furthermore, Chen's study shows that exceptions to the phonetic pattern take still another form. For example, Chen found a vowel-duration difference in Russian completely comparable to that in other languages, although a footnote indicates that all the final consonants determining the vowel durations were voiceless, Russian having a rule of final devoicing.[4] The duration pattern was apparently determined by underlying values of the voicing feature. A similar difference was found for German and was shown to be marginally perceptible by Port *et al.* (1981). In the same way, vowel duration for speakers of some English dialects varies before voiced flaps according to underlying stop-voicing values (Fox & Terbeek 1977). Clearly, if vowel durations can be determined by underlying phonological values for voicing, then the relation between vowel duration and voicing cannot be automatic and physiological. It is important to realize that these cases are actually counterexamples to the pattern at the systematic phonetic level, since in Russian longer vowels occur before voiceless consonants, and in the English dialects shorter vowels occur before voiced consonants. The pattern is clear only at some point in the derivation before the phonetic transcription.

At the same time, there is obviously a trend across languages and across phonological rules that must be accounted for. We can summarize the possibilities as follows: Languages can show no vowel durational differences, or they can show some kinds of differences that relate shorter vowels to following voiceless obstruents. If they do show such a pattern, they can do so at either the phonetic or phonological level. No language shows durational effects in which vowels are shortened before all voiced consonants and lengthened before all voiceless consonants. It is as if there were a possible patterning available to languages: Vowels may be shorter before voiceless consonants. The reverse pattern is not available in this way. Thus we find languages like Polish and Czech with no difference, languages like French and some English dialects with shorter vowels before phonetically voiceless consonants, and languages like Russian and German with a phonologically conditioned pattern.

This example of extrinsic vowel-duration patterning shows that a supposed phonetic universal is not in fact universally attested. Because of this fact, and because the extent and level of duration differences varies across those languages with the pattern, the pattern cannot be automatic or predictable. Each language must specify its own phonetic facts by rule. Possibly, following Fromkin (1977), we could say that languages with an exaggerated pattern and languages with no pattern must include a rule in their grammars. In addition, languages whose patterns are not exaggerated but operate on phonological representations must also include a rule in their grammars. This leaves languages with an unexaggerated duration difference that is entirely phonetically conditioned. Following Fromkin, this pattern could be provided by the phonetic component.

Obviously, however, such a treatment entails a change in the conception of the phonetic component. Rather than a phonetic universal that is predictable and automatic, that phonetic statement would represent one special case, simply a kind of "elsewhere" condition on phonetic detail. Alternatively, the phonetically conditioned cases could be treated exactly like the phonologically conditioned cases, by a grammatical rule.

As in the intrinsic duration case, it appears that the role of the phonetics is to provide a pattern that might be preferred. Within any one language, however, vowel duration is controlled by the grammar, even though it is a low-level phonetic phenomenon. While it is a good idea to continue looking for phonetic universals that would support a model of automatic phonetic interpretation, it seems more likely that our eventual model will incorporate phonetic rules of timing into the phonology.

4. VOICING TIMING

In the case of the occurrence and timing of stop-consonant voicing, each of the investigative methods considered above has been employed by a number of people. Cross-language surveys have revealed patterns that must be explained, and modeling studies have tried to provide some explanations. What is interesting is that none of the patterns found is universal, yet each is a good example of phonetic naturalness. Thus these patterns are a key to the relation among physical motivations, phonetic rules, and the grammar.

The sort of patterns I have in mind are exemplified as follows. Surveys of phoneme inventories (e.g., Maddieson 1984) produce two major observations. First, voiceless stops are generally preferred to voiced stops, especially for geminates. Second, the extent of this stop-consonant preference with regard to voicing varies according to place of articulation, with further front stops more likely to be voiced. Thus some languages have /b/ but no /p/ (labials favor voicing), or /k/ but no /g/ (velars favor voicelessness). Surveys of allophone occurrence and detail lead to similar conclusions. In most environments, voiceless unaspirated stops are favored, even in intervocalic position, contrary to popular belief (Houlihan 1982; Keating, Linker, & Huffman 1983). Place-of-articulation effects on the duration of voicing and of aspiration can be observed across languages (Lisker & Abramson 1964), although various exceptions have been noted. In this section I confine discussion to the more categorial effects on voicing discussed in Keating *et al.* (1983), namely, the position-in-utterance preferences seen in unrelated languages.

The best-known work on physiological motivations for voicing patterns in general is probably that of Ohala (much of it summarized in Ohala 1983). Ohala has used a simple model of breath-stream dynamics to illustrate the common observation that voicing requires glottal airflow, while stop occlusion impedes such airflow; in this sense stop occlusion and voicing are at odds with each other. Thus it is understandable that voiceless stops should be more common than voiced. He also used the model to reason about the further patterns found. Drawing on other modeling work by Rothenberg (1968) and Muller and Brown (1980), Ohala stressed the role of passive and active expansion of the vocal tract walls in allowing airflow, and hence voicing, to continue during stop occlusion. Wall expansion is related to findings about place of articulation in that the further front the occlusion, the more expandable vocal tract wall area there is between glottis and occlusion. Thus we should expect further-front places to allow voicing continuation more easily than further-back places.

Westbury and I, together and separately, have looked in more detail at effects of place of articulation, position in utterance, and stress on Voice Onset Time (VOT) and closure voicing duration. A model of voicing based on Rothenberg's was devised and is described in more detail in Westbury (1983). It allows us to vary over time the subglottal pressure, the position of the vocal cords, the oral constriction in three dimensions, and the stiffness of the vocal tract walls. We use results from an x-ray study (Westbury 1979) and a tracheal puncture study (conducted by Westbury and others at the University of Texas Phonetics Lab) for constriction and pressure data, and other published data on factors such as glottal opening as inputs (see Westbury 1983 for references). The computer program takes these inputs and calculates the resulting airflows and air pressures in the vocal tract. From the airflow through the larynx we can see exactly when voicing should occur. In the case of position-in-utterance effects, our results (Westbury & Keating 1984) were clear. We compared initial, intersonorant, and final positions, assuming that the only difference across them was the subglottal pressure being generated. We assumed that the vocal cords were equally ready to vibrate in all three positions and that the closures and velocities of the oral gestures were the same, except (noncrucially) that initial closures were longer. Such modeling showed that the pressure differences result in three different acoustic patterns. In initial position, voicing does not occur until after consonant release with these inputs; in medial position, voicing continues from the preceding sonorant through most but not all of the stop occlusion; in final position, voicing continues into the beginning of the occlusion but ceases earlier than in medial position.

A preference of languages for voiceless unaspirated initial and final allophones is thus seen to arise from the physical operation of the speaking device. What does this preference explain? It may be useful to compare our account of final stop voicelessness with Dinnsen's (1980) discussion of supposed aerodynamic explanations of phonological rules of final devoicing. He distinguishes explaining the structural description of a rule (here, that it affects final stops) from explaining its structural change (here, that it devoices them) and from explaining why there should be any rule in the first place (here, some difficulty posed by final voiced stops); he says that only the structural description is explained by, for example, the work of Ohala. Our explanation is different from Ohala's,[5] however, and goes further in illuminating the structural change of the final devoicing rule and arguably its motivation. This improvement comes from carefully quantifying the articulatory conditions that hold before the stop consonant, the acoustic characteristics of a stop in which those conditions are changed only minimally, and the acoustic characteristics of stops in which those conditions are changed more drastically. A devoicing rule specifies a structural change most in accord with the result of a minimal change in articulatory conditions.

However, as Dinnsen emphasizes, a phonological rule exists independently of such a phonetic motivation. That this must be so in the case of final devoicing is shown by the fact that our motivation applies only to position-in-utterance effects. Position in utterance is not the same as position in word, and many linguistic rules and constraints operate in the word domain. For example, instances of word-final devoicing in utterance-medial position are phonetic counterexamples to the patterns generated by the model. They may serve to demarcate word boundaries in running speech, for example, but are no longer directly physically motivated. At best, then, physiology motivates one basic case that can be incorporated arbitrarily into phonological rules.

Does that mean that those cases where a linguistic voicing pattern does correspond directly to outputs of the model are in fact automatic? The answer must be, only if controlling articulation in the way we have assumed is automatic. It is important that specific sets of articulatory inputs are required to produce the outputs discussed here. The speech production system must be controlled by a real speaker in a way that ensures those inputs and no others. Possibly, as was suggested for the extrinsic vowel duration case, such control of the phonetic pattern is provided outside the phonology, with only the exceptions given in the phonology. But already that means that some very low-level phenomena of timing are to be included in the phonology. Consider, for example, the pattern for place of articulation to correlate with VOT, presumably due in part to differences in the movement velocity of the various articulators. Suppose that in some language this pattern were counterex-emplified by having apical stops with lower VOT values than labials, and that the reason was that the upper lip did not participate in the labial gesture (giving a lower net labial-movement velocity). This would mean that in this language the place of articulation counterpattern would be specified in the grammar, though it is concerned with mere milliseconds of timing difference. Thus, if every time we find an exception to a phonetic generalization we state that exception in the grammar, our notion of grammar will be much expanded. In fact, the grammar will include all the kinds of statements that remain in the phonetic component, for no kind of generalization appears to be exceptionless.

On analogy with the use of an articulatory model, we can think of preferred articulatory values as being "default" values of the articulatory system and the outputs that result from these inputs as default outputs of the system. Speakers are not physically constrained to use these default inputs, and it is clear that across languages a wide variety of articulatory values are used.[6] In those cases the language has chosen to override the default settings and substitute more marked settings. Possibly the more substitutions a given output requires, the more marked it will be. Nonetheless, the default settings, where found, must still be specified at some point in the production of an utterance.

5. DISCUSSION

Three candidates for inclusion in the set of phonetic universals have been considered: intrinsic vowel duration, extrinsic vowel duration, and voicing timing. None of them is an automatic consequence of articulatory biomechanics, the strongest view of what a set of universals might be. None of them is necessarily universal. Thus it cannot be the case that a segmental phonetic transcription is automatically interpreted by phonetic conventions, at least with respect to such timing variables. Rather, language-specific rules extend further into phonetics than was assumed in the constrained SPE model. There are two ways that the model can be revised. If the phonetic component still consists of universals, or even just default cases, then almost everything is in the phonology, and the phonetic transcription will be quite narrow. If the phonetic component can include language-specific rules, then the phonetic transcription need not be so narrow, but some independent way of deciding what is in the phonetic component is needed, for example, all timing rules. Phonetic experiments will not determine which of these possibilities is preferable. Only actually trying to devise grammars to include new phonetic data is relevant to that question.

What phonetic experiments can do is identify those parameters that must be controlled by the speaker and default values for those parameters, by studying recurrent phonetic patterns. These patterns exist as options available to languages as physical conveniences but not necessities. Languages must choose whether to incorporate the default and at what level of the grammar. It is not the phonetic patterns themselves that constitute universals; rather, what is universal are the general principles that dictate the default articulatory settings.

Lindblom (1983), in discussing the concept of economy of effort as a factor in the development of sound systems, arrives at a similar overall conclusion. He stresses that speech typically underexploits the capabilities of the speech production system. In his view, more economical speech gestures are favored but are not inevitable. Thus the occurrence and extent of consonant–vowel coarticulation, for example, may differ across speakers or be specified phonologically. Patterns found across languages are due to minimizing the expenditure of energy per unit time; lack of a pattern in a given language indicates a greater level of performance effort of the speech system. Lindblom also concludes that the physiological mechanisms underlying economy of effort are not yet understood.

Previous approaches to language-specific exceptions to phonetic patterns have given a special grammatical role to the exceptions. Stampe (1973) proposed that a child begins acquisition with a set of phonetic processes and replaces some of them with rules on the basis of learning. Hyman (1975) developed the idea of phonologization, that some universal phonetic processes get incorporated into the phonologies of certain languages by being made arbitrary in some way and then play a role in the grammar. But it seems more plausible that every aspect of phonetic control must be learned, for example, the patterns of rise and fall of subglottal pressure that give rise to consonant voicing patterns. I am suggesting here that we consider all phonetic processes, even the most low level, to be phonologized (or grammaticized) in the sense that they are cognitively represented, under explicit control by the speaker, and once-removed from (that is, not automatic consequences of) the physical speaking machine.

Where this account seems unmotivated, as discussed before, are those cases where the default pattern actually occurs without exception phonetically. In these cases it would be possible to say that the default pattern is not controlled by a phonologized rule but that a value is filled in by a phonetic component after all rules have applied. Consider, however, such a phonologization account of extrinsic vowel duration in various languages. That account will distinguish languages like Russian and German (with final devoicing and opaque vowel-length differences) from languages like French (with phonetically transparent vowel-length differences). Russian and German will have phonologized vowel length, while French will not; it will have durations supplied by the phonetics. Suppose now that French acquires a rule of final-consonant devoicing like that of German or Russian, and that, as in German and Russian, vowel length is sensitive to phonological voicing. The phonologization account would have to say that at the moment the devoicing rule is added to the French grammar, vowel length also becomes a grammatical rule, as opposed to a default option or pattern. Since the only change in the vowel-length pattern is that it has changed from phonetically transparent to opaque, then rule transparency must be criterial in assigning phonetic patterns to the phonetics or the phonology. On the other hand, if all phonetic patterns, including transparent vowel length, are represented in the grammar, then the only change in the French grammar is the addition of the devoicing rule. In the absence of arguments for the transparency criterion, then, the phonologization account seems more complex than required.

The view that all phonetic phenomena are controlled by rule has a further interesting implication. Anderson (1981) argued that phonological rules by definition are not natural; they are what is left when everything else is factored out. As a response to various theories of natural phonology, this argument is valid. But it leaves the frequent phonetic naturalness of rules—even rules with exceptions on the surface—unexplained. It sounds ad hoc that some rules (most low-level ones) should actually be natural, while other rules (the opaque ones) only look natural. But once we recognize that all phonetic patterns are rule governed and once-removed from the physical machine, then naturalness can be seen as a more abstract and general property of rules, wherever they are in the phonology. Various rules will have in common the fact that they embody default patterns. Some of these rules will apply transparently; others will apply opaquely. Naturalness is not directly a fact about the speaking machine. It is a fact about the phonological component: The phonology values highly rules that in form indulge the preferences of the speaking machine.

Patterns of phonetic detail are interesting, then, not because they constitute a special universal component outside of grammars, one whose workings are quite different from those of phonology, but rather because they are an integral part of phonology. It seems likely that there are no true linguistic phonetic universals and that the grammar of a language controls all aspects of phonetic form.

NOTES

1. Also taken into account at this stage are nongrammatical suprasegmental parameters, both for languages (base of articulation) and for individuals at a given moment (voice quality, rate of utterance).

2. It does not matter for this discussion whether the pattern is seen as shortening of vowels before voiceless obstruents or lengthening of vowels in converse environments.
3. Chen's comparisons confounded language and position of the vowel + consonant in a word: Some languages were represented mainly by monosyllables, others mainly by disyllables with a medial vowel + consonant. The degree of vowel-duration difference is known to vary even within a single language according to position (compare Sharf 1962 and Klatt 1973 with Lehiste 1970).
4. The rule of devoicing does not guarantee that the neutralized consonants themselves are identical (Dinnsen 1982).
5. Ohala links final devoicing to an observed lengthening of final consonants, that is, they devoice for the same reason geminates do. Notice that in our modeling we have not lengthened final consonants, showing that such lengthening is not required, though of course it would have the enhancing effect Ohala describes.
6. Although these settings have some absolute limits in the physical world (e.g., how fast the tongue can move), it is interesting that these limits are not typically approached in speaking. For example, the changing volume of the oral cavity is relevant in any consideration of voicing maintenance for stop consonants, as we have seen, and obviously there is some finite limit on how large an individual's oral cavity can become. But this limit is probably never approached in speaking. Westbury (1983) shows that the set of possible maneuvers to expand the oral cavity makes so much expansion possible that from the point of view of speaking the oral cavity seems to have unlimited potential volume. When a speaker exploits these maneuvers is a separate question, of course.

REFERENCES

Anderson, S. (1974). *The organization of phonology*. New York: Academic Press.
Anderson, S. (1981). Why phonology isn't 'natural'. *Linguistic Inquiry, 12*, 493–589.
Chen, M. (1970). Vowel length variation as a function of the voicing of consonant environment. *Phonetica, 22*, 129–159.
Chomsky, N. (1964). Current issues in linguistic theory. In J. A. Fodor & J. J. Katz (Eds.), *The structure of language* (pp. 50–118). Englewood Cliffs, NJ: Prentice Hall.
Chomsky, N., & Halle, M. (1968). *The sound pattern of English*. New York: Harper & Row.
Dinnsen, D. A. (1980). Phonological rules and phonetic explanation. *Journal of Linguistics, 16*, 171–191.
Dinnsen, D. A. (1982). *Abstract phonetic implementation rules and word-final devoicing in Catalan*. Talk presented at the annual meeting of the Linguistic Society of America, San Diego.
Flege, J. E. (1979). *Phonetic interference in second language acquisition*. Unpublished doctoral dissertation, Indiana University.
Fowler, C. A. (1980). Coarticulation and theories of extrinsic timing. *Journal of Phonetics, 8*, 113–133.
Fox, R. A., & Terbeek, D. (1977). Dental flaps, vowel duration and rule ordering in American English. *Journal of Phonetics, 5*, 27–34.
Fromkin, V. A. (1977). Some questions regarding universal phonetics and phonetic representations. In A. Juilland (Ed.), *Linguistic studies offered to Joseph Greenberg on the occasion of his sixtieth birthday* (pp. 365–380). Saratoga, CA: Anma Libri.

Fujimura, O., & Lovins, J. (1978). Syllables as concatenative phonetic units. In A. Bell & J. Hooper (Eds.), *Syllables and segments* (pp. 107–120). Amsterdam: North-Holland.

Hooper, J. B. (1976). *An introduction to natural generative phonology*. New York: Academic Press.

Houlihan, K. (1982). *Is intervocalic voicing a natural rule?* Talk presented at the annual meeting of the Linguistic Society of America, San Diego.

Hyman, M. (1975). *Phonology: Theory and analysis*. New York: Holt, Rinehart and Winston.

Keating, P. A. (1979). *A phonetic study of a voicing contrast in Polish*. Unpublished doctoral dissertation, Brown University.

Keating, P., Linker, W., & Huffman, M. (1983). Patterns in allophone distribution for voiced and voiceless stops. *Journal of Phonetics, 11*, 277–290.

Klatt, D. (1973). Interaction between two factors that influence vowel duration. *Journal of the Acoustical Society of America, 54*, 1102–1104.

Ladefoged, P. (1971). *Preliminaries to linguistic phonetics*. Chicago: University of Chicago Press.

Ladefoged, P. (1980). What are linguistic sounds made of? *Language, 56*, 485–502.

Lehiste, I. (1970). *Suprasegmentals*. Cambridge, MA: MIT Press.

Lindblom, B. (1967). Vowel duration and a model of lip mandible coordination. *STL-QPSR, 4*, 1–29.

Lindblom, B. (1983). Economy of speech gestures. In P. F. MacNeilage (Ed.), *The production of speech* (pp. 217–246). New York: Springer-Verlag.

Lisker, L. (1957). Closure duration and the intervocalic voiced-voiceless distinction in English. *Language, 33*, 42–49.

Lisker, L., & Abramson, A. (1964). A cross-language study of voicing in initial stops: Acoustical measurements. *Word, 20*, 384–422.

MacNeilage, P. (1970). Motor control of serial ordering of speech. *Psychological Review, 77*, 182–196.

Maddieson, I. (1984). *Patterns of sounds*. Cambridge: Cambridge University Press.

Muller, E. M., & Brown, W. S., Jr. (1980). Variations in the Supraglottal Air Pressure Waveform and their Articulatory Interpretation. In N. Lass (Ed.), *Speech and language: Advances in basic research and practice:* Vol. 4 (pp. 317–389). New York: Academic Press.

Nelson, W. L. (1980). Performance bounds in speech motor control of jaw movements. *Journal of the Acoustical Society of America, 68*, Suppl. 1, S32 (A).

Ohala, J. J. (1983). The origin of sound patterns in vocal tract constraints. In P. F. MacNeilage (Ed.), *The production of speech* (pp. 189–216). New York: Springer-Verlag.

Pierrehumbert, J. (1980). *The phonology and phonetics of English intonation*. Unpublished doctoral dissertation, Massachusetts Institute of Technology.

Port, R. (1977). *The influence of speaking tempo on the duration of stressed vowel and medial stop in English trochee words*. Doctoral dissertation, University of Connecticut, published by the Indiana University Linguistics Club.

Port, R., Mitleb, F., & O'Dell, M. (1981). *Neutralization of obstruent voicing in German is incomplete. Journal of the Acoustical Society of America, 70*, Suppl. 1, S13(A).

Postal, P. (1968). *Aspects of phonological theory*. New York: Harper and Row.

Rothenberg, M. (1968). *The breath-stream dynamics of simple-released-plosive production* (Bibliotheca Phonetica 6). Basel: Karger.

Sharf, D. (1962). Duration of post-stress inter-vocalic stops and preceding vowels. *Language and Speech, 5*, 26–30.

Stampe, D. (1973). *A dissertation on natural phonology.* Doctoral dissertation distributed by Indiana University Linguistics Club as Stampe (1979).

Westbury, J. R. (1979). *Aspects of the temporal control of voicing in consonant clusters in English. Texas Linguistic Forum, 14,* 1–304.

Westbury, J. R. (1983). Enlargement of the supraglottal cavity and its relation to stop consonant voicing. *Journal of the Acoustical Society of America, 74,* 1322–1336.

Westbury, J., & Keating, P. (1980). Central representation of vowel duration. *Journal of the Acoustical Society of America, 67,* Suppl. 1, S37 (A).

Westbury, J., & Keating, P. (1984). On the naturalness of stop consonant voicing. Unpublished manuscript.

9

Computation of Mapping from Muscular Contraction Patterns to Formant Patterns in Vowel Space*

Yuki Kakita
Osamu Fujimura
Kiyoshi Honda

1. INTRODUCTION

In previous papers (Fujimura & Kakita 1978; Kakita & Fujimura 1977), we demonstrated that a three-dimensional static model of the tongue can be used to explain basic characteristics of vowels. At that time we specifically discussed some characteristics of the vowel [i]. In the present chapter we present some preliminary results of our study of various vowels, in particular the five tense vowels of American English, /i/, /e/, /ɑ/, /o/, /u/. This study is in part based on the emg data reported by Alfonso et al. [1982]. The computational method, after Kiritani's original work, is an application of the finite-element method (Kiritani, Miyawaki, & Fujimura 1976). The anatomical data on which the design of our model is based are largely due to Miyawaki (1974).

2. A COMPUTATIONAL MODEL OF THE TONGUE

Figure 9.1 shows our tongue model in three different views. The anatomical structure in the front view (to the right) shows a frontal section in the plane indicated by the vertical line in the top view (upper left)

* We are grateful to our colleagues at Haskins Laboratories for their permission to use the emg and speech data that originally appeared in Alfonso, Honda, Baer, and Harris (1982) and in Alfonso, Baer, and Honda (1983), respectively.

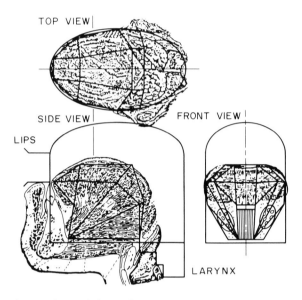

Figure 9.1 Three orthogonal views of the anatomical structures and the computational model of the tongue. The cavity walls, lip, and larynx are also shown.

and in the side view (lower left). Surrounding tissues considered in the model are added by hand drawing. This model of the tongue uses 86 tetrahedra to represent one-half of the tongue body, assuming a symmetry with respect to the midsagittal plane. The entire set of tetrahedra is subgrouped into 30 functional units, giving rise to 33 functional node points.

The wall structures housing the tongue are approximated by an elliptic vertical cylinder connected to the upper half of an ellipsoid, representing the side walls and the palatal ceiling, respectively. The shape of the labial section is specified by two parameters of a cylinder, representing lip opening and protrusion. The laryngeal cavity consists of three cylinders.

3. THE ANATOMY OF TONGUE MUSCLES AND THEIR IMPLEMENTATIONS IN THE MODEL

The muscles related to the tongue control can be classified in four categories: (1) intrinsic, (2) extrinsic, (3) suprahyoid, and (4) infrahyoid muscles. The division of the model into a set of functional units is designed in such a way that any of the relevant muscles can be simulated effectively by a few units. In Figures 9.2–9.7 we show the anatomical structures of the individual muscles and how each muscle is simulated in the model. Each muscle is simulated by a combination of a few functional units.

There are four intrinsic muscles. Figure 9.2 shows two of the four, the superior longitudinal (SL) and the inferior longitudinal (IL) muscles. The anatomical structure is shown in the left panel, and the model in the right panel. Directions of muscle fibers are shown with thick lines in the anatomical illustrations. The direction of the muscle contraction force for each of the muscles is indicated by a double-headed arrow. Unlike our previous model (Kakita & Fujimura 1977), the model now can specify any direction in the three-dimensional space.

Figure 9.3 shows the remaining two intrinsic muscles, the transverse (T) and the vertical (V) muscle. Contraction of the transverse muscle reduces the width of the tongue, and this causes a slight elevation of the tongue body due to the volume incompressibility of the substance composing the tongue.

SL: SUPERIOR LONGITUDINAL

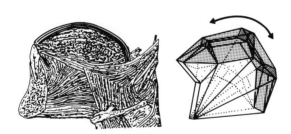

IL: INFERIOR LONGITUDINAL

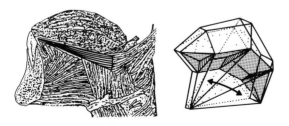

INTRINSIC MUSCLES I

Figure 9.2 Intrinsic lingual muscles (I): the superior longitudinal (SL) and the inferior longitudinal (IL) muscles.

T : TRANSVERSUS

V : VERTICALIS

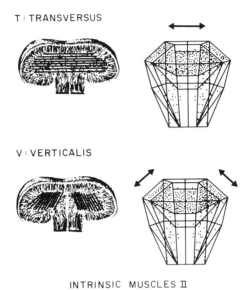

INTRINSIC MUSCLES Ⅱ

Figure 9.3   Intrinsic lingual muscles (II): the transverse (T) and the vertical (V) muscles.

There are four extrinsic muscles. Figure 9.4 shows the fan-shaped genioglossus (GG) muscle. It has been reported that the emg activity of different parts of this muscle varies, depending on the vowel in question (Miyawaki, Hirose, Ushijima, & Sawashima 1975). Therefore, in our model, this muscle is divided into three functional parts: the anterior (GGA), the middle (GGM), and the posterior (GGP) portions. In our

GG : GENIOGLOSSUS
  GGA : ANTERIOR   GGM : MIDDLE   GGP : POSTERIOR

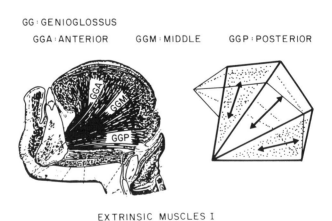

EXTRINSIC MUSCLES I

Figure 9.4   Extrinsic lingual muscles (I): the genioglossus muscle (GG).

previous paper (Fujimura & Kakita 1978), we discussed their roles in producing front vowels.

Figure 9.5 shows the remaining four extrinsic muscles: the styloglossus (SG), the hyoglossus (HG), the palatoglossus (PG), and the pharyngeal constrictor (PC) muscles. Each of these muscles is represented as a set of pulling forces exerted on selected node points. The styloglossus muscle is discussed in some detail later. Pharyngeal constrictors (PC) are shown by two straps and corresponding arrows. These muscles are, in reality, continuously distributed along the pharyngeal walls, and they squeeze the pharyngeal walls inward as well as pull the tongue backward.

Figure 9.6 shows four suprahyoid muscles. In the model, the total

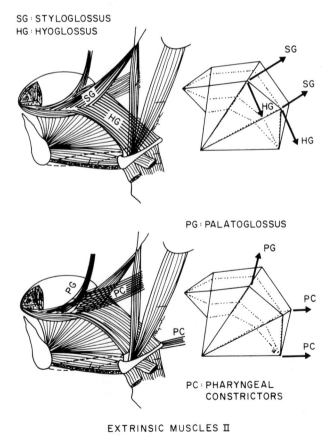

EXTRINSIC MUSCLES II

Figure 9.5 Extrinsic lingual muscles (II): the styloglossus (SG) and the hyoglossus (HG) muscles in the upper drawing, and the palatoglossus muscle (PG) and the pharyngeal constrictors (PC) in the lower drawing.

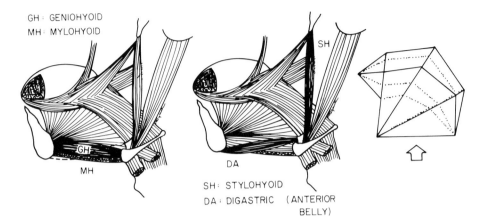

SUPRAHYOID MUSCLES

Figure 9.6 Suprahyoid muscles. The geniohyoid (GH), the mylohyoid (MH), the stylohyoid (SH) muscles, and the anterior belly of the digastric (DA) muscle.

effect of all these muscles is simulated by an elevation of the tongue body. These muscles are only indirectly represented in our model. We come back to this issue later.

Figure 9.7 shows three infrahyoid muscles. These muscles act to pull down the bottom of the tongue. This effect is simulated in our model by adjusting what we call "jaw height."

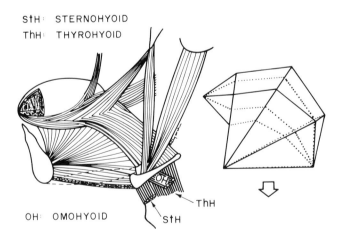

INFRAHYOID MUSCLES

Figure 9.7 Infrahyoid muscles. The sternohyoid (StH), the thyrohyoid (ThH), and the omohyoid (OH) muscles.

4. A NEW IMPLEMENTATION OF THE STYLOGLOSSUS MUSCLE

The styloglossus muscle is simulated by three effective components of forces as shown in Figure 9.8. Component 1 is a force that acts on the lateral surface of the tongue body, pulling it back toward the styloid process. This force is exerted by those fibers ending in this region of the tongue body. Component 2 pulls the tip of the anterior part of the tongue backward and slightly downward. This force is due to the fibers ending in this region. The same muscle also produces an effective force, component 3, which pulls the tongue body around the middle of the muscle upward. It was implemented for the following reasons: (1) The upper fibers of this muscle are curved in this region. (2) There is no termination of these muscle fibers between the tip of the tongue and the styloid process. (3) When the muscle fibers contract, achieving an equilibrium, the surrounding tissues around the portion of the largest curvature receive, in effect, an upward force as shown by the dashed arrow in b.

Thus, the contraction of the styloglossus muscle results in bunching of the tongue (c) along the line suggested by Ladefoged, Harshman, Goldstein, and Rice (1978). Without the second and the third components, it is very difficult, in our experience, to simulate the vowel /u/ properly.[2]

5. Emg DATA VERSUS MODEL PARAMETERS

Electromyographic data of the tongue muscles during the production of American vowels were reported by Alfonso et al. (1982). We used their data as a reference for producing (static) vowel qualities representing the relatively stationary portions of the five tense vowels /i/, /e/, /ɑ/, /o/, and /u/ of American English. Figure 9.9 shows bar graphs comparing model parameters with the measured emg data, muscle by muscle. Emg data (left) and model parameters (right) are semiquantitatively scaled for the convenience of comparison. A linear relation between the emg voltage and the muscle force is assumed.[3] Jaw-height values are also from Alfonso et al. (1982). In this figure, the scale is adjusted so that the lowest jaw height, for the vowel /ɑ/, exhibits the same value for the measured height and the optimal model parameter used for our simulation.

A trial-and-error procedure obtained a suitable consistency among (1) emg magnitudes reported, (2) tongue shapes expected from x-ray data, and (3) formant frequencies observed (simultaneously recorded wih the emg data) and those computed.

Our results may be summarized as follows:

1. For the intrinsic and extrinsic muscles in general, our model parameters agreed quite well with the emg magnitudes for those muscles

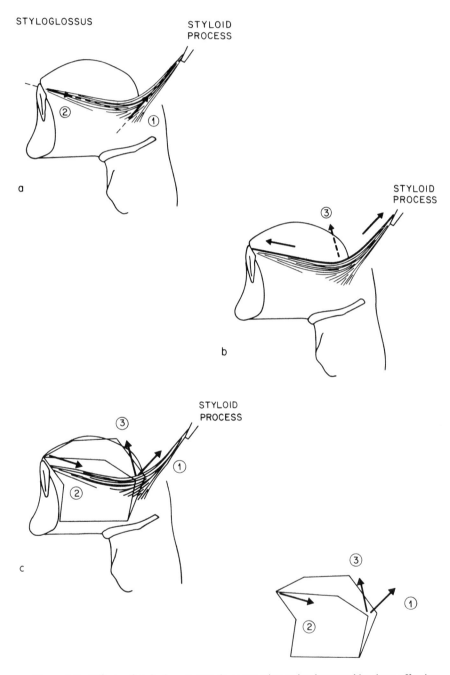

Figure 9.8   Effects of styloglossus muscle contraction as implemented by three effective components of forces.

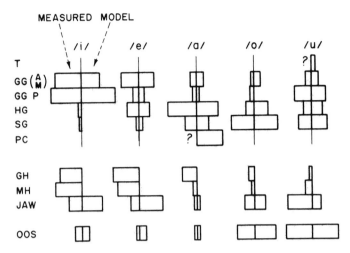

Figure 9.9 Comparison between the measured values (the left side of the bars) and the model parameters (the right side of the bars) for five tense vowels of American English.

observed in the emg experiment. The model simulation, however, predicted that additional muscles must be active: the pharyngeal constrictors for /ɑ/ and the transverse muscle for /u/. For these muscles, emg data were not available. For the vowel /ɑ/, we could not obtain a satisfactory result without contracting the pharyngeal constrictors. For the vowel /u/, the styloglossus muscle plays the main role in forming the appropriate tongue shape. When the transverse muscle is added, however, the force for the styloglossus can be reduced to 75%. This latter value for the styloglossus agrees well with the measured emg value.

2. Jaw height for the model qualitatively agrees well with the measured value for the vowel /o/. However, the model-based value is greater for the vowels /i/ and /e/, and smaller for the vowel /u/, than reported measurements. On the other hand, for the vowels /i/ and /e/, the geniohyoid (GH) and the mylohyoid (MH) muscles show greater emg activities than for other vowels. This suggests that the jaw-height parameter that was used in the model in part reflected the effects of elevating the floor of the tongue, as a result of geniohyoid and mylohyoid activities.[4]

6. MEASURED AND COMPUTED FORMANT DATA

Figure 9.10 shows a F_1 versus F_2 plot. F_1 increases downward and F_2 increases leftward, so that a conventional vowel triangle is seen. Crosses indicate the measured formant values in the emg experiment cited above, and filled circles are the computed formant values using our model. The

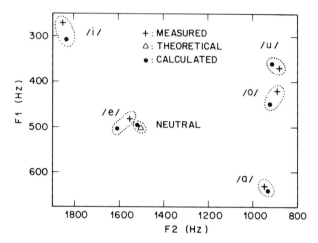

Figure 9.10 F_1–F_2 diagram for measured (crosses) and computed (circles) values. The acoustic signals used here were simultaneously recorded with emg shown in Figure 9.9.

triangle shows the theoretically defined neutral vowel, that is, a uniform acoustic tube. The closed circle next to this triangle is the computed value using an intermediate jaw-height value and no muscle contractions.

In Figure 9.11, a good comparison of model-based computer values (long lines) with values obtained by acoustic measurements as reported by Peterson and Barney (1952) (short lines) is demonstrated for the three lowest formant frequencies. The third formant frequency values for our subject, whose F_1–F_2 data are shown in Figure 9.10, were not available.

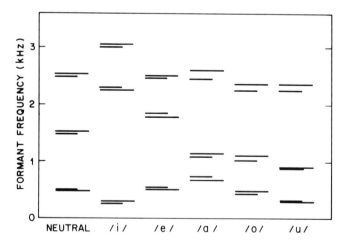

Figure 9.11   Comparison between the measured (short lines) and computed (long lines) values for the three lowest formant frequencies.

7. CONCLUSION

Based on our three-dimensional computational model of the tongue, we have successfully mapped plausible combinations of muscle contractions onto formant patterns of five different vowels (and a neutral vowel). Our feeling is that the phonetic vowel space can be covered more or less completely by this model as far as the static characteristics of vowels are concerned. Eventually, with minor improvements, we should be able to pursue a muscle-to-formant mapping and its inverse, in a manner discussed previously by Mathews *et al.* (1976) and Atal *et al.* (1978) concerning formant to area-function mapping.

NOTES

1. When one of the authors visited Professor Ladefoged at the UCLA Phonetics Lab almost 20 years ago, he was taken to the Faculty Club. Professor Ladefoged pointed to the slices of smoked beef tongue being served in the buffet and demanded that the visitor name all the muscles appearing in the cross-section of the tongue before he could be treated for lunch. Having gone through some anatomical dissection sessions at the University of Tokyo Medical School, the young visitor managed to escape starvation, but this experience imprinted in his mind a strong motivation to study what the tongue actually did in speech articulation. For this reason, this preliminary report is submitted to Professor Ladefoged on his 60th birthday in partial fulfillment of the long-term homework requirements for joining his school of experimental phonetics.

2. The muscle fibers causing the third component of the muscle contraction effect are assumed to be separate from those fibers causing the first two effects. Whether the third component should be treated separately from the second is an empirical question, but the answer does not affect our conclusion, as long as the effect of modeling is concerned. Even if such independent fibers cannot be observed in the actual anatomical structures, it is still reasonable to interpret those as virtually separate components, representing a part of the effect of the relatively loose connection between the muscle fibers in question and the surrounding tissues. In other words, if the general assumption that tissues comprising the tongue are homogenious (within each unit of the model) is violated in some parts of the system, then we can approximately represent the deviation by an additional component.

An obvious anatomical case of this nature is known, namely, human digastric muscle. The tendon concatenating the anterior and posterior bellies of this muscle is coupled through a freely sliding hook to the hyode bone.

3. In Figure 9.9, bars on the left indicate normalized magnitudes of the measured emg signals, whereas those on the right indicate normalized magnitudes of the computed model parameters. Values cannot be compared between different muscles.

To obtain normalized magnitudes of the emg signals, (1) an interval of 100 ms up to the voice onset was selected, considering the delay mainly due to the muscle contraction time, and the average value for the 100-ms interval was computed. Then, (2) the minimum value among the five vowels was scored as 1 and the maximum value as 9. Values between were scored in linear proportions between 1 and 9. (3) For ease of comparison with the model values, the total magnitude of left bars for the five vowels was normalized to be the same as the total of the right bars.

The orbicularis oris muscle (OOS) is related to lip protrusion. To compare with its emg magnitude, we used the logarithm of the ratio of the length to the lip opening area of the model, with a similar normalization procedure as above.

4. In other words, the natural system, due to the compliance of the support of the floor of the tongue, tends actually to have a lower floor position than the mandible height prescribes. This happens when the posterior genioglossus contracts and makes the floor yield downward, unless there is a reinforcement of the support system by stiffening and thickening the geniohyoid and mylohyoid muscles. There is a trading relation, therefore, between the amounts of the GH–MH contraction and jaw height when GGP contracts. This is actually what we observe when we compare the measured and model-prescribed values in Figure 9.9 for the vowels /i/, /e/, and /u/. The trading, presumably, has to be artifactually strong in our computation because the model does not have GH or MH implemented directly.

It may be suggested that in natural gestures, also, there may be significantly negative correlations between GGP and GH–MH, and between GH–MH and mandible height for the same vowel among different instances of articulation. Our preliminary data actually show a negative correlation between observed GGP activities and mandible height values in the case of /i/.

REFERENCES

Alfonso, P. J., Baer, T., & Honda, K. (1983). Lingual control and vowel articulation. *Proceedings of 11th ICA*, 3–10.

Alfonso, P. E., Honda, K., Baer, T., & Harris, K. S. (1982). Multichannel study of tongue emg during vowel production. *JASA, 71*, S54(A).

Atal, B. S., Chang, J. J., Mathews, M. V., & Tukey, J. W. (1978). Inversion of articulatory–acoustic transformation in the vocal tract by a computer-sorting technique. *JASA, 63*, 1535–1555.

Fujimura, O., & Kakita, Y. (1978). Remarks on quantitative description of the lingual articulation. In B. Lindblom & S. Ohman (Eds.), *Frontiers of speech communication research* (pp. 17–24). London: Academic Press.

Kakita, Y., & Fujimura, O. (1977). Computational model of the tongue: A revised version, *JASA, 62*, S15(A).

Kiritani, S., Miyawaki, K., & Fujimura, O. (1976). A computational model of the tongue. Research Institute of Logopedics and Phoniatrics, University of Tokyo, *Annual Bulletin, 10*, 243–252.

Ladefoged, P., Harshman, R., Goldstein, L., & Rice, L. (1978). Generating vocal tract shapes from formant frequencies. *JASA, 64*, 1027–1035.

Mathews, M. V., Atal, B. S., Chang, J. J., & Tukey, J. W. (1976). Computer-sorting procedure for inverting functions. *JASA, 60*, S77(A).

Miyawaki, K. (1974). A study of the musculature of the human tongue (Observations on transparent preparations of serial sections). Research Institute of Logopedics and Phoniatrics, University of Tokyo, *Annual Bulletin, 8*, 23–50.

Miyawaki, K., Hirose, H., Ushijima, T., & Sawashima, M. (1975). A preliminary report on the electromyograhic study of the activity of lingual muscles. Research Institute of Logopedics and Phoniatrics, University of Tokyo, *Annual Bulletin, 9*, 91–106.

Peterson, G. E., & Barney, H. L. (1952). Control method used in a study of the vowels. *JASA, 24*, 175–184.

10

Rhythm of Poetry, Rhythm of Prose

Ilse Lehiste

This chapter constitutes a pilot study for a pilot study. It is dedicated to Peter Ladefoged in the hope that he will be as interested in an imperfect attempt to open up a new line of research as in a traditional presentation of the results of research following well-established (and perhaps more reliable) patterns.

1. INTRODUCTION

I have been interested for some time in the rhythmic structure of spoken language (see summary in Lehiste 1983a); a parallel interest has been the metric structure of poetry (Lehiste 1973, 1977, 1983b). I have now started on a research project devoted to exploring the similarities and differences between the rhythm of spoken language and the rhythmic structure of orally recited poetry. I have believed for some time that the essence of the suprasegmental structure of a language is crystallized in the meter of its traditional poetry. Rhythm is part of the suprasegmental structure. In poetry, rhythm is one of several possible organizing principles; in many languages, a poetic line is structured in terms of rhythm, while in others, a poetic line may be structured in terms of, for example, number and type of syllables. One aspect of the problem I intend to explore is the difference between prose and poetry on the one hand, and poetry composed in free verse versus poetry composed in one of the classical meters (e.g., trochaic) on the other hand. Comparison of the realization of similar meters in different languages is another aspect of the planned research.

As is well known, classical meters are being used in many languages with varying success, the degree of success depending partly on the degree of closeness between the prosodic structure of the language and the prosodic patterns implied by the classical meters. As disyllabic metric

PHONETIC LINGUISTICS

feet are employed in the poetry of several languages in which I am interested, my initial studies focus on disyllabic metric feet consisting either of a sequence of long syllable + short syllable (the classic definition of a trochaic foot) or stressed syllable + unstressed syllable (the version usually found in so-called stress-timed languages such as English).

2. METHODOLOGY

As a first step, I recorded two sets of materials in English: poetry read both as poetry and as prose by two authors, each reading his or her own texts. I decided that at least one potential source of error would be eliminated by asking the poets to read their own texts: The question of whether the reader reproduced the author's intention in an acceptable way could not arise. The materials consisted of five short poems by Arnold M. Zwicky (AMZ) and two shorter poems and one longer one by Catherine A. Callaghan (CAC) (the poems are given in the appendix). The seven short poems were typed on white 8½" x 11" sheets in two ways. To be read as poetry, each poem was typed on a separate sheet, with division into lines as intended by the author. To be read as prose, the poems were typed continuously with the punctuation marks provided by the poet in the original version. The five short poems of AMZ were typed on a single page, each poem constituting a single paragraph. The two short poems of CAC were likewise typed on a single page; "Dark Twin" was typed as a single paragraph, while "Last Day" was typed in three paragraphs. The longer poem by CAC consists of alternating stanzas of free verse and regular trochaic lines; this poem was included in its original form, without attempting to present it in a form that could be conducive to the poem being read as prose.

Each reader was first given the materials prepared to be read as prose; after the first reading, they were given the separate sheets containing the poems printed in poetic form. The process was repeated, so that the recordings consist of two readings of the materials as prose and two readings of the same materials as poetry. The long poem by CAC was likewise read twice, at the end of each prose cycle. The recordings were made in the anechoic chamber of the Linguistics Laboratory of the Ohio State University, using high-quality equipment. Broad-band spectrograms were made of all productions. The tapes were also processed through a Honeywell Model 1858 Visicorder, which produced a continuous oscillogram. Segmental durations were measured primarily from spectrograms, while the duration of longer utterances and of pauses was measured from oscillograms. All measurements were made by the author of this chapter.

The paper speed was 10 cm/sec; 1 mm thus corresponds to 10 msec. An attempt was made to measure with a precision of .5 mm, which would correspond to 5 msec. Averages are presented with an apparent accuracy of .1 milliseconds, but I do not claim to have measured with such precision. Only a part of the measurements is presented in this context.

I started out with a set of expectations, which may develop into hypotheses during a later stage of this investigation. One of the expectations was that the rhythm of read poetry would be more regular than that of materials read as prose. This I expected to be reflected in durational variability: I anticipated that the duration of metric feet contained in texts read as poetry would be less variable than the duration of the same verbal material read as prose. One measure of variability is standard deviation; the expectation would be fulfilled if the standard deviations of metric feet contained in texts read as poetry were smaller than the standard deviations of the same verbal material contained in texts read as prose.

3. RESULTS

Table 10.1 contains average durations (in msec) and standard deviations of trochaic initial and medial feet in the materials read as poetry and as prose by the two speakers. The decision as to which feet to include was made on the basis of an admittedly subjective procedure: I listened to the recordings, established the position of stresses, and selected sequences that consisted of a stressed and an unstressed syllable. Those trochaic feet that occurred in final position in the written lines of the poems were not included, even though when the materials were read as prose they often occurred in the middle of a sentence rather than in final position. (E.g., the trochaeus *roses* from the sentence *These plastic roses are not perfect* was excluded, since it occurred in final position in the poetic

Table 10.1

AVERAGE DURATION OF TROCHAIC INITIAL AND MEDIAL FEET IN TEXTS READ AS POETRY AND AS PROSE

Speaker	Number of trochaic feet	Poetry		Prose	
		Duration (msec)	Standard deviation	Duration (msec)	Standard deviation
AMZ	104	452.5	106.3	382.7	97.1
CAC	56	543.5	170.1	404.2	107.3

version.) The duration of an initial consonant was included in the duration of the metric foot, with the exception of the unmeasurable duration of plosive consonants occurring in absolute initial position.[1] I calculated the average durations and standard deviations of 104 such trochaic feet as they occurred in the two sets of readings by AMZ and 56 trochaic feet that occurred in readings of the two short poems by CAC (both readers producing the materials twice as poetry and twice as prose). As is apparent from Table 10.1, the expectation was not met: The difference between the standard deviations is in the opposite direction, the reading as poetry showing a larger standard deviation.

The average durations of the metric feet were greater in texts read as poetry than in the same texts read as prose. This resulted in greater length for the lines read as poetry, as may be seen from Table 10.2. This table contains average durations of lines read as poetry and the same verbal material measured from the corresponding text read as prose. (E.g., the duration of *These plastic roses* taken from the reading from a typed text in which it constituted the first line of the poem and the duration of the same partial utterance taken from the reading of a typed text in which it constituted the first part of the full sentence *These plastic roses are not perfect.*)

Table 10.2 shows that for both readers the lines read as poetry were longer than the same texts read as prose. The table shows also that the standard deviations were larger in the case of poetry. The observation made with regard to metric feet thus can be extended to whole lines: Materials read as poetry do not appear to have been read with greater regularity than the same materials read as prose, if indeed the standard deviation is an appropriate measure of variability in these cases.

The longer poem by CAC consists of alternating free verse and trochaic stanzas. There are three free-verse stanzas of five lines each and three stanzas consisting of six four-foot lines, each containing three trochaic feet and a final monosyllabic foot. I measured the durations of all metric feet in the two productions of the poem. The averages are presented in

Table 10.2

AVERAGE DURATION OF LINES READ AS POETRY AND AS PROSE

Speaker	Poem	Lines read as poetry			Lines read as prose		
		N	Duration (msec)	Standard deviation	N	Duration (msec)	Standard deviation
CAC	"Dark Twin"	36	1660.8	498.9	36	1245.0	306.5
	"Last Day"	40	1930.4	892.9	40	1354.9	514.5
AMZ	Five poems	114	1246.6	350.0	114	1085.0	339.0

Table 10.3

AVERAGE DURATIONS OF METRIC FEET CONTAINED IN TWO READINGS
OF A 33-LINE POEM

Position	N	Average duration (msec)	Standard deviation
Metric feet in 30 free-verse lines			
Anacrusis	26	188.8	80.0
Trochaic initial and medial	34	572.9	193.0
Trochaic final	8	665.0	144.0
Monosyllabic medial	8	513.1	158.0
Monosyllabic final	22	589.1	128.8
Other	6	950.8	199.1
Free-verse line	30	1858.7	605.6
Metric feet in 36 trochaic lines			
Trochaic initial	36	501.1	161.1
Trochaic second	36	747.1	291.8
Trochaic third	36	596.1	287.9
Monosyllabic final	36	526.8	91.0
Trochaic line	36	2371.1	464.0

Table 10.3, which consists of two parts, one section containing the results
of measurements made from the three free-verse stanzas, the other offering
the results of measurements made from the three trochaic stanzas. My
expectation was to find greater regularity in the duration of metric feet
in the regular trochaic lines as compared to the duration of metric feet
in the free-verse lines, which may be considered more similar to prose.
As can be seen from the standard deviations, there was greater variability
in the durations of trochaic feet in the regular lines than in the free-verse
part of the poem. However, the sum of the standard deviations of the
metric feet is in both cases larger than the standard deviation of the
duration of the line, which (in the case of the trochaic lines) would
indicate a certain amount of temporal coordination between the durations
of the metric feet constituting the line. As might have been expected,
the standard deviation of the trochaic lines is smaller than the variability
of the lines composed in free verse and containing unequal numbers of
metric feet.

Above I characterized this chapter as a pilot study for a pilot study.
In approaching the problem of comparing the rhythm of spoken language
with the rhythm of orally presented poetry, I found that the first task is
to develop an appropriate methodology. Such a methodology was un-
available to me when I started out.[2] The present study of the durations
of poetic lines and metric feet represents a first attempt on my part to
develop the necessary methodology. With all its imperfections, the study

has produced some surprising results. I have always felt that if the results of my experiments surprise me, they must be right: Unexpected results indicate that the experiment was not designed, even unconsciously, to confirm a hypothesis, but to test one. While the study described above does not constitute a proper experiment, it has already been helpful in suggesting approaches future studies may take—future studies that are currently in the planning stage.

One interesting conclusion did emerge from the current study: The difference between the rhythmic units used in English prose and poetry is not really very great. The trochaic feet that were in the focus of this study appear to be realized in very similar ways, regardless of whether the materials are produced as poetry or as prose. Perhaps this is also an indication that even though poetic form superimposes a set of rhythmic constraints on spoken language, these constraints operate within the possibilities provided by the suprasegmental structure of the language.

NOTES

1. I am fully aware of the problems connected with establishing a stress beat that could be considered to constitute the beginning of a metric foot defined with reference to stress. (For a recent summary of several views, see Fowler 1983.) In the absence of a generally accepted definition of the phonetic correlates of a perceived stress beat, inclusion of the duration of the initial consonant of the stressed syllable seemed reasonable.
2. I am grateful to Professor A. Cohen for calling my attention to the dissertation of his student Marijke E. Loots (1979) and for making it available to me. Some of the methods of analysis employed in this dissertation will be adapted for use in later stages of the investigation.

REFERENCES

Fowler, C. (1983). Converging sources of evidence on spoken and perceived rhythms of speech: Cyclic production of vowels in sequences of monosyllable stress feet. *Journal of Experimental Psychology: General, 112*, 386–412.

Lehiste, I. (1973). The well-formedness of an Estonian folk song line. In A. Ziedonis, Jr., et al. (Eds.), *Baltic literature and linguistics* (pp. 135–139). Columbus, OH: AABS.

Lehiste, I. (1977). Quantity in Estonian language and poetry. *Journal of Baltic Studies, 8*, 130–141.

Lehiste, I. (1983a). "The Role of Prosody in the Internal Structuring of a Sentence." *Proceedings of the XIIIth International Congress of Linguists*, Tokyo 1982 (Shirô Hattori and Kazuko Inoue, eds., Tokyo 1983), pp. 220–231.

Lehiste, I. (1983b). "The Estonian Translation of the Elder Edda: Problems of Metric Equivalence." *Journal of Baltic Studies, 14*, 3 (1983), 179–184.

Loots, M. E. (1979). *Metrical myths. An experimental-phonetic investigation into the production and perception of metrical speech.* Dissertation, Utrecht, Drukkerij Elinkwijk BV, Utrecht.

APPENDIX

UNNATURAL BEAUTY

ARNOLD M. ZWICKY

These plastic roses
Are not perfect;
Each has a flaw,
Neither glaring
Nor subtle. Their
Imperfections never
Alter; they are
Immortal.

NEQUE SEMPER TENDIT ARCUM APOLLO

ARNOLD M. ZWICKY

Apollo will not keep
  His bowstring taut.
His eye will turn away
  From present prizes
To scan the land and air
  For other music,
And leave you unrewarded.
  You gaze upon his distant arc;
If you would have him hunt for you,
  Tender offering to his song.

CENTRAL PARK WEST

ARNOLD M. ZWICKY

Such a hot dog, with mustard,
Could never be so good
As on this bench in this
Amazing hot sun. What should
We do now, go back to
  Our padding
    On museum floors,

Or take in March 1st
On the street, out of doors?

MY VEGETABLE LOVE

ARNOLD M. ZWICKY

Poems on vegetables,
Poems on weeds.
Bean-writing. Parsley
Trisected. You celebrate
The minor plants that
Feed and flavor, modest
Greens, common places. You
See their intricacy, more
Marvelous than the rose, for
Parsley branches three
Times three, acutely
Hints at infinite
Trifoliation.
You love it
For its verdant
Subtlety.

UNION

ARNOLD M. ZWICKY

A school of fish, a flock
Of birds, wheel as one.
Ethologists explain that each creature
Senses subtle messages from his neighbors—
Some movement, maybe,
A click, some kind of
Chemical messenger.

You sat apart, that night,
Yet turned together as we talked—
Not like puppets, poor
Manipulated things,
But like the fish, the flock,

Moving in unison
For the common good.

LAST DAY

CATHERINE A. CALLAGHAN

I remembered when the sun was soft
and flowers bloomed
but for two years we'd barely
seen a cloud—even the cactus
had begun to wilt.
The riverbed was thick and scaly
like a tea kettle boiled dry.

Instead of the tractor,
I heard a SPIK   SPIK
from behind the house.
I rushed out back,
found my father chipping the earth,
straining his thin arms
to hoist the pick,
sweat gleaming on his lined face.

"We've got to hurry
and dig our graves."
He pointed to a great crack
opening
in the sky.

DARK TWIN

CATHERINE A. CALLAGHAN

The dark twin
is at the wrong end of the scale,
a balance point
for proper bell curves.
My twin shared my bench
in the first grade.
I led the class

while she scored bottom,
then lower and out
till she grew tall,
was sent forever back to school
with children her own age.
They play on swings,
make large simple things
and lock the world out each night.
I visit her sometimes—
she smiles at me,
her dark twin.

TO THE GODDESS

CATHERINE A. CALLAGHAN

I come a pilgrim
to Your way of power,
leaning on a willow staff,
my night path lit
by the Triple Moon.

Western Crescent, maiden thin,
Let our sacred dance begin.
Now a matron, round and full
Like our circle on this hill.
Shrunken orb, now bent and lone—
Grant us wisdom, Kindly Crone.

I stir with You
to the sun's warm wand,
breathe incense from new buds,
rise to incantations
of March wind.

Whirling wind and climbing sun,
Hunter's hope, the Hornèd One—
Let the Lord of air and fire
Fill the Goddess with desire.
Gracious priestess, loving priest,
Bless this fruit, our summer feast.

I revel-in high autumn,
roll in its blood-red leaves,
look inward under spreading ice,
the winding sheet, the womb
You will rip with spring.

> Dance is worship, so is wine,
> Joy is sacrament divine.
> Let us face the altar stone,
> Raise a mighty power cone—
> Death is done, now comes rebirth
> In our holy temple, Earth.

11

The Story of /r/*

Mona Lindau

1. INTRODUCTION

In standard feature theory, features are taken to be identical on the phonological and phonetic levels. Each feature is related to a single articulatory or acoustic parameter. This makes it possible to describe contrasts in binary terms and phonetic differences between languages in terms of different values along a particular phonetic parameter. This chapter investigates rhotics; it argues that the feature for the class of r-sounds is associated with the phonetic level in a complex way, and that this relation is considerably different from what is generally assumed.

Rhotics are quite common in the languages of the world. About 75% of all languages contain some form of /r/ phoneme (Maddieson 1984). These languages mostly have a single /r/, but 18% of languages with /r/s contrast two or three rhotics.

Phonologically, rhotics tend to behave in similar ways and participate as a class in phonological rules, so there is a need for a phonological feature of r-sounds that may be labeled "rhotic." For example, rhotics occupy the same place in consonant systems and in syllable structures of different languages. In languages with consonant clusters, rhotics tend to occur close to the syllable nucleus. Postvocalic rs tend to become vowels or disappear altogether, as happens in Southern British English with its postalveolar approximant [ɹ], and in German, Danish, and Southern Swedish with their uvular r-sounds. Rhotics have similar effects on environments: vowels before r tend to lengthen, as in English and Swedish.

* Many thanks to members of the linguistics and phonetics groups at the University of Ibadan, the University of Port Harcourt, the University of Lund, and the University of California, Los Angeles for help with data collection, and to Peter Ladefoged and Ian Maddieson for comments and discussion. This work was supported by the National Science Foundation and the Swedish Council for Research in the Humanities and Social Sciences.

PHONETIC LINGUISTICS

Vowels before or after *r* tend to lower, as in French and Danish with their uvular *r*-sounds, as well as in Standard Swedish with its apical *r*-sound. Rhotics often alternate with other rhotics. In Persian, a trilled /r/ has a tap allophone in intervocalic position and a voiceless trill variant in word–final position. In Fula (West Atlantic), a trill is realized as an approximant [ɹ] before a consonant, as a trill elsewhere. In Hausa, /r/ is realized as a tap or approximant between vowels and as a trill before a consonant or in initial position.

Phonetically, the rhotics form a heterogeneous group. Most *r*-sounds are voiced, but contrasting voiceless *r*-sounds do occur in a few languages, for example Irish, Hmar (Tibeto-Burman), and Konda (Dravidian). Voiceless allophones are quite common. A wide variety of manners and places of articulation is exhibited by the class of rhotics. We find fricatives, trills, taps, approximants, and vowels as realizations of /r/. The most common places of articulation are in the dental–alveolar area. Postalveolar, retroflex *r*s are not unusual. In some languages *r*s have a uvular articulation and are referred to as back *r*-sounds: [ʀ, ʁ, χ]. Uvular *r*-sounds are quite rare, in spite of what one may imagine from the languages of Western Europe (Maddieson 1984). A more complex articulation occurs in the so-called bunched *r* in American English with simultaneous constrictions in the lower pharynx and at the palate.

Given this articulatory variation, it is difficult to imagine a single articulatory correlate of a rhotic feature. Instead, the invariance may be sought in the acoustic domain. Based on data mainly from English, Ladefoged (1975) and Lindau (1978) suggested a lowered third formant as a common acoustic factor.

2. PROCEDURE

In order to test this claim and study the phonetics of rhotics closer, I investigated *r*-sounds in four Indo-European languages and in seven languages spoken in West Africa. These languages represent many phonetically different *r*-sounds. The four Indo-European languages were American English as spoken in California, Swedish, Spanish, and French. Swedish has one /r/, pronounced as a uvular in the southern parts of the country and as a lingual in other parts. Speakers representing both types of /r/ were included. Spanish has two *r*s, a trill and a tap. The Spanish data consist partly of Chicano Spanish as spoken in Los Angeles, partly of other forms of Spanish from Latin America. The French data come from Parisian speakers, except for one speaker from the South of France. Hausa is a Chadic language, belonging in the Afro-Asiatic family, spoken

Table 11.1

LANGUAGES USED IN THE ACOUSTICS INVESTIGATION

Language	Number of speakers	Main allophones of /r/
California English	9	/r/ [ɹ]
Standard Swedish	6	/r/[r,ɾ,ɹ]
Southern Swedish	10	/r/ [ʀ,ʁ,χ.ə]
French	4	/r/ [ʀ̆,ʁ,χ]
Chicano Spanish	6	/r/ [r], /ɾ/ [ɾ]
Other Spanish (Mexico, Colombia, Argentina)	8	/r/ [r,z̧], /ɾ/ [ɾ]
Kano Hausa	20	/r/ [r,ɾ] /ʈ/ [ʈ,ɾ]
Ẹdoid ⎰ Degema	4	/r/ [r ɾ ɹ]
Ẹdo	4	/r/ [r,ɾ], /rh/[r], /ɹ/[ɹ]
Ghotuọ	6	/r/ [r,ɾ,ɹ]
Ịjọ ⎰ Kalaḅari	7	/r/ [r,ɾ,ɹ]
Bụmọ	4	/r/ [r ɾ ɹ]
Ịzọn	4	/r/ [ɹ]

in Northern Nigeria and used as a lingua franca over large parts of West Africa. Hausa has two *r*s, a trill–tap and a retroflex flap. The Ẹdoid languages are spoken in the Midwest part of Nigeria, and the Ịjọ languages in the Delta area of Nigeria. Both groups are classified as Niger–Congo languages. Ẹdo (Bini) has three *r*-phonemes, /r/, /ɹ/, and /ɾ/. The other Nigerian languages have one /r/. Each language or dialect was represented by several speakers, so the results reflect sound properties in the languages rather than in individual speakers. Table 11.1 is a list of the languages used, the number of speakers, and the rhotic phoneme(s) and main allophone(s) in each language. The speakers from these languages were recorded in a sound studio, where available, and otherwise in the field with a good portable tape recorder. The recorded utterances consisted of words illustrating the *r*-sounds, said in a frame. The principle was to find words with the rhotics in a similar vocalic environment, between open vowels, in the different languages. These data were analyzed from wide-band spectrograms. In addition, cinefluorographic data from six Midwestern American English speakers were used. These speakers said *say* herd *again*.

3. RESULTS

Figure 11.1 illustrates apical trills in Chicano Spanish, Standard Swedish, and Degema, a voiceless trill from Ẹdo, and uvular trills from one male

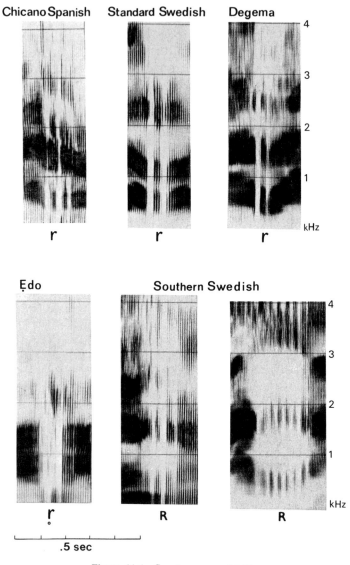

Figure 11.1 Spectrograms of trills.

and one female speaker of Southern Swedish. (Spanish *carro* /karo/ 'cart';
Swedish *kárra* /çɛrra/ 'cart'; Degema *mọ kạra* /mọ kara/ 'hard'; Ẹdo *o
gha raa* /o ɣa raa/ 'he will steal'; Southern Swedish *kärra* /çɛrra/ 'cart.')
Apical trills typically consist of two to three pulses. The mean rate of
vibration is 25 Hz (range 18–33 Hz, standard deviation 4.5, 25 speakers
of Ẹdo, Degema, Ghotuọ, Kalabari, Bụmọ, Spanish, and Standard Swed-

ish). The mean rate of vibration for the voiceless trill is somewhat slower, 22.5 Hz for three speakers of Ẹdo. The uvular trills tend to be longer and consist of four to six pulses. Their mean rate of vibration is 30.5 Hz (range 29–33 Hz, standard deviation 2.5, nine tokens each of three speakers of Southern Swedish). The uvula thus vibrates somewhat faster than the tip of the tongue, which is not surprising since it is a smaller organ. These rates of vibration for trills are consistent with the results in Ladefoged, Cochran, and Disner (1977), although the differences in rate of vibration between the apical and uvular trills are larger in my data. The spectral patterns of the open phases of the trills may differ considerably between languages. As expected from acoustic theory (Fant 1968), with a constriction in the velar–uvular area, the uvular trill has a high third spectral peak. For the last, female, speaker, the third spectral peak is very high (around 3200 Hz). But the apical trills are not produced with the same place of constriction in different languages. The third spectral peak is quite low in Chicano Spanish (around 2000 Hz), higher in Standard Swedish (2300 Hz), and even higher in Degema (2500 Hz). The other forms of Spanish from Argentina, Colombia, and Mexico display a much higher third spectral peak than the Chicano Spanish, indicating a more dental place of articulation. The low third spectral peak in Chicano Spanish may be due to influence from English.

An actual trill realization of an /r/ is not as common as might be expected from descriptions of languages, where an /r/ is often labeled as a "trill." Even in languages where a possible realization is a trill, not all speakers use a trill, and the speakers that do, have tap and approximant allophones as well as the trill. In the languages used in this study that were described as having an apical trill, about half the speakers produced trills, but not for every token. In Spanish, however, most of the speakers did produce trills for /r/ most of the time. The uvular r-sound in Southern Swedish was produced as a trill by only three of the ten speakers.

Figure 11.2 shows a common variant of the trill (Swedish kärra /çɛrra/ 'cart'; Bụmọ ara /ara/ 'she.'). Instead of several pulses, it consists of a single closure followed by a prolonged opening phase. This variant occurs in all the languages that have trills.

Figure 11.3 shows taps from Spanish (Argentina), Hausa, and Bụmọ (Spanish caro /karo/ 'expensive'; Hausa, bara /bara/ 'begging'; Bụmọ ara /ara/ 'she'). The taps are not produced in the same way in different languages nor are they always produced in the same way by different speakers of the same language. Some taps, like the one from Bụmọ, show a certain amount of acoustic energy during the closure; others, like the ones from Spanish and Hausa in Figure 11.3, do not. The precise articulatory location of the closure also varies, so the loci for the formants differ between languages and between speakers.

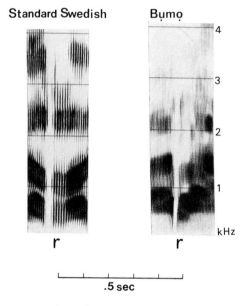

Figure 11.2 Spectrograms of a variant of apical trills in Standard Swedish and Bumọ.

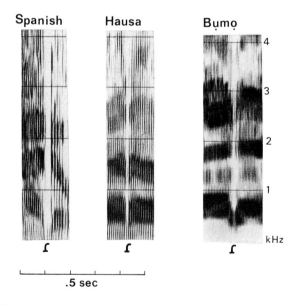

Figure 11.3 Spectrograms of taps in Spanish (Argentina), Hausa, and Bumọ.

Figure 11.4 shows other types of *r*-sounds, usually labeled "approximants" (English *(a) year a(go);* Izon *ara ama* /arama/ 'her home town'; Degema *(ar)ara(r)* /ararar/ 'things'; Swedish *kärra* /çɛrra/ 'cart'). The left spectrogram is an American English [ɹ]. It has formants like a vowel, indicating that the vocal tract has no constriction smaller than those for vowels. All the American English speakers had a lowered third formant, as in Figure 11.4. Acoustic theory for vowels predicts a relatively low third formant, close to the second formant, when there are vocal tract constrictions in the lower pharyngeal region or in the post-alveolar–palatal region (Fant 1968). Both second and third formants are also lowered by lip rounding. Figure 11.5 shows the /r/ in *herd* for six speakers of American English. This American English bunched *r*-sound has constrictions in both the low pharynx and at the palate. Three of the six speakers, P3, P4, and P5, add liprounding. Other speakers of American English use a more or less retroflex articulation for /r/, which is also combined with a constriction in the lower pharynx, as well as liprounding (Delattre & Freeman 1968). This also produces a low third formant. Thus it seems that speakers of American English combine all available articulatory mechanisms to produce a low third formant for /r/.

The approximants of all four speakers of Ịzọn show a considerably lowered third formant very similar to that of American English. The

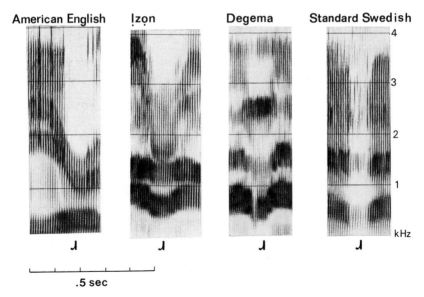

Figure 11.4 Approximant *r*-sounds from American English, Ịzọn, Degema, and Standard Swedish.

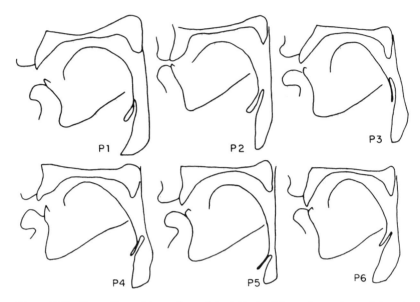

Figure 11.5 Cineradiographic tracings of the /r/ in *herd* from six speakers of American English.

apical approximant in Degema has spectral peaks, but the low amplitude of the second peak indicates that this sound was not produced with a vowel-like vocal tract but had a smaller constriction somewhere. The third spectral peak is relatively high, around 2500 Hz, and with a high amplitude, so the place of constriction was not like those that produced the type with the lowered third formant. The rightmost spectrogram in Figure 11.4 shows an apical *r*-sound of Standard Swedish. This [ɹ] contains some fricative component has spectral peaks with low amplitude, so it has a fairly narrow constriction somewhere.

Figure 11.6 shows uvular *r*-sounds from French and Southern Swedish (French *errer* /ɛre/ 'to wander'; Swedish *kärra* /çɛrra/ 'cart'). They all have a third spectral peak over 2500 Hz, but otherwise they are quite different from each other. The French *r*-sound contains fricative noise, but trill-type closures and openings are also visible. This French *r*-sound is thus a uvular fricative trill. Other French *r*-sounds have a clear formant pattern with no friction, indicating that they are more vowel-like. One type of uvular nontrill *r*-sound in Southern Swedish is a vowel-like uvular approximant, as in the middle of Figure 11.6. The last uvular rhotic illustrates that a low intensity fricative is another possible manifestation of the uvular rhotic in Southern Swedish.

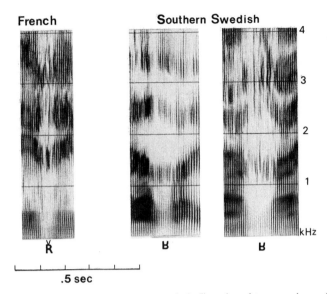

Figure 11.6 Spectrograms of uvular *r*-sounds in French and two speakers of Southern Swedish.

4. DISCUSSION

A lowered third formant is a well-justified specification for the American English /r/, particularly when considering that speakers use all available articulatory mechanisms to achieve this acoustic effect. The Ịzọn /r/ is similar. The open phase of the trills in Chicano Spanish also shows a lowered third formant. But a lowered third formant is not a pervading property of rhotics. The rapid closure of a tap is mostly realized as an (almost) empty space on a spectrogram without any formants. Both voiceless and fricative *r*-sounds contain acoustic noise, sometimes with spectral peaks, but these peaks are not, strictly speaking, formants (Fant 1968). The location of formants in the approximant *r*-sounds depends on the constriction location. Uvular *r*-sounds have a high third formant, sometimes close to the fourth formant. Dental *r*-sounds also have a relatively high third formant, though not as high as the uvulars (Fant 1968). A lowered third formant is in fact rather unusual and thus not a good candidate for a correlate of the rhotic feature.

But if the phonetic correlate is not the proposed lowered third formant, then what property is there that makes us recognize all these different sounds as rhotics? The uvular trill used in Southern Swedish and the American English approximant do not seem to have much in common.

The uvular trill is, however, strikingly similar to other trills in the pattern of pulses of closures and openings (Figure 11.1). Trills sound similar. The similar pulsing patterns in apical and uvular trills could explain the changes from tongue-tip trills to uvular trills that occurred in French, German, and Southern Swedish. Once the *r*-sound is established as uvular, it often weakens, and there is free variation between uvular trills, fricatives, and approximants. All uvular rhotics have similar spectral shapes in that they have some spectral peak in the area of a high third formant. Dental trills and approximants also have fairly high third formants. There is an acoustic similarity between these rhotics that is demonstrated in some areas in Sweden that are on the border between tongue tip *r*s and uvular *r*s. In these areas, members of the same family may use either front or back *r*-sounds, and other family members never notice the difference (Ohlsson, Nielson, & Schaltz 1977).

Acoustic similarities between trills and taps are evident in Figures 11.1 and 11.3. The taps look very much like the closure phase of a trill. An average apical tap lasts 20 msec. This average was calculated from about 50 speakers of Swedish, Spanish, Hausa, Degema, Edọ, and Kalaḅari. Each closure phase of an apical trill also lasts about 20 msec, based on the average from twenty-five speakers of six languages. From an acoustic point of view, a trill can be regarded as a series of taps. A tap is also frequently a variant of a trill, particularly in intervocalic position.

The French uvular *r*-sound in Figure 11.6 shows that frication and trilling may co-occur. This may result in fricative–approximant variants of the French *r*-sound. The variant of an apical trill in Swedish in Figure 11.3 was produced with a closure followed by an open phase that is prolonged as a single long approximant instead of alternating shorter openings with closures. This production of an apical trill with a prolonged open phase could explain why trilled *r*-sounds vary with, or change into, approximants.

But there is no physical property that constitutes the essence of all rhotics. Instead, the relation between members of the class of rhotics are more of a family resemblance (Wittgenstein 1958). Each member of the rhotic class resembles some other member with respect to some property, but it is not the same property that constitutes the resemblance for all members of a class. Trills and taps are alike as to closure duration, the open phase of a trill resembles an approximant in the presence of formants, and tongue-tip trills and uvular trills resemble each other in their pattern of rapid pulses. Rhotics produced with the same constriction location(s) are alike in the distribution of spectral energy. In the class of *r*-sounds, member r1 resembles r2, which resembles r3, which resembles r4. Although members r1 and r4 may not be much alike, it is entirely possible to express their relationship as a set of steps across other members. Such steps show that some members are more closely related than other members. Apical trills are more like taps than uvular fricatives. This may be a reason why some alternations within the rhotic class are more common than others. Figure 11.7 illustrates this notion in a simplified way as a diagram of sets and relations.

Clearly, searching for a single phonetic correlate underlying a whole class of sounds may not always be a profitable task. It is doubtful that any phonological class can be characterized in this simple way. Instead, the reasons for membership of sounds in phonological classes must be sought in the phonological behavior of the sounds, and the relation between phonological and phonetic classes is considerably more complex than the one-to-one relation that is generally assumed. In the class of rhotics, this relation can profitably be described in terms of the notion of family resemblance.

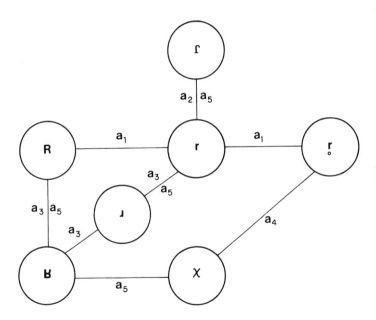

Figure 11.7 Parameter relations among *r*-sounds. Lines indicate parameters that relate types of *r*-sounds to each other; a_1 = pulse pattern (trill); a_2 = closure duration; a_3 = presence of formants (sonorant); a_4 = presence of noise; a_5 = distribution of spectral energy (place of articulation).

REFERENCES

Delattre, P., & Freeman, D. C. (1968). A dialect study of American r's by x-ray motion picture. *Linguistics, 44,* 29–68.
Fant, G. (1968). Analysis and synthesis of speech processes. In B. Malmberg (Ed.), *Manual of phonetics* (pp. 171–277). Amsterdam: North-Holland.
Ladefoged, P. (1975). *A course in phonetics.* New York: Harcourt Brace Jovanovich.
Ladefoged, P., Cochran, A., & Disner, S. (1977). Laterals and trills. *Journal of the International Phonetic Association, 7,* 46–54.
Lindau, M. (1978). Vowel features. *Language, 54,* 541–563.
Maddieson, I. (1984). *Patterns of sounds.* Cambridge: Cambridge University Press.
Ohlsson, S. Ö., Nielsen, J. P., & Schaltz, K. (1977). Om r-gränsen pa öland: på östfronten intet nytt?'' *Arkiv för Nordisk Filologi, 92,* 177–199.
Wittgenstein, L. (1958). *The blue and brown books. Preliminary studies for the philosophical investigations.* New York: Harper & Row.

12

The Speech Homunculus and a Problem of Phonetic Linguistics

Björn Lindblom
James Lubker

Sensations are set by the encoding functions of the sensory nerve endings and by the integrated neural mechanics of the central nervous system. Afferent nerve fibers are not high fidelity recorders, for they accentuate certain stimulus features, neglect others. The central neuron is a story-teller with regard to the nerve fibers, and it is never completely trustworthy, allowing distortions of quality and measure . . . sensation is an abstraction, not a replication of the real world.

(Mountcastle 1975)

1. INTRODUCTION

In the neurophysiological literature spanning the period from the 1950s (Penfield & Rasmussen 1950) to the 1980s (Kandel & Schwartz 1981), it is common to find descriptions of the motor and sensory homunculi of the human brain of the sort shown in Figure 12.1. The homunculus demonstrates the amount of brain tissue associated with the sensory or motor functions of various parts of the body. Quite clearly, the motor and sensory representations of these parts do not correspond at all well to their actual physical size. For example, by means of electrical stimulation of the brain it has been demonstrated that movements of the thumb or of facial structures (e.g., lips or tongue) can be elicited from cortical areas that, in relative terms, are much larger than are those for leg and trunk movements. The relative size of the cortical area appears to be related to the degree of precision and fine control with which the movement can be executed.

PHONETIC LINGUISTICS

Copyright © 1985 by Academic Press. Inc.
All rights of reproduction in any form reserved.
ISBN 0-12-268990-9

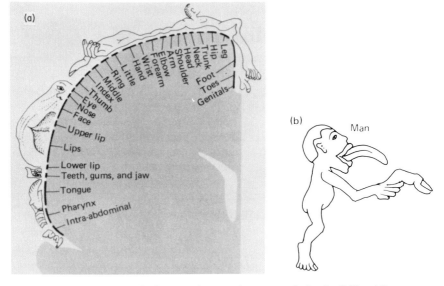

Figure 12.1 (a) The standard sensory homunculus patterned after Penfield and Rasmussen (1950); and (b) the somewhat different representation suggested in Kandel and Schwartz (1981).

Some natural questions for phoneticians would be the following: What do the homunculi for speech look like? Are they similarly distorted in relation to the physical characteristics of articulatory and phonatory structures? Are certain aspects of the vocal tract favored over others in terms of extent of cortical representation? If so, or if not, what are the phonetic implications of such findings?

At the present stage of development of neurophonetics, direct answers to such questions are not readily available. They require further analysis and must be reformulated in somewhat more specific terms before relevant experiments can be designed. The value of introducing the notion of a motor or sensory homunculus in the context of research on speech consists chiefly in reminding ourselves that physical information on speech movements, as provided by laboratory measurements, may be different from the information used by our brains in generating, as well as in monitoring, such movements. Conceivably there may be differences with respect to both the dimension selected and the scaling of a given dimension.

Ladefoged (1980) has proposed a universal phonetic framework for describing articulatory aspects of speech sounds that uses approximately 17 parameters. Two of these, back raising and front raising (see Figure 12.2), are derived from a factor analysis of the tongue shapes observed

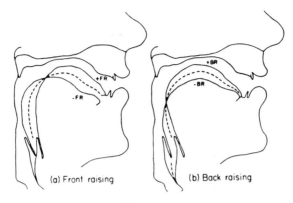

Figure 12.2 Midsagittal drawings of the parameters front raising and back raising as described by Ladefoged (1980).

in English vowels (Harshman, Ladefoged, & Goldstein 1977). Ladefoged (1980: 488) asks "whether descriptions of the body of the tongue in terms of front raising and back raising parameters are simply mathematical abstractions, or whether they can really help us explain why vowels are as they are." We can develop this point, in a similar vein, by asking whether the dimensions he proposes are neurophysiologically real. Are they, in fact, the attributes that a speaker's nervous system monitors in vowel production? For the sake of argument, let us assume that they are.

Such an assumption leads instantly to the problem of relating two types of scales, namely, physical and neurophysiological. In Ladefoged's (1980: 487) work both parameters are formally defined as "deviations (in centimeters) of the tongue position of an average speaker from the position of that speaker's tongue in a reference position." They are physical scales. From the speaker's point of view, however, front and back raising represent sensory scales. What is the nature of the transformation that converts a speech movement expressed as a physical quantity into a numerical estimate correctly reflecting how large this movement appears to the speaker?

We can further illustrate the problem by the following analogy. Consider the frequency and the pitch of a pure tone. We describe the former in terms of cycles per second or Hz and the latter in terms of mel or Bark units. There exists a unique transformation that relates the Hz and the Bark scales. In the articulatory domain we can calibrate parameters physically in terms of centimeters, but we lack the equivalent of a mel or Bark scale (see Table 12.1) for describing articulatory movements in subjective terms.

Table 12.1
THE PHYSICAL AND SUBJECTIVE DIMENSIONS OF PITCH COMPARED TO
THE PHYSICAL AND SUBJECTIVE ASPECTS OF ARTICULATORY MOVEMENT

	Physical	Subjective
Perception	Hz	Bark
		?
Articulation	centimeters	"sensimeters"

Nevertheless, we feel that although the problem of phonetic-movement perception may be a great deal more difficult to solve than that of pitch perception, it certainly merits attention.

Porter and Lubker (1980) investigated physical and subjective estimates of tongue movement in the horizontal plane during nonspeech tasks and found that subjects were able to bisect, reproduce, and transpose tongue movements with ease and great accuracy. Their subjects' abilities in these tasks were surprisingly linear; for example, when bisecting a two-centimeter space in the horizontal dimension, subjects made the bisection very close to one centimeter, although very consistently with slight over-shoot, no matter where along the horizontal dimension the two-centimeter space was located. This experiment suggests that speakers have an accurate and perhaps even linear representation of "tongue space" in the brain. Porter and Lubker stress, however, the nonspeech nature of their experimental task and warn against extending the observations to speech.

On the basis of a review of the neurophysiological literature, Hardcastle (1970) hypothesized a direct relationship between the diversity of speech sounds in the languages of the world and the density and variety of sensory mechanisms along the vocal tract. He noted that languages seem to favor the front part of the oral region over the back (e.g., the non-uniform distribution of place of articulation among the IPA series of voiceless fricatives). Hardcastle also noted that the anterior part of the vocal tract has a richer sensory supply than does the posterior part. If correct, his observations shed some indirect light on the sensory speech homunculus and suggest, perhaps in contrast with Porter and Lubker, that it imposes a certain degree of warping on the physical scaling of the articulatory space.

In what follows, we make a preliminary approach to the relation between physical and neurophysiological scales in vowel production. We restrict our attention to jaw and tongue spaces and to very simple production tasks. In doing so we believe that we may also be able to approach the important question asked by Ladefoged (1980) as to whether articulatory descriptions can "really help us explain why vowels are as they are."

2. METHODS

2.1. Some Preliminary Comments

The questions posed above quite clearly bring us to that area of experimental psychology concerned with the quantification of sensory experiences: sensory psychophysics. Psychophysical techniques, in general, provide quantitative methods for investigating sensory phenomena, or, somewhat more specifically, the relationship between physical stimuli and sensory responses. We have chosen a particular psychophysical technique, based upon the power law principle proposed by Stevens (1975), which states that the relationship between a subjective sensation and the physical magnitude of the stimulus is a power function described by the formula: $y = lx^k$ where y = the sensation magnitude, l = a constant, x = the stimulus magnitude, and k = the exponent, or power, describing the relationship. Stevens (1975: 16) sums up the stimulus–response relationship in the following way: "Equal stimulus ratios produce equal subjective ratios."

Although Stevens (1975) describes a very wide application of his power law principle, we here consider it only as it may be used to describe the particular relationships that we have discussed above. We later return to a more detailed discussion of the application of a power law principle to our particular needs as well as some of its more general applications within neurophysiology. Now we simply point out that in developing the conceptual scheme of the power law, Stevens also produced a very convenient and powerful experimental procedure, specifically, Direct Magnitude Estimation (DME).

DME procedures involve presenting subjects with a standard stimulus to which they assign a number of their own choice (or, in some cases, to which the experimenter assigns a number in an arbitrary fashion). Test stimuli that vary randomly around the standard are then presented. The task of the subjects is to assign numbers to the test stimuli that reflect their subjective impressions of the relation of the test to the standard stimulus. If the test is one-tenth as big or as loud in the subject's view, then the subject assigns .10 to that test stimulus; if the next test appears to be 25 times as big or as loud as the standard, then the number 25 is assigned to it. When this procedure is used for a great many types of stimulus–response situations, the result is a power function relationship, which is, by definition, linear when plotted on log–log paper.

In the present experiment, we use the DME procedure to investigate a speaker's subjective impression of articulatory distances, specifically jaw-opening movements during vowel productions, and then attempt to make some theoretical extensions of those observations to the same speaker's subjective impressions of tongue movements during vowel productions.

2.2. Subjects

Seven adult speakers, five male and two female, all with normal speech and hearing, were subjects in this experiment. Three of the subjects were experienced phoneticians and the other four naive with regard to matters such as vowel charts. Five speakers were native Swedes. Two had American English as their first language but were fluent in Swedish; they were among the experienced phoneticians.

2.3. Experimental Tasks

Each subject took part in a series of tasks, being tested individually in the order of tasks as given below. Except as noted, each subject performed all the tasks in one session of approximately one hour.

2.3.1. Circle Area Judgment. Stevens (1975) suggests that when relatively difficult magnitude-estimation tasks are to be required of subjects it is wise to begin with a very simple training task to familiarize them with the technique. Accordingly, each subject was presented with a "standard" circle and told to assign the number "1" to this standard. They were then presented with eight test circles, four larger and four smaller than the standard, and were told to assign numbers to the test circles that reflected their judgment of the area of each circle relative to the standard. All subjects performed this task with ease.

2.3.2. Arm Movement Judgment. The subject was seated, blindfolded, at a table with the right elbow held on a fixed point on a board lying flat on the table. The forearm was free to move in an arc on that board from a fixed block at zero degrees until the back of the hand encountered a second, adjustable block. The second block could be positioned at any of eight positions in approximately 11-degree steps from the fixed zero degree block. The standard was set at 33 degrees, so there were two locations below and five above the standard. The subjects were first presented with the standard and were told to assign a number to that movement, that is, the movement of the forearm in the 33-degree arc from the zero position. The test movements were then presented in random order, and the subjects assigned numbers to the tests reflecting the amount of movement of the forearm relative to the standard. Again, the subjects performed the task with ease.

This task was included for two reasons: (1) it provided the subjects with a second familiarization task somewhat more difficult than the circle area judgments, and (2) the neurophysiological systems used by an individual to judge movements of the forearm about the elbow might be similar to those used to judge movements of the jaw, since both systems would be expected to make use of joint-capsule, muscle-stretch, and tendon-organ information. This point is discussed further below.

In all the remaining tasks, jaw movement, in both the vertical and horizontal dimensions, was monitored by a custom-made magnetometer system (Lubker, Lindblom, Gay, Lyberg, Branderud, & Holmgren in press). Briefly, a very small (5 × 4 × 3 mm) coil was attached to the jaw, just below the lower central incisors, with a small piece of dental wax. Two generator coils were attached, one to the forehead on a headband and the other to a plastic plate suspended from the headband and located approximately 10 cm from the subject's mouth. The sensor coil on the jaw thus moved within two magnetic fields simultaneously, and in this way fine movements of the jaw in the horizontal and vertical dimensions were recorded.

A practice session occurred after the first two experiments to introduce the subjects to the remaining experiments and permit them to practice for each. The magnetometer coils were then attached, and the subject and one of the experimenters were seated in a sound-insulated and electrically shielded testing booth. During each of the following experimental tasks, the audio signal and the jaw movements of the speaker were recorded on three channels of an FM tape recorder.

2.3.3. Jaw Movement: Nonspeech. The subjects were required to produce the syllable /æ/ silently and then to make jaw movements that were double and then one-half as great as the jaw movement they made in the silent production of the syllable. This task was then repeated with the silent production of the syllables /ja/ and /je/ serving as standards. Subjects found this task to be somewhat more difficult than the first two but still were able to carry it out.

In this experiment, the subjects were engaged in a magnitude-estimation task that made use of structures that, as noted above, must be neuroanatomically quite similar to the elbow–forearm system in the second experiment and that subserve speech. However, only their ability to estimate the magnitude of jaw movements for the nonspeech task of fractionating spaces was tested.

2.3.4. Jaw Movement: Speech. The speech sample used in this experiment is shown in Table 12.2. The jaw movement required to go from

Table 12.2
SPEECH SAMPLE

Syllables used in jaw-speech task	Syllables used in tongue experiments	
jɛ	jɛ	jɑ
ji	çi	ju
jɑ	ça	ço
jo	jo	jæ
je	çæ	je
ju	çu	ji
jæ	çe	çɛ
ja	ja	çɑ

/j/ to a following vowel can be considered to be about the same as that required for going from /i/ to the following vowel, and thus the sample shown in Table 12.2 is essentially a series of vowel–vowel syllables. The standard syllable for each subject was /jɛ/, and the subject was asked to assign a number to the jaw movement required for the production of that syllable. After presentation of the standard syllable, each of the test syllables was presented in random order and numbers were assigned relative to the standard movement. The standard syllable was then repeated and the list presented a second time with the subjects now required to produce the syllables with great vocal intensity, thus increasing their jaw movement considerably (Lindblom & Schulman 1982). The use of the loud productions extended the range of magnitude of the jaw movements for the subjects to estimate, thus providing more data points for evaluation of their success in making those estimations. All subjects judged this task to be more difficult but were nevertheless able to perform it with relative ease.

2.3.5. Tongue Movements. The speech sample is also given in Table 12.2. The subjective impressions of the tongue movements required for the production of the syllables were elicited in a separate experimental session several days to a week following the completion of the first four experiments. Two separate judgment tasks were required.

1. Movement of the tongue as a whole. In this task, the syllable /jɛ/ was presented as a standard and the subject was to estimate the movement of the tongue as a whole and assign a number to that standard movement. The remaining syllables were then presented in random order. The relative movements of the tongue as a whole were estimated and appropriate numbers assigned relative to the standard. We assume that use of the palatal /ç/ phoneme alternated with /j/ does not significantly alter the

essential /i/-to-vowel quality of the syllables while it does effectively expand the number of data points available.

2. Movement of a specific point on the tongue. In this task, just prior to the presentation of the standard, a sharp metal point was used to stimulate the subject's tongue on the midline at approximately two centimeters back from the tip. The subjects were then asked to concentrate on this point and to estimate the movement of the point rather than the tongue as a whole. This standard-point movement was given a number and the experiment proceeded as above with the point stimulation being reapplied periodically.

All subjects found these tongue-judgment tasks to be quite difficult.

Two general comments should be made with respect to the tongue-movement experiments. First, for several speakers, especially during the point-movement task, when the standard /jɛ/ syllable was produced, no movement was sensed. For these subjects the syllable /ja/ was substituted as the standard, and normalization procedures were applied to the resultant data.

Second, and more important, no actual measurements of tongue movements were made during the experiments. Instead, we used x-ray data available for sustained vowels produced by one of the subjects (RL). These are the data used by Lindblom and Sundberg (1971) in the construction of an articulatory model. Tracings of the following vowel articulations were made: /i, e, ɛ, a, o, u/. For /æ/ and /a/, the profiles generated by the Lindblom-Sundberg model were used. The following measures were explored from the tracings: (1) Average displacement of blade, dorsum, and root landmarks. In Table 12.3, average displacement

Table 12.3

PHYSICAL MEASURES OF TONGUE MOVEMENT IN [jV] SYLLABLES (IN mm)[a]

	Average		Blade		Dorsum		Root	
	1a	1b	2a	2b	3a	3b	4a	4b
ji	1	1	1	1	1	1	1	1
je	5	5	3	4	7	7	5	4
jɛ	6	7.5	4.5	6	7	8	6.5	8
jæ	17	9.5	6	7.5	7	10	8	11
ja	17.5	21	17	21	18	18	17	24
jɑ	18.5	24	17	22	20	24	18	25
jo	16.5	19	17	20	17	19	16	18
ju	11	10	8	5	12	13	12	13

[a] a indicates mandible-based definition; b indicates maxilla-based definition.

is shown in column 1, blade, dorsum, and root in columns 2, 3, and 4 respectively. That is, column 1 represents a physical estimate of the displacement of the tongue *as a whole* in relation to both mandible and maxilla. (2) Displacement of point on the anterior surface of the tongue (blade landmark) in relation to both mandible and maxilla. (3) and (4) Measures corresponding to (2) for dorsum and root landmarks respectively. (These were used together with (2) only to derive (1)). (5) Shift of location of the point of maximum constriction.

For the first and second of these measures, the positions of the apex and the valecula were determined on each profile. The midsagittal outline of the tongue between these points was defined as the tongue contour. The length of each contour was measured and then divided into three segments of equal length. The point located one third of the distance from the apex is called the "blade"; the point two thirds away, the "dorsum"; and the point near the valecula, the "root."

To derive measures 1 and 2, the displacement of each landmark was measured for all vowels using the /i/ configuration as a reference approximating the initial /j/, as discussed above. Since this procedure generates zero displacement for /ji/, irrespective of the specific definition chosen, and since in the presentation of results we use logarithms, an arbitrary value of one millimeter tongue movement was assigned to /ji/ everywhere. The results of this procedure are presented in Table 12.3. It appears reasonable to assume that the displacements of these individual points should be correlated with changes in fiber length of the extrinsic tongue muscles and therefore only occasionally exceed 15 mm.

The third measure gives numbers that are several magnitudes greater and is defined as follows: Articulatory profiles were generated for /i, e, ε, æ, a, ɑ, o, u/. Using the procedures developed by Lindblom and Sundberg (1971), area functions and formant frequencies were derived. The area functions were inspected for the place of maximum constriction. Tongue displacement was then defined as a shift in the location of this point. Values for this parameter are denoted by ΔX_{Amin} and are given in Table 12.4 for all the vowels relative to /i/. Also shown are other characteristics of these model vowels. As can be seen, this measure reaches a maximum value of nearly 80 mm in the syllable /ja/.

3. DATA REDUCTION AND ANALYSIS

The recorded jaw movements were later played, along with their calibration signals, onto a mingograph T34 ink-writing oscillograph. Hand measurements of all appropriate vertical jaw movements were made directly from mingograph printouts.

Table 12.4

MODEL PARAMETER VALUES USED IN DERIVING TONGUE
DISPLACEMENT MEASURE $(\Delta X_{Amin})^a$

	Jaw	Degree of deviation from neural	Place of Constriction	X_{Amin}	ΔX_{Amin}	F_1	F_2	F_3
i	9	1	−1	118	1	255	2135	2826
e	11	1	−1	123	−5	305	1880	2650
ε	23	1	−1	133	−15	456	1800	2566
æ	23	0	—	48	70	623	1702	2524
a	23	.75	1	40	78	702	1100	2572
ɑ	15	1	1	53	65	600	1075	2590
o	11	1	.5	65	53	420	770	2440
u	5	1	0	110	8	220	700	2200

[a] From Lindblom & Sundberg 1971. X_{Amin} = place of minimum cross-sectional area (mm) rel to glottis; ΔX_{Amin} = displacement of X_{Amin} with [i] as reference (mm).

In accordance with the fact that power functions appear as straight lines when plotted on log–log paper, all jaw movements (in millimeters) and subjective evaluations (in arbitrary units) were converted to log scales during calculation of correlation coefficients.

4. RESULTS

Table 12.5 summarizes the results for individual subjects for the non-speech tasks. Since all data were converted to log scales, the high correlations noted here and in subsequent data suggest straight-line relationships between the subjective estimations and the objective stimuli when they are plotted on log–log paper. That is to say, these data strongly suggest power function relationships of the type described by Stevens (1975). In addition, the power functions themselves show remarkable similarity across subjects but not across tasks, to the extent that the k columns in Table 12.5 could be averaged, as Stevens suggests for the treatment of such data, and three separate power functions could be calculated to describe each of these three relationships. That the power functions for the three tasks are different is not especially surprising since the objective measures in each task are quite different: circle area, elbow–forearm movement in degrees of arc, and jaw movement in the vertical plane. What is important is that all seven subjects show such high, positive correlations. They were clearly able to perform these non-speech estimation tasks with ease and accuracy. The power functions

Table 12.5

RESULTS OF CORRELATING SUBJECTIVE ESTIMATES AND PHYSICAL
MEASURES OF CIRCLE AREA, FOREARM MOVEMENT, AND JAW–
NONSPEECH TASKS

Subject	Circle task		Forearm task		Jaw–nonspeech	
	r^a	k^b	r	k	r	k
RL	1.00	4.45	0.98	1.76	0.91	0.68
RM	0.99	4.82	0.97	1.25	0.96	1.42
LE	0.98	4.13	0.93	1.21	0.97	0.78
SU	0.99	4.13	0.97	1.53	0.89	1.20
RS	0.99	3.75	0.99	1.48	0.96	1.46
MA	1.00	4.24	0.90	1.38	0.89	0.95
ST	0.99	6.32	0.98	1.63	0.96	0.89

[a] The correlation coefficient.
[b] The value of the exponent in Stevens' equation.

noted for the jaw–nonspeech task range around 1.0 (the mean of all
seven subjects is 1.05), suggesting some support for the tongue-nonspeech
data reported by Porter and Lubker (1980).

In a similar manner, Table 12.6 summarizes the data for the individual
subjects during the speech tasks. The subjective estimations of jaw movements show essentially as high correlations with actual jaw movements
during speech tasks, as were noted between the subjective and objective
nonspeech tasks. However, the power functions for the jaw–speech task
are lower than are those for the jaw–nonspeech task.

Table 12.6

RESULTS OF CORRELATING SUBJECTIVE ESTIMATES AND PHYSICAL
MEASURES OF JAW AND TONGUE MOVEMENT

Subject	Jaw movement		Tongue displacement			
			Point		As a whole	
	Correlation	Slope	Correlation	Slope	Correlation	Slope
RL	.94	.79	.54 (.64)	.31 (.25)	.70 (.96)	.56 (.41)
RM	.92	.68	.90 (.92)	.49 (.47)	.90 (.92)	.49 (.48)
LE	.95	.67	.82 (.91)	.63 (.50)	.86 (.91)	.71 (.49)
SU	.94	.69	.61 (.69)	.71 (.55)	.67 (.93)	.77 (.59)
RS	.95	1.27	.16 (.25)	.15 (.17)	.33 (.48)	.29 (.28)
MA	.72	.56	.64 (.71)	.56 (.43)	.53 (.52)	.46 (.29)
ST	.96	.86	.64 (.69)	.37 (.33)	.42 (.66)	.17 (.18)

The tongue data, derived from mandible-based tongue movement, present a somewhat different picture. Six judgments were made on each of eight syllables: [ji, je, jɑ, jæ, ja, jo, ju]. For these data two sets of numbers are shown for each column. In each case, the first number shows the correlation and the slope for the estimations of tongue movement versus our calculations of tongue movement with the calculations based upon the total set of data points available; the second number, in parentheses, represents the correlation and slope calculated from averaged data. In almost every case there is a difference, often a large one, in the direction of larger rs for the averaged data, and in this way the relative "noisiness" of the unaveraged data is demonstrated. In spite of this noise, all subjects, with the exception of RS, show a remarkably high correlation between their estimates and our calculations of tongue movement. We should note parenthetically that subject RS is one of the three experienced phoneticians. Five of the subjects show a slight advantage for estimations of point movement. The slope of the power function describing the tongue relationship is somewhat more variable across subjects than is that for the jaw relationship and is everywhere lower than that for the jaw.

The data shown in Tables 12.5 and 12.6 for the individual speakers may be summarized as follows:

1. The DME technique does allow the generation of power functions with ease and consistency for all of the nonspeech tasks and for the jaw-movement tasks during speech.
2. The averaged tongue data also show a clear tendency toward the effective use of DME and its resultant power functions.
3. For the tongue data, the correlations based upon individual observations demonstrate the much noisier character of the tongue experiment.
4. The extremely high correlation between "point" and "tongue as an entity" might suggest that (a) subjects subconsciously judge an entity movement in terms of anterior tongue movement, (b) point results may be roughly equal to entity results, and (c) therefore, evidence is supplied for homunculus warping or, more cautiously, for the nature of the introspective tapping of the homunculus (see Hardcastle's hypothesis discussed above).
5. The power function slopes for the jaw–speech experiment are greater than are those for the tongue experiment and less than for the jaw–nonspeech experiment.

Table 12.7 shows the estimated and averaged jaw movement during speech averaged across subjects for each syllable. The normal and loud intensities are shown separately. These averaged data are plotted along

Table 12.7

MEASURED AND SUBJECTIVELY ESTIMATED EXTENT OF JAW MOVEMENT
AVERAGED ACROSS SUBJECTS (MEDIAN VALUES) FOR SELECTED jV
SYLLABLES

Syllable	Normal		Loud	
	millimeters	subject	millimeters	subject
/ji/	3.5	0.5	5	0.5
/je/	4.0	0.9	8	1.5
/jɛ/	7.8	1.0	10.2	1.5
/jæ/	13.6	2.0	19.5	2.1
/ja/	15.1	2.0	22.5	2.5
/jɑ/	10.1	1.5	15.4	2.0
/jo/	5.0	0.8	7.8	1.5
/ju/	1.9	0.5	5.2	0.5

linear scales in the upper left corner of Figure 12.3. The strong relationship
between the estimations and the objective measurements is obvious.

Table 12.8 shows the tongue data averaged across subjects for each
of the syllables. Shown are the subjective estimates of as-a-whole movement
and movement of a point on the anterior tongue surface, as well as three
different methods for predicting tongue movement. Some of the data

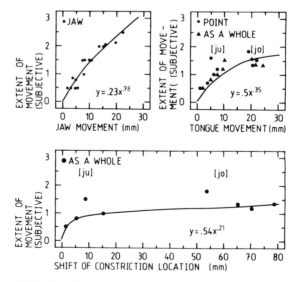

Figure 12.3 Graphic summary of data shown in Tables 12.7 and 12.8.

Table 12.8

SUBJECTIVELY ESTIMATED EXTENT OF TONGUE MOVEMENT AVERAGED
ACROSS SUBJECTS (MEDIAN VALUES) IN jV SYLLABLES

Syllable	Tongue displacement			Subjective	
	Average	Point	ΔX_{Amin}	Point	As a whole
/ji/	1.0	1.0	1	0.5	0.5
/je/	5.0	4.0	$\lvert -5 \rvert$	0.7	0.8
/jɛ/	7.5	6.0	$\lvert -15 \rvert$	1.0	1.0
/jæ/	9.5	7.5	70	1.2	1.2
/ja/	21.0	21.0	78	1.3	1.3
/jɑ/	24.0	22.0	65	1.5	1.3
/jo/	19.0	20.0	53	1.6	1.8
/ju/	10.0	5.0	8	1.6	1.5

from Table 12.8 are plotted graphically, also along linear scales, in Figure 12.3: subjective estimation of movement against the calculation of movement in the upper right hand corner and subjective estimation against shift of the location of the tongue constriction in the lower graph. Again, the strong subjective–objective relationship is clear. Figure 12.3 also makes clear that judgment of movement from /j/ to the rounded vowels /u/ and /o/ shows a systematic deviation. It is possible that the addition of the rounding feature increases the complexity of the judgment task, thus causing such a deviation.

5. DISCUSSION

In the next few paragraphs we make frequent reference to the concept of feedback. We assume that if individuals are able to make accurate estimations of where a body part is in space or of how extensive a movement has been, then they must have some sort of feedback systems providing them with the appropriate information for making such estimations. Others have, of course, also made this assumption (e.g., Hardcastle 1970; Sussman 1972).

Three different systems are used to convey information about the functioning of the body to the central nervous system: the exteroceptive, proprioceptive, and interoceptive systems. The third provides signals of internal bodily events such as blood pressure and is of little interest to the questions considered here. The exteroceptive systems are sensitive to stimuli from the external environment and include vision, hearing, and skin sensation, or touch. In the experiments performed here, none of these is likely to have provided much, if any, information to our subjects, although it is clear that touch and pressure are likely to be important sources of information under many natural and experimental speech conditions (see, e.g., Dubner, Sessle, & Storey 1978, Sussman 1972). Proprioceptive systems specifically provide information about the relative position of body segments to one another and the position of the body in space, and thus are the systems we can assume the subjects used in their estimations of jaw and tongue movements. Proprioceptive information, or position sense, arises from mechanical disturbances in muscles and joints. That is, our subjects were most likely dependent upon two information sources in their estimations: (1) muscle receptors, specifically muscle spindles and Golgi tendon organs, and (2) joint afferents.

Martin (1981) points out that when we make use of these sensory systems we tend to believe that our perceptions are precise and direct when, in fact, this is not the case. He also points out that a scientist wishing to investigate the relation between the information supplied by these systems and our perception of that information must make use of psychophysical techniques, an important one being the power function of Stevens. There have been a number of experiments reported that demonstrate a power-function relation between physical stimuli and neurophysiological behaviors. A good example of such work is that by Mountcastle and his associates (e.g., Mountcastle, Poggio, & Werner 1962), in which power-function relations were found between joint angle in monkey limbs and the firing of third-order neurons in the brain. Another is the work by Franzén and Offenloch (1969) demonstrating a power-function relation between tactile pulses on the finger and evoked cortical potentials.

There is little to argue about in the preceding. There are, however, several issues about which there has been some debate. One of these is the question of whether it is movement (e.g., amplitude, acceleration, velocity) or position that is being sensed by the proprioceptive systems. That is, do we estimate movement in terms of such information as amplitude, acceleration, and velocity, or change of position? The second question is whether the most important information is provided by muscle receptors or by joint receptors.

Whatever disagreement there may be regarding the role of the muscle receptors in the control of movement, there is little disagreement as to what kinds of information they input to the central nervous system. It has been accepted since the work of Matthews (1933) and up to more recent research (e.g., Carew 1981) that muscle receptors convey information regarding changes in muscle length, tension, and velocity of stretch. It is also generally agreed that joint receptors are capable of providing information about the position of the joint (i.e., its angle), and the direction and velocity of its movement (see, e.g., Davson & Segal 1978; Dubner et al. 1978; Martin 1981). It is how these separate pieces of information are used by the organism that is questioned.

In our instructions to the subjects in this experiment, we placed emphasis upon asking them to report on their sensation of movement. As has been noted above, they were able to estimate with good accuracy the actual physical movements of the elbow–forearm, jaw, and tongue, but the difficulty of the task increased in the following order: elbow–forearm, jaw–nonspeech, jaw–speech, tongue. It is of interest to see if these findings are related to the questions stated above.

In an extensive review of the literature, Russell (1976) concludes that the evidence is in favor of position or location being coded in memory and that it is joint receptors, particularly in single-joint movements, that supply the most important information about location. He also stresses that the problem becomes more complex in multiple-joint movements. In a more recent review, Martin (1981) states that the joint afferents may not play a dominant role in limb-position sense. Dubner et al. (1978), speaking specifically of temporomandibular joint (TMJ) function, cite conflicting evidence on the muscle versus joint-receptor primacy and conclude as follows: "Attempts to assign the mechanism of mandibular kinesthesia to either the joints or the muscles may be unwise in light of studies by Millar (1973) demonstrating that the sensitivity of joint receptors in limb joints is modulated by the degree of activity of the muscles acting on the joint. Further work will be needed to clarify the interaction between the TMJ and jaw muscle receptors. In the meantime it may be wise to consider muscles and joints as contributing complementary kinesthetic inputs" (p. 169).

In the present experiment we have concluded that when subjects are asked to estimate amount of movement of a single joint structure they are able to do so with considerable accuracy; in addition, they are able to estimate amount of movement of a structure that involves no joints at all, the tongue, although not quite as easily or accurately. This suggests support for the position of Dubner et al. (1978) that we must make use of both muscle and joint-receptor information, since our speakers were able to make reasonable but degraded estimations with only muscle-receptor information available to them.

It is of certain interest to examine somewhat more closely the movements that we have investigated. In Figure 12.4 we show extent of measured jaw movement (averaged over normal and loud productions) versus tongue displacement (as defined by the maxilla-based and mandible-based measures of tongue movement described above). Alternative definitions of both

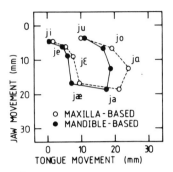

Figure 12.4   Extent of tongue movement versus extent of jaw movement.

opening and anterior–posterior movement would be possible, but the present choice is acceptable for making the following point: The measures of tongue movement that we have employed give numerical estimates of extent of movement that are either drastically larger (shift of constriction location) or roughly comparable (displacement of tongue as a whole or of a point on the tongue) in magnitude to observed jaw movements. As a result, the articulatory space, when examined in the perspective of the present /jV/ syllables, becomes centered around a straight line through the origin and with a slope of −1 and thus appears warped in relation to more conventional geometrical arrangements such as vowel quadrilaterals. For instance, we note that the opening dimension defined by the front series /i, e, ɛ, æ/ and the back series /u, o, ɑ, a/ appears rather extended in relation to front–back articulatory distances, for example, /i/–/u/ and /ɛ/–/o/. Had we used shift of constriction for tongue movement, this asymmetry would have been further reinforced, the opening dimension dominating that of front–back movement.

Our selection of parameters for producing Figure 12.4 is clearly arbitrary and needs independent justification before firm conclusions can be drawn about a psychologically correct articulatory calibration of the phonetic space. However, it should be in principle possible to use the present DME experiments to shed some light on that topic.

For the judgment of jaw movement we were able to establish power functions describing the relation between physical measurement and subjective response with very good accuracy. To obtain a set of numerical values representing perceived degrees of opening in the present syllables, let us take the median values of the jaw-movement measurements and apply them to the formula summarizing the results from all subjects ($y = .23x^{.78}$). The numbers thus derived are plotted along one of the dimensions of Figure 12.5, a diagram that is intended to represent a subjective version of the physical space described by Figure 12.4.

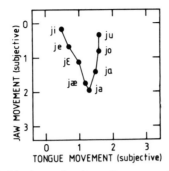

Figure 12.5 Subjective estimations of tongue and jaw movement.

In the case of the tongue, a similar procedure is not used since certain syllables, those with rounded vowels, exhibited systematic deviations from the best-fitting power law. Rather, for the tongue we simply plot the median scores of the subjective estimates along a second dimension of the subjective articulatory space. The result of these operations is shown in Figure 12.5. Again, we observe that opening spans a wider range than does front–back.

Comparing Figures 12.4 and 12.5, are we entitled to conclude that our psychological representation of the articulatory space retains the relation between opening and front–back observed for a physical interpretation of these parameters? Before drawing any conclusions, let us critically examine some of the qualifications that must be made with regard to using the information in Figure 12.5 in that way.

It might be objected that in our experiments we never asked our subjects to compare jaw and tongue movements directly. Therefore, we should not equate the subjective units, although numerically identical, along the y and x axes of Figure 12.5. This objection can be handled by reminding ourselves of the meaning of the two scales. The subjects' estimates are relational numbers. They imply that, for instance, our subjects judged movement of /jɛ/ to be twice that of /ji/ and approximately two-thirds that of /ja/. Comparing the extremes we thus find that the jaw dimension spans a range from 0.2 to 2, or approximately a tenfold increase, whereas the tongue numbers cover the range of 0.5 to 1.6, a three- or fourfold increase. As long as we use ratios as the relevant information, the absolute values of x and y coordinates are unimportant, and we are, indeed, entitled to compare jaw opening and tongue movements. Therefore, our conclusion is that, according to the subjective impressions of our subjects, jaw opening spans a wider psychological range than tongue movements in the present set of /jV/ syllables.

Suppose we were to express the formant frequencies of some typical

reference vowels in terms of similar scales. What would an acoustic
vowel diagram then look like?

	F_1		F_2	
/i/	250	1.0	2400	1.00
/ɛ/	500	2.0	1800	0.75
/a/	750	3.0	1200	0.50
/ɔ/	500	2.0	840	0.35
/u/	250	1.0	600	0.25

Using /i/ as a standard for both F_1 and F_2, we obtain the ratios above
and the configuration shown in Figure 12.6. We conclude that F_2, a
correlate mainly of anterio–posterior tongue movement (Lindblom &
Sundberg 1971) exhibits a range equal to four times its smallest value,
whereas F_1, a dimension controlled primarily by degree of (jaw) opening
(Lindblom & Sundberg 1971) shows a ratio of three between maximum
and minimum frequencies. F_2 covers two octaves while F_1 covers one
and one-half octaves. In perceptual terms, this implies that tongue movement spans a wider range than does the opening dimension, a result that
is opposite to that we have just reported for the perception of articulatory
movement.

Before pursuing the comparison of articulatory and acoustic–perceptual
spaces, we review some typological facts about vowel systems. Let us
study the use of a peripheral vowel series such as /ɪ, e, ɛ, æ/ and /ʊ, ɔ,
ɑ/ and investigate how frequently those qualities occur in the languages
of the world in relation to maximally high vowels such as /y, ü, ɨ, ɯ,
u/. Since /i, a, u/ are likely to be favored by most languages, our question
amounts basically to establishing the vowels functioning as /i, a, u/ and

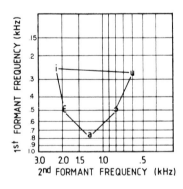

Figure 12.6 F_1–F_2 plot of vowel formant frequencies.

Table 12.9

PERCENTAGE OF LANGUAGES HAVING 0–3 PERIPHERAL VOWELS
INTERSPERSED BETWEEN THE VOWELS FUNCTIONING AS /i, a, u/

	High series				Front series				Back series			
Number of vowels	0	1	2	3	0	1	2	3	0	1	2	3
Percentage of languages	72.7	24.2	0.1	0	16.7	61.1	20.2	2.0	26.8	60.1	11.1	2.0

then counting the number of qualities interspersed between /i/ and /u/ (the high series), between /i/ and /a/ (the front series), and between /u/ and /a/ (the back series). Consulting a study of 198 languages having three through nine vowels by Crothers (1978), we obtain the frequencies shown in Table 12.9.

This exercise teaches us that in Crother's sample the high series is clearly disfavored relative to the front and back peripheral vowels.

Liljencrants and Lindblom (1972) attempted to predict the phonetic qualities of vowel systems on the basis of a hypothesis about the universal vowel space (an articulatorily based definition of possible vowel) and a principle of maximal perceptual contrast. An unsuccessful but instructive result of their work was the tendency of the predictions to produce too many high vowels for systems with more than six vowels. Lindblom (1980) has pointed out that psychoacoustically better-motivated distance measures (Bladon & Lindblom 1981) than the one used by Liljencrants and Lindblom have the consequence of reducing the perceptual distance between /i/ and /u/ relative to those derived for /u/–/a/ and /i/–/a/. Such measures do improve the predictions. Nevertheless, serious errors remain. In particular, both the Liljencrants and Lindblom model and its revised version (Lindblom 1980) fail to handle certain typological facts correctly. For instance, they both fall short of accounting for the patterning often observed in systems containing seven vowels. Ignoring detailed phonetic differences for the moment (Disner, 1983) we can approximate the systems of Italian, Yoruba, and several others as follows:

$$
\begin{array}{lll}
& i & u \\
(1) & e & o \\
& \varepsilon & \mathfrak{o} \\
& \quad a &
\end{array}
$$

The original and revised versions of the dispersion theories (2a and

2b, respectively) give us as optimal cases

(2)   a.   i   ü/ʉ   ɨ   u
                  ɛ   ɔ
                        a

(2)   b.   i   ü   ɯ   u
                  ɛ   ɔ
                     a

When we look for the reasons why perceptual contrast measures appear, so far, to make systematically incorrect predictions about the gross characteristics of vowel systems, several lines of future research suggest themselves. Perhaps the most obvious one begins with the fact that a great deal of research on the perceptual calibration of distance metrics remains to be done (Klatt 1982). As empirically more satisfactory frameworks appear, the verification or refutation of dispersion theories of vowel systems should be facilitated.

Another natural approach would be to envision the emergence of vowel systems as governed not only by demands for perceptual distinctiveness (and other listener-based criteria) but also by factors optimizing the production of speech. It would be along that line of inquiry that the present results might merit attention. Taking such an approach we might begin by considering the following observations:

1. Vowel systems favor the dimension of opening over front–back contrasts.
2. So far no entirely successful phonetic explanation for 1 has been proposed. Thus, perceptually motivated theories of vowel systems have failed to predict 1 satisfactorily.
3. The present DME experiments on jaw opening and tongue movement should be replicated with more subjects and with systematic variations of the basic task before firm conclusions can be drawn. Nevertheless, these experiments suggest, by way of hypothesis, a possible characteristic of speakers' psychological space of articulatory movement that parallels the distribution of vowel qualities in the languages of the world. In this subjective articulatory space there appears to be more room for opening distinctions than for front–back contrasts.

If substantiated by further experimentation, this coincidence of neuropsychological data and linguistic-typological facts forces us to ask: Is it merely fortuitous or does it reflect a certain degree of genuine causal connection?

6. SUMMARY

We have had three aims in this chapter. First, we have drawn attention to a research problem that we believe merits attention, the problem of establishing a neuropsychologically valid calibration of the articulatory space for vowels. Second, as a preliminary contribution toward that goal, we have reported on some direct magnitude-estimation experiments for jaw and tongue movement and have presented results in the form of a power function relating subjective judgments of movements and physical measurements of those movements. Two of our findings deserve particular highlighting.

In an introductory series of experiments subjects were asked to make DME judgments of nonspeech tasks; they were able to do this with ease. A second series of tests involved judging extent of jaw and tongue movements in /jV/ syllables. While the subjects performed consistently and without difficulty on the jaw task, they all found the estimation of tongue movement to be much more difficult. Thus, one striking fact about the results is how relatively inaccessible, on introspection, tongue positioning and movement seem to be as compared with nonspeech movements and jaw–speech movements.

However, when given opportunity to get used to the tongue judgment task, subjects were able to make consistent and for the most part quite accurate responses, and it was possible to compare the relative magnitudes reported for tongue gestures with those given for jaw movements. This comparison produces our second major finding, which is that jaw-opening estimates span a wider numerical range than do tongue judgments. We interpret this observation tentatively as an indication that in the psychological space of vowel articulations the dimension of opening dominates that of lingual front–back movement.

As a third major point, we have discussed the implications of this finding for the understanding of some general properties of vowel systems such as the tendency to favor contrasts along the dimension of opening over that for front–back distinctions.

REFERENCES

Bladon, R. A. W., & Lindblom, B. (1981). Modeling the judgement of vowel quality differences. *Journal of the Acoustical Society of America, 69,* 1414–1422.

Carew, T. J. (1981). Spinal cord I: muscles and muscle receptors. In E. Kandel & J. Schwartz (Eds.), *Principles of neural science* (pp. 284–292). London: Arnold.

Crothers, J. (1978). Typology and universals of vowel systems. In J. H. Greenberg (Ed.), *Universals of Human Language* (Vol. 2) (pp. 93–152). Cambridge, MA: MIT Press.

Davson, H., & Segal, M. B. (1978). *Introduction to physiology* (Vol. 4). London: Academic Press.

Disner, S. F. (1983). Vowel quality: The relation between universal and language specific factors. *UCLA Working Papers in Phonetics, 58*, 1–158.

Dubner, R., Sessle, B., & Storey, A. (1978). *The neural basis of oral and facial function*. New York: Plenum.

Franzén, R., & Offenloch, K. (1969). Evoked response correlates of psychophysical magnitude estimates for tactile stimulation in man. *Experimental Brain Research, 8*, 1–18.

Hardcastle, W. J. (1970). The role of tactile and proprioceptive feedback in speech production. *Work in progress* (No. 4). Department of Linguistics, Edinburgh University.

Harshman, R., Ladefoged, P., & Goldstein, L. (1977). Factor analysis of tongue shapes. *Journal of the Acoustical Society of America 62*, 693–707.

Kandel, E. R., & Schwartz, J. H. (Eds.). (1981). *Principles of neural science*. London: Arnold.

Klatt, D. (1982). Speech processing strategies based on auditory models. In R. Carlson, & B. Granström, (Eds.), *The representation of speech in the peripheral auditory system*. Amsterdam: Elsevier Biomedical Press.

Ladefoged, P. (1980). What are linguistic sounds made of? *Language, 56*, 485–502.

Liljencrants, J., & Lindblom, B. (1972). Numerical simulation of vowel quality systems: The role of perceptual contrast. *Language, 48*, 839–862.

Lindblom, B. (1980). Phonetic universals in vowel systems. (To appear in J. Ohala (Ed.), *Experimental phonology*. New York: Academic Press.

Lindblom, B., & Sundberg, J. (1971). Acoustic consequences of lip, tongue, jaw and larynx movement. *Journal of the Acoustical Society of America, 50*, 1166–1179.

Lindblom, B., & Schulman, R. (1982). The target theory of speech production in the light of mandibular dynamics. *Proceedings of the Institute of Acoustics: Autumn Conference, Bournemouth, England*.

Lubker, J., Lindblom, B., Gay, T., Lyberg, B., Branderud, P., & Holmgren, K. (forthcoming) Compensatory articulation in the control of speech timing.

Martin, J. H. (1981). Somatic sensory system I: Receptor physiology and submodality coding. In E. Kandel, & J. Schwartz (Eds.), *Principles of neural science* (pp. 157–169). London: Arnold.

Matthews, B. H. C. (1933). Nerve endings in mammalian muscle. *Journal of Physiology, 78*, 1–53.

Millar, J. (1973). Joint afferent fibers responding to muscle stretch, vibration and contraction. *Brain Research, 63*, 380–383.

Mountcastle, V. B. (1975). The view from within: Pathways to the study of perception. *Johns Hopkins Medical Journal, 136*, 109–131.

Mountcastle, V. B., Poggio, G. F., & Werner, G. (1962). The neural transmission of the sensory stimulus at the cortical input level of the somatic afferent system. In R. W. Gerard, & W. Duyff (Eds.), *Information processing in the nervous system* (pp. 196–217). Amsterdam: Exerpta Medica Foundation.

Penfield, W., & Rasmussen, T. (1950). *The cerebral cortex of man*. New York: MacMillan.

Porter, R., & Lubker, J. (1980). The 'linguameter': a device for investigating tongue–muscle control. *Journal of Speech and Hearing Research, 23*, 490–494.

Russell, D. G. (1976). Spatial location cues and movement production. In G. E. Stelmach (Ed.), *Motor control: Issues and trends*. New York: Academic Press.

Stevens, S. S. (1975). *Psychophysics*. New York: Wiley.

Sussman, H. (1972). What the tongue tells the brain. *Psychological Bulletin, 77*, 262–272.

13

Serial-Ordering Errors in Speech and Typing*

Peter F. MacNeilage

1. INTRODUCTION

Peter Ladefoged's work can be primarily characterized as a number of seminal contributions to the area of paradigmatic phonetics. He has done more than anyone in the modern era to specify and describe the properties of the sound elements of spoken languages. No comparably important contributions have been made to the understanding of syntagmatic aspects of phonetics—the serial origination of spoken languages. It is to this relatively neglected area that I turn my attention. While this area is not one in which I can benefit directly from Ladefoged's contributions, I can at least aspire to the high scientific standards that have informed his work.

Some light may be cast on syntagmatic aspects of speech by directly comparing it with other complex serial-output systems. It certainly seems desirable to make such a comparison, because the widespead claims that speech and language are unique can best be evaluated by direct comparison with other functions. The direct comparison I have in mind is in terms of error patterns. It is well accepted that much can be learned about the operation of a mechanism by observing the ways in which it goes wrong. A good deal of work has been done on speech errors from this standpoint, but to my knowledge no systematic comparison has ever been made between speech errors and errors in any other complex voluntary output process. This chapter presents a comparison of errors in speech and typing.

* Preparation of this paper was supported by Grant NS 15336-05 from the Department of Health and Human Services, Public Health Service. I wish to thank Judase Hutchinson and Harvey Sussman for comments on an earlier draft of this paper.

2. ERROR PATTERNS

At the phonological level of language, with which this chapter is most concerned, the element most involved in serial-ordering errors is the single segment (Fromkin 1971). In an otherwise correct utterance, a single segmental element can be (1) replaced by another (substitution error), (2) added, (3) omitted, (4) shifted in location, or (5) exchanged in location with another element in the sequence.

A rough equivalent of the segment in typing is the letter. With the exception of shift errors, analogs to all the above error types occur in typing. However substitution errors are not considered here, because typed substitution errors seem to primarily involve spatial contingencies (typing a letter spatially adjacent to the correct one) rather than temporal factors.

Table 13.1 shows the frequencies of various types of serial-ordering errors observed in a study of typing errors (MacNeilage 1964) involving 5 undergraduates of moderate skill whose typing speeds ranged from 30 to 45 words per minute. They were typing final drafts of laboratory reports from rough written drafts. The descriptive labels used in the study are given at the left of the table and equivalent terms for speech errors, where available, are given on the right. An equivocal error is one in which a letter one stroke ahead of the correct letter is typed, after which the typist stops typing. (Students were instructed to stop as soon as they noticed an error.) An anticipation error involves typing one or more strokes ahead of the place where the mistake began. Examples of errors and error types are shown in Table 13.2.

The central difference between serial-ordering errors in speech and typing is that while there are severe serial (syntagmatic) restrictions on erroneous sequences of speech segments, there are no such restrictions on erroneous sequences of typed strokes. It is widely attested that, with

Table 13.1

TYPING-ERROR FREQUENCIES[a]

Typing-error term	Speech-error term	Number of errors
Reversal	Exchange	32
Omission	Omission	26
Interpolation	Addition	11
Equivocal	—	88
Anticipation	—	33
Total		190

[a] MacNeilage (1964).

Table 13.2
ERRORS RESULTING IN LETTER SEQUENCES NOT PERMISSIBLE WITHIN SYLLABLES

Reversals	Equivocals
part ⟶ patr	high ⟶ hg
and ⟶ adn	perhaps ⟶ perhp
experiment ⟶ experiemtn	criterion ⟶ crt
together ⟶ togeht	behavior ⟶ behv
conditioning ⟶ condtii	conditioned ⟶ condt
phenomenon ⟶ peh	reconditioning ⟶ recondti
reconditioning ⟶ recondtii	generally ⟶ gn
evidence ⟶ evidne	much ⟶ mc
experiment ⟶ experimnet	Interpolations
shown ⟶ shwo	fixed ⟶ firxed
unnecessary ⟶ unnce	had previous ⟶ hadh
despite ⟶ desptie	Anticipations
intended ⟶ intedn	training ⟶ traing
Omissions	
conditioned ⟶ cnd	
qualitatively ⟶ qul	
persevering ⟶ persver	

few exceptions, erroneous speech sequences conform to the phonotactic rules of the language (e.g., Fromkin 1971). It is important to note that these rules apply primarily to the internal structure of syllables. There are relatively few sound sequences that are not possible across syllable boundaries.

Table 13.2 is a list of erroneous letter sequences observed in the errors summarized in Table 13.1, in which within-syllable letter sequence constraints have been violated. They constitute approximately 14% of the total number of errors and show that there is no obvious constraint against such sequences in typing.

A further instance of syllable-structure constraints on speech errors is observed in exchange errors. Speech segments involved in exchanges virtually always move to a position in syllable structure identical to the one from which they migrated. Syllable-initial consonants exchange with syllable-initial consonants, vowels with vowels, and syllable-final consonants with syllable-final consonants (e.g., MacKay 1969). No such constraint is observable in typing errors. Exchange errors in typing virtually always involve adjacent letters in the text. This was true in the MacNeilage (1964) study and in a more recent study of expert typists by Grudin (1981). In addition, unlike speech, there is no prohibition of exchanges between consonants and vowels in typing. The left side of Table 13.3

Table 13.3

FREQUENCIES OF EXCHANGE OF VOWELS AND CONSONANTS IN
REVERSAL AND EQUIVOCAL ERRORS

Reversal		Equivocal	
Within class			
C ↔ C	6	C ← C	21
V ↔ V	2	V ← V	11
Total	8	Total	32
Cross class			
V ← C	15	V ← C	22
C ← V	9	C ← V	33
Total	24	Total	55

shows the participation of vowel and consonant letters in the 32 reversal errors of the MacNeilage (1964) study. These frequencies are close to the expected frequencies of about 9 and 23 for within-class and cross-class sequences based on a digraph frequency count of English text by Baddeley, Conrad, and Thompson (1960). The right side shows a classification of equivocal errors in terms of the frequency with which vowel and consonant letters were advanced into positions intended for vowel and consonant letters. Again there is no sign of a prohibition on exchanges between vowel and consonant letters.

It appears that while speech-segment exchanges are a result of placement of segments in the wrong syllables, typing exchanges may result primarily from a failure to coordinate the two hands. In the MacNeilage corpus, two different hands were involved in the exchanges on about 70% of the occasions. This can be compared with an expected frequency of cross-hand sequences of 58% based on the count by Baddeley et al. (1960). Furthermore, in Grudin's (1981) study of expert typists, two different hands were involved in about 80% of exchanges.

A further constraint on serial-ordering errors of speech segments is that vowels are much less likely to participate in errors that change the number of segments (additions and omissions) than are consonants (Shattuck-Hufnagel, personal communication November 1983). The factors underlying this constraint may perhaps be inferred from a consideration of the effects of the various possible consonant and vowel errors on output structure.

Consonant omissions would probably leave a permissible syllable structure in most cases. On the other hand, vowel omissions would not only reduce the number of syllables in the output by one, but the resultant bringing together of the consonants that were scheduled to surround the vowel might often result in impermissible syllable structures. Consonant additions are in principle possible up to a maximum of three prevocalic and four postvocalic consonants. Adding a single consonant where no consonant was scheduled would probably almost always result in a permissible syllable structure. Adding consonants where one or more was already present might often result in a permissible syllable structure. Vowel additions would always increase the number of syllables by one. But it would seem that adding a vowel would seldom produce an impermissible syllable structure. In fact, such additions are often observed in children and adults with speech problems as they apparently attempt to simplify syllable structure; for example, [ple] might become [pəle].

In summary, neither consonant additions nor omissions change syllable number, and neither typically has severe repercussions on syllable structure. On the other hand, both vowel additions and omissions change syllable number, and vowel omissions may result in impermissible syllable structures.

In contrast to the situation in speech, there appears to be no constraint against the addition or omission of vowel letters in typing. Table 13.4 shows the frequency with which vowel and consonant letters were involved in interpolation (addition) and omission errors in the 1964 study. These frequencies are about what would be expected from the fact that about 70% of written text consists of consonant letters and 30% of vowel letters (Baddeley et al. 1960).

There is no equivalent in speech errors to the anticipation errors observed in typing. But such errors are informative in that they give some idea of the extent to which letters ahead of the correct letter being typed are available in temporary storage prior to output. The number of letters skipped in anticipation errors ranged from 1 to 6 with a mean of 3.6 letters. These data suggest that the letter(s) in the corresponding position in the next syllable to the letter currently being typed might often be available to participate in an exchange error of the kind frequently observed in speech. For example *k* in *taken* would be available to reverse with *t*

Table 13.4

FREQUENCIES OF VOWEL AND CONSONANT OMISSIONS AND
INTERPOLATIONS

	Vowels	Consonants
Omissions	9	17
Interpolations	3	8
Total	12	25

in a syllable-initial consonant reversal. The fact that analogs of such characteristic speech-sound reversals do not occur in typing can therefore probably not be attributed to short-term storage limitations in typing.

The general conclusion from this comparison of segmental speech errors and typing errors is that while the pattern of speech errors is constrained by syllable number and syllable structure factors, no such constraints are observable in typing errors. One implication of the absence of syllable structure constraints in typing is that the presence of such constraints in speech is not simply a result of the relative frequency with which certain sequences have been produced in the past. As letter-sequence contingencies are derived from sound-sequence contingencies, any practice-related constraining effects of relative frequency of sequences on the buildup of preferences in serial output patterns would be expected to be at least roughly analogous in both types of output tasks, even though it must be conceded that speakers are more practiced than typists.

Another conclusion to be drawn from differences in error patterns in the two types of task is that the constraints observed in speech are probably introduced primarily at a relatively late stage of phonological organization—a stage specific to speech output. This conclusion is based on the assumption that there is a considerable commonality between speaking and typing in earlier stages of phonological organization, stages involving lexical representation. The likelihood that lexical representations are indeed involved in typing—even copy typing—is suggested by Grudin (1981) who found that on 11 of 15 occasions copy typists spontaneously corrected the spelling of a misspelled word with which they were inadvertently presented. To the extent that speaking and typing share earlier stages of the output process, differences in error patterns between speakers and typists must be attributed to differences in later stages of the two output processes.

An analogy between the operation of freight trains and conveyor belts may be useful in characterizing the contrasting modes of operation of speech and typing suggested by the error patterns reviewed here, particularly the patterns of exchange errors. For speech, imagine a small number of freight trains (syllables), each composed of the same short sequence of different freight cars (say a flatcar, a gondola, a boxcar, a tank car, and a hopper car). These trains are being loaded more or less simultaneously but are scheduled to travel in a particular order to their common destination, where the contents of each train will go to a different recipient. In loading the trains, a particular commodity (segment) is occasionally loaded into a correct car but on the wrong train (e.g., wheat intended for the hopper car of train 1 is put into the hopper car of train 2, and simultaneously, perhaps, the corn intended for the hopper car of train 2 is placed in the hopper car of train 1.) It is much less likely, though perhaps occasionally possible, for a commodity to be successfully loaded onto the wrong car on the right train (e.g., wheat onto a flat car). In this analogy, the loading of the commodity onto the wrong train is an error with respect to semantic intention, and the use of the correct type of car for the misplaced segment is analogous to adherence to syllable-internal structural constraints.

In contrast, compare typing to two workers (the two hands) placing items on a single conveyor belt. The items come to the workers in an order corresponding to the order of letters in written language. Occasionally one worker puts his next item on the belt when the other worker should have put the next item on. Consequently, a pair of items are placed on the belt in the wrong order. The belt itself exercises no constraint on the order in which things can be placed on it, and so sequences of items that could not have occurred as part of the (language-constrained) input to the two workers are observed with some frequency in the output.

3. IMPLICATIONS FOR THE ORGANIZATION OF SPEECH

Why should there be such a difference in output organization in speech and typing? My colleagues and I have argued elsewhere that many aspects of speech error patterns are indicative of the evolution of a novel mode of organization for speech, a mode we describe by the phrase "frame/content" (Lindblom, MacNeilage, & Studdert-Kennedy, in preparation; MacNeilage, Studdert-Kennedy, & Lindblom 1985). Perhaps the most important observation leading to that conclusion was made by Shattuck-Hufnagel (1979). As she noted, the fact that speech segments in exchange errors move into the same position in syllable structure as the one they were scheduled to occur in means that syllable structure must be represented in production independently of segmental content elements. In our terminology, the production process involves insertion of segmental content elements into syllabic frames. It is our contention that the frame/content mode of organization evolved at the phonological level as a means of generating a large message set at high output rates within the constraints imposed by articulatory ease and perceptual distinctiveness. The alternating opening and closing of the vocal tract associated with the alternation between vowels and consonants, embodied in the notion of syllable, involves a phylogenetically old, basically rhythmic operation that produces, with each opening and closing, acoustic discontinuities to which the auditory system is sensitive. The separation of frame from content allows an explosive increase in the segmental concatenative possibilities while maintaining the simple open–close sequence.

In defense of the frame/content hypothesis it should be noted that it is not just an ad hoc attempt at explanation of patterns of segmental speech errors but part of a more comprehensive view of the evolution of language. According to this view, the frame/content mode of organization of phonology was a precursor to a similar mode of morphosyntactic organization and, in turn, had a precursor in a particular form of bimanual coordination. The hypothesis that the morphosyntactic level of language may have a frame/content mode of organization comes primarily from Garrett's conclusion that large numbers of language errors can be accounted for in these terms. For example, errors such as

McGovern favors busting pushers ⟶ *McGovern favors pushing busters*

suggest a mode of organization in which content-word stems (*push, bust*) are placed into syntactic frames (*ing, ers*). The particular mode of bimanual coordination suggested as a precursor to language organization is the one in which an object is held in the nonpreferred hand (the frame) and operated on by the preferred hand (content).

From the standpoint of the frame/content hypothesis for the evolution of language, it comes as no surprise that typing errors do not show constraints related to syllable structure. In typing, there is no functional analog to the frame/content mode of spoken syllable organization. Therefore, there are no prominent output constraints related to syllable structure in typing, even though typing involves the same language as speaking, and printed language does include sequential patterns related to syllable structure.

4. SUMMARY

In accordance with the conviction that light can be cast on syntagmatic aspects of speech by comparing it with other complex output systems, a comparison was made between patterns of serial-ordering errors in speech and typing. It was found that while there are severe syntagmatic constraints on speech-error patterns, related to syllable structure and number, there are no such constraints on typing errors. The syllable-structure constraints on speech errors are considered to result from the evolution of a frame/content mode of organization for speech whereby segmental content elements are inserted into syllabic frames. This frame/content mode may have evolved from bimanual coordination and may be the precursor of an analagous mode of morphosyntactic organization.

The absence of syllable structure constraints in typing is considered to result from the absence, in typing, of a functional analog to the frame/content mode of phonological organization.

REFERENCES

Baddeley, A. D., Conrad, F., & Thompson, W. E. (1960). Letter structure of the English Language. *Nature, 186*, 414–416.

Fromkin, V. A. (1971). The nonanomalous nature of anomalous utterances. *Language, 47*, 27–52.

Garrett, M. (1975). The analysis of sentence production. In G. Bower (Ed.), *Psychology of learning and motivation* (Vol. 9) (pp. 133–177). New York: Academic Press.

Grudin, J. T. (1981). *The organization of serial order in typing.* Unpublished doctoral dissertation, University of California, San Diego.

Lindblom, B., MacNeilage, P. F., & Studdert-Kennedy, M. B. (in preparation). *Biological bases of spoken language.* Orlando: Academic Press.

MacKay, D. G. (1969). Forward and backward masking in motor systems. *Kybernetik, 6*, 57–64.

MacNeilage, P. F. (1964). Typing errors as clues to serial ordering mechanisms in language behavior. *Language & Speech, 7*, 144–159.

MacNeilage, P. F., Studdert-Kennedy, M. G., & Lindblom, B. (1984). Functional precursors to language and its lateralization. *American Journal of Physiology, 246*, 912–914.

MacNeilage, P. F., Studdert-Kennedy, M. B., & Lindblom, B. (1985). Planning and production of speech: An overview. In J. Lauter (Ed.), *Proceedings of the Conference on Planning and Production of Speech by Normally Hearing and Deaf People, A.S.H.A. Reports.*

Shattuck-Hufnagel, S. (1979). Speech errors as evidence for a serial ordering mechanism in sentence production. In W. E. Cooper & E. C. T. Walker (Eds.), *Sentence processing: Psycholinguistic studies presented to Merrill Garrett* (pp. 297–342). Hillsdale, NJ: Erlbaum.

14

Phonetic Cues to Syllabification

Ian Maddieson

1. INTRODUCTION

Ladefoged (1982:219) states simply that "there is no agreed phonetic definition of a syllable." That such a definition is lacking can be readily seen in any reading of current phonetic literature. Earlier optimism over defining the syllable (see, e.g., Pike 1943, Stetson 1951) has largely given way to pessimism. Yet despite the difficulty of defining it, the syllable has been given a major role in recent developments in phonological theory (e.g., Cairns & Feinstein 1982; Clements & Keyser 1983; Kahn 1976; Kiparsky 1979; Selkirk 1980; Steriade 1982). Views differ as to how complex the internal structure of the syllable is, for example, whether a syllable node dominates higher-order elements with their own constituent structure such as onset and rhyme, dominates C and V elements, or directly dominates segments (i.e., feature matrices). However, all accounts essentially agree that in some way segment-like elements are grouped into syllables.

Moreover, there may be rules that change the membership of a segment from one syllable to another (resyllabification rules). For example, Harris (1983) states a common observation about Spanish as follows: "In casual speech a word-final consonant syllabifies with the initial vowel of the following word" (p. 43). He formulates a rule that reassigns a consonant before a word boundary and a vowel to an onset rather than a rhyme and exemplifies the effect of the rule with the sentence:

(1)   *Los otros estaban en el avión.*

After this rule applies, this sentence is syllabified as follows (a syllable boundary is represented by a period):

(2)   *Lo.so.tro.ses.ta.ba.ne.ne.la.vión*

Elsewhere, Marlett and Stemberger (1983) argue that resyllabification of

PHONETIC LINGUISTICS

a somewhat different sort applies in Seri after vowel deletion in certain forms with prefixes. The prefixes have the form 'consonant + /i/,' as in the irrealis /si-/. When a consonant follows this prefix, the vowel /i/ is dropped so that

(3)   σ   σ   σ
      | Λ   Λ
      i – s i – k a

becomes

(4)   σ   σ   σ
      | | Λ
      i – s – k a

Since a syllable containing only /s/ is not well formed, a rule of resyllabification applies that attaches /s/ to the onset of the following syllable, giving /i.ska/.

With the ability to define a syllable phonetically in doubt, questions obviously arise concerning the basis on which selection between plausible alternative syllabifications is made. These questions apply as much to any initial (lexical) assignment to syllables as to cases where resyllabification is posited across word boundaries, as in the Spanish example above. Likewise, in the Seri example, the syllabification of /s/ with /ka/ is obviously only one of two potential ways that the faulty syllabic structure could have been remedied. The output of resyllabification could have been /is.ka/, with the syllable boundary between the consonants as in the Spanish /es.ta.ban/.

2. DETERMINING SYLLABIFICATION

When syllabification is at issue, what is the basis on which linguists have determined that their view in any given case is the correct one? There are sometimes formal arguments that can be made to justify particular syllabifications, for example, those related to input to reduplication rules advanced in Steriade (1982). These seem more likely to relate to initial syllabification, leaving surface syllabification to be determined from other kinds of evidence. If it is accepted that languages differ in their surface syllabification,[1] it is reasonable to assume that there must be some indications of the differences in syllable structure in the phonetic string. Note that the lack of a phonetic definition of the syllable does not prevent the recognition of phonetic markers of syllable constituency.[2] Their presence would enable a resolution to be made in situations where alternative syllabifications might be posited.

Of course, in many languages there are extrinsic allophonic rules that select allophones based on their position in the syllable. A well-known example is the difference between syllable-initial and syllable-final /l/ in both British and American English. Acoustic data on this phenomenon in American English are provided in Lehiste (1964). Since it is syllable based, this allophonic difference is capable of providing evidence of constituency of syllables in potentially ambiguous cases. An example is *holy* versus *holey* (i.e., *hole* + adjectival suffix *-y*). *Holy* is syllabified [hou.li] with the syllable-initial (clear) allophone of /l/. In the monosyllable *hole*, a syllable-final allophone of /l/ occurs, and, in my speech as well as that of many other speakers of British English, a special allophone of the preceding vocalic element that appears only before a tautosyllabic lateral also occurs. That both of these features occur in the derived form *holey* provides evidence that the syllabification of this word retains the lateral as a constituent of the first syllable (cf. Faure 1972). Tokens of *holy* and *holey* showing these syllable-bound properties from my speech are given in Figure 14.1.

Such an allophonic difference in laterals (and in vowels preceding laterals) is a particular fact about my dialect of English and is not general across languages.[3] Many languages lack such salient cues for syllable constituency in their allophonic rules. And in the languages that do show them, they are not present in all segment types. It follows that if there

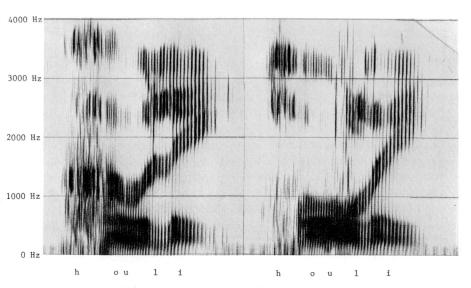

Figure 14.1 Syllable-dependent allophones of /l/ in the near-homophones *holy* (left) and *holey* (right) in the author's speech. Note F_2 above 1000 Hz in *holy* but below 1000 Hz in the vowel /ou/ and the lateral in *holey*.

are cues to syllabic constituency in these other situations, they must be more subtle ones. Linguists (not to mention native speakers) may well be responding to these cues when they make judgments about syllabic constituency in their data.

An explicit appeal to these more subtle cues can be made in the attempt to determine syllabic constituency in ambiguous circumstances. For example, Maddieson (1983) claims that most word-initial consonant sequences in the Chadic language Bura are resyllabified when a vowel precedes. Thus, the first element of the sequence becomes a coda to the syllable containing that vowel, and the syllable boundary falls between the elements of the sequence. For example, the verb /bda/ when preceded by the person–aspect marker /tsa:/ is syllabified as /tsa:b.da/. Part of the evidence for this view is that the vowel preceding one of these sequences tends to be shorter than that before a single word-initial consonant. Figure 14.2 shows waveforms of utterances containing /tsa:/ before [ptsi] and [pi]. A substantially shorter vowel can be seen before the sequence consisting of [p] preceding the affricate /ts/[4] than before the single consonant /p/ in the form /pi/.[5] As is shown below, vowel shortening in closed syllables is a relatively common phenomenon across languages. Its ocurrence in this Bura example thus provides some objective support for the intuitive feeling that the syllable boundary falls where it is shown in /tsa:b.tsi/.

However, the appeal to vowel shortening in Bura carries no weight unless the phenomenon of vowel shortening in closed syllables is in fact a general cross-linguistic one. Since there are no Bura words that contain unambiguous syllable-closing obstruents (e.g., word-final stops), the argument cannot be extended to the between-word cases on the basis of language-internal evidence from within-word cases. Unless closed-syllable vowel shortening can be shown to be quite widely found in other languages, the Bura data are unconvincing evidence for any particular syllabification, since the mere fact of a difference could reflect a language-particular rule of vowel shortening under some other circumstances.

The topic of universal bases for recognition of syllable constituency seems to have been rather neglected since an early and unconvincing experiment on formant transitions with the Haskins pattern-playback synthesizer by Malmberg (1955/1967). Although the vowel shortening referred to above has previously been mentioned as common (e.g., Abercrombie 1967; Jones 1950), there does not seem to be any study that has explicitly shown that it tends towards universality and hence has value as evidence. The remainder of this chapter is dedicated to showing that vowel shortening associated with syllable structure is widely found. For convenience, the phenomena being investigated are referred to under the name Closed Syllable Vowel Shortening (CSVS).[6]

(a)

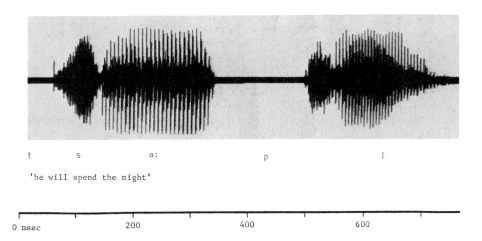

t   s   a: p   i

'he will spend the night'

0 msec   200   400   600

(b)

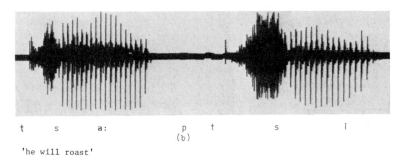

t   s   a: p   t   s   i
                                (b)

'he will roast'

Figure 14.2 Vowel duration in the morpheme /tsa:/ before word-initial (a) single consonant, and (b) consonant sequence in Bura (from Maddieson 1983).

3. VOWEL DURATION

Of course, many factors in addition to syllable constituency affect the duration of a vowel, including lexical vowel quantity and other inherent properties of the vowel itself, various suprasegmental factors (stress, tone, intonation, etc.), and contextual effects such as the nature of surrounding segments and position in units such as the word and sentence. However, when these factors are controlled for, many languages prove to have a vowel duration difference that relates to the syllabification of the following consonant. It is shown below that there are quite a few languages in which this effect seems to have been phonologized, for example in the form of rules that require only short vowels in closed syllables or forbid them in open syllables.

4. PHONETIC VOWEL DURATION BEFORE SINGLE AND GEMINATE CONSONANTS

The best test for a relationship between vowel length and syllabification is to be found in languages that allow word-internal geminated intervocalic consonants. It is assumed that these geminates are a sequence of two identical consonants with a syllable boundary falling between them. The vowel in a syllable closed by the first of a pair of geminated consonants can be compared with the vowel preceding a single consonant of the same type that is the onset to a second syllable, that is, $C_1V_1C_2.C_2V_2$ compared with $C_1V_1.C_2V_2$. In this way the contrast is limited to only the syllabic structure, and all other variables are controlled for.

A shorter vowel before geminate than before single consonants is known to occur at least in Kannada, Tamil, Telugu, Hausa, Italian, Icelandic, Norwegian, Finnish, Hungarian, Arabic, Shilha, Amharic, Galla, Dogri, Bengali, Sinhalese, and Rembarrnga. I review below some of the phonetic data from these languages, reporting principally on studies in which measurements from several speakers are provided.

Mona Lindau (personal communication February 1984) has measured the duration of lexically short vowels before single and geminate consonants in three pairs of words in the Chadic language Hausa. The results, given in Table 14.1, show that vowels are distinctly shorter before geminates. Long vowel duration is provided for comparison.

Table 14.1
SHORT VOWELS BEFORE SINGLE AND GEMINATE PLOSIVES IN HAUSA[a]

VC–		VCC–		V:C–	
Word	V duration (msec)	Word	V duration (msec)	Word	V duration (msec)
cítàa	67	cíttàa	46	líitàa	106
wátàa	71	báttàa	64	fáatàa	118
gádàa	67	háddàa	50	táadàa	125
means	68		53		116
difference		15			

[a] Each value is the mean of two or three tokens from 9 or 10 speakers, except for the third set for which data from only six speakers is available.

Table 14.2
VOWEL DURATION (IN MSEC) BEFORE
SINGLE AND GEMINATE AFFRICATES IN
ITALIAN[a]

	Slow speech rate	Fast speech rate
VC–	208	153
VCC–	132	112
Difference	76	41

[a] Each value is a mean of ten tokens from each
of eight speakers.

Italian also has shorter vowels before geminate consonants (Antonetti & Rossi 1970; Bertinetto & Vivalda 1978). The difference in duration is greater in Italian than it is in Hausa. Some measurements of /a/ before single and geminate affricate /tʃ/ were made at two different speech rates by Maddieson (1980). The results are reproduced in Table 14.2.

Ghai (1980) recorded data from five speakers of Dogri, an Indo-Iranian language related to Panjabi. He reports that the short vowels /ə/, / ɪ /, and /ɒ/ before the geminates were 27 msec on average shorter than the vowels before single consonants in the three word pairs in Table 14.3, and the long vowels /oː/ and /ɑː/ were 36 msec shorter before geminates in the two word pairs in Table 14.3. (The mean values themselves are not reported, only the differences.) It should be noted that there is a tendency for single medial stops to become fricatives in this language. The examples cited here, with the possible exception of /ɟɑːdaː/, are exempt from this trend.

In the variety of Icelandic labeled Norðlenzka (Northern Icelandic) by Orešnik and Pétursson (1977), vowel quantity can be predicted. For our purposes, what is important is that the vowels are about half as long before long voiceless stops (orthographic *bb, dd, gg*) than before single voiceless stops (orthographic *p, t, k*). The mean duration of all vowels

Table 14.3
WORD PAIRS WITH SINGLE AND
GEMINATE CONSONANTS IN DOGRI[a]

Short vowels	Long vowels
'kəcaː / 'kəccaː	'boːli / 'boːlli
'kɒli / 'kɒlli	'ɟɑːda / 'ɟɑːddaː
'kɪla / 'kɪlla	

[a] From Ghai (1980).

classed as short is 81 msec, the mean duration of long vowels is 163 msec. Data are from two speakers, but results are not given separately for vowels before geminates as opposed to other clusters or environments in which short vowels are found. (The facts in the more standard Southern Icelandic are different and call for vowel length to be taken as an underlying contrast; see Orešnik and Pétursson 1977:163–167.) In another North Germanic language, Norwegian, Fintoft (1961) found that vowels before geminate consonants have a mean duration 94 msec shorter than vowels before single consonants in a set of nonsense words (eight speakers). That CSVS also operates in Finnish can be deduced from a remark by Wiik (1965): "The same amount of lengthening [as is found when comparing final open syllables with final closed syllables] is found in words like *muuta, puuta* as compared with *muutta, puutta*" (p. 118). Wiik has data from five speakers but does not publish these measurements separately.

Less extensive data are available on several additional languages. Length differences consistent with CSVS can be seen in spectrographic data from the Dravidian language Telugu, although this evidence is only from a single speaker (Peri Bhaskararao, personal communication, December 1983). Balasubramanian (1972) indicates that shorter vowels occur before the geminate sonorants that remain in Tamil. Applegate (1958:13) reports shortening of vowels before geminates in Shilha (Berber) on the basis of spectrographic data from one speaker. McKay (1980:346) found in spectrograms of one speaker of the Australian language Rembarrnga that "in general shorter vowels occurred before the geminate stops than before the single stops." Informal examination of material in the language data archives of the UCLA Phonetics Laboratory confirms that the same phenomenon is found in Amharic, Galla, Kannada (cf. Gowda 1970), Bengali, Sinhalese, and Arabic. Surprisingly, no published measurements on this question in Arabic could be located, although a few spectrograms are included in Al-Ani (1970) showing shorter vowels before /ʔʔ/ and /ʕʕ/ than before /ʔ/ and /ʕ/.

Thus the reality of CSVS can be demonstrated in data from languages of several diverse language families that provide the most controlled environment for its observation, namely, before geminate and single consonants. It can be shown to occur in languages with and without a lexical vowel length contrast, in different speech rates, and under different prosodic conditions.

In at least one language, the phonetic length difference before single and geminate consonants is in the process of being converted into what is essentially a phonological contrast of vowel length. In the cornouaillais dialect of Breton studied by Bothorel (1982), the distinction between single and geminate sonorants, preserved in the léonais dialect, has been reduced to insignificance. Measurements of both consonant and preceding

Table 14.4

MEAN VOWEL LENGTH BEFORE FORMER SINGLE AND
GEMINATE SONORANTS AND DURATION OF
FOLLOWING CONSONANT IN A BRETON DIALECT[a]

	–VC–		–VCC–
V duration	C duration	V duration	C duration
127	48	87	53

[a] Computed from data provided in Bothorel (1982).

vowel durations are given in Table 14.4 for three speakers, using five words of each type. The difference in consonant duration is an insignificant 5 msec, but the vowels before the former geminates are 40 msec shorter than before the historical single consonants.

In some Dravidian languages, such as Tamil and Malayalam, the formerly general contrast between single and geminate consonants has been eliminated from obstruents and replaced by a contrast between long voiceless stops and short voiced fricatives (Lisker 1958; Velayudhan 1971). In these languages, the vowel length difference before the former contrasting single and geminate stops is retained. Tamil data from four speakers (about 60 tokens per speaker) are given by Balasubramanian (1981). Means from his results are reproduced as Table 14.5.

In the case of Swedish, a different phonological consequence has ensued from the restructuring of length contrasts originally related to syllable structure into both quantitative and qualitative distinctions between sets of "tense" and "lax" vowels. Elert (1964) provided measures across different vowel pairs before single and geminate consonants from eight speakers. His results before /t/ and /tt/ in the two Swedish word-accent patterns are reproduced in Table 14.6. Each value represents a mean of 10 tokens for each of nine vowels in their "tense" and "lax" variants.

Table 14.5

MEAN DURATIONS (IN MSEC) OF SEVEN LONG AND SHORT VOWELS
BEFORE SINGLE AND GEMINATE VOICELESS PLOSIVES IN TAMIL[a]

	Short vowels				Long vowels			
	VC–	VCC–	CVC–	CVCC–	V:C–	V:CC–	CV:C–	CV:CC–
Mean	112	97	93	80	221	188	184	152
Difference		15		13		33		32

[a] After Balasubramanian (1981).

Table 14.6
VOWEL DURATION (IN MSEC) BEFORE SINGLE
AND GEMINATE ALVEOLAR STOPS IN TWO
ACCENT PATTERNS OF SWEDISH[a]

	Accent I	Accent II
–VC–	140	134
–VCC–	90	92
Difference	50	42

[a] Data recalculated by Mona Lindau from Elert's
(1964) raw measures.

5. PHONOLOGICAL CONSTRAINTS ON VOWEL QUANTITY AND CONSONANT GEMINATION

Elsewhere, other reflections of the association between shorter vowel
and geminate consonant can be found in phonotactic constraints. Quite
commonly those languages with both long and short vowels and single
and geminate consonants restrict the vowels before geminate consonants
to being phonologically short.[7] This rule is found in Arabic (Al-Ani 1970),
Hausa (Abraham 1959), Hindi (Ohala 1972), Estonian (Lehiste 1966), and
apparently in both Gowda and Standard dialects of Kannada (Gowda
1970) and Ulithian (Sohn & Bender 1973). In Koya, long vowels do not
occur before geminates (Tyler 1969), and this language also has mor-
phophonemic rules that shorten an underlying long vowel when geminates
are derived. In Punjabi, the set of "lax" centralized vowels, which tend
to be shorter than the peripheral vowels, are the only vowels that may
precede geminate consonants (Gill & Gleason 1963:12). In a Bavarian
dialect of German, Bannert (1972) reports that a long vowel can only
precede a short consonant and a short consonant can only precede a long
consonant (in the minimal pair [vi:sn] vs. [vis:n], vowel length is 190
msec vs. 110 msec).

We thus see that both on the phonetic level and in phonological constraints shorter vowels frequently precede a geminate consonant that
contrasts minimally with a single consonant within a word. In other
words, the shorter vowel is in the closed syllable. An apparent counterexample, Japanese, is discussed below. Otherwise all the languages on
which data are to hand show the occurrence of a shorter vowel in a
syllable closed by a geminate consonant.

6. VOWEL DURATION IN OPEN AND CLOSED SYLLABLES IN GENERAL

In a fairly wide range of other languages there are phonetic measurements available or brief descriptive remarks that indicate a difference between vowel length in open syllables and closed syllables in general. Jones (1950:126–128) was among the first to measure such differences in English, comparing, for example, *see* with *seed* and *seat*. Jones also comments on a similar difference for Russian. Wiik (1965) confirmed Jones' findings on a larger scale for English and extended them to Finnish, using five speakers from each language. Han (1964:57–61) reported that in a set of Korean data (29 words from each of 4 speakers) the mean duration of /a/ in CV syllables was 266 msec, whereas in CVC syllables it was 127 msec. In Standard Chinese the only possible syllable-final consonants are nasals. Mean values for a set of vowels and diphthongs measured by Ren Hong-Mo (personal communication, February 1984) before /n/ and /ŋ/ are 238 and 200 msec respectively, whereas these syllable nuclei without a final nasal are 363 msec long (means of data from four speakers). Phonologically long vowels in closed syllables in Thai are reported as substantially shorter than the same vowels in open syllables (Abramson 1962). Listeners' judgments of vowel quantity reflect an awareness of this fact in that a shorter vowel is judged to be phonologically longer in a closed syllable than is the case in an open one.

Brief remarks on vowel duration and syllabification in other languages include the following. For Assamese, Goswami (1966:114) reports that stressed vowels are longer in open syllables than elsewhere in nonfinal syllables. Buth (1981) reports that long vowels are lengthened slightly in open syllables in the Nilotic language Jur Luo.

A phonologization of the kind of distribution of vowel duration discussed here can be found in several languages, as either a synchronic or historical process. For example, vowels in Ngizim in closed syllables must be phonologically short (Schuh 1978:255). In an earlier period of English, short vowels in open syllables were lengthened, in some cases merging with existing phonologically long vowels (the lower vowels /ɛ, a, ɔ/ were principally affected). The phonetic basis of this change, namely the correlation of length and syllable structure, inspired the thirteenth-century monk Orrm to devise an orthography in which all short vowels were indicated by writing a geminate consonant after them. (For a convenient brief summary of these facts see Strang 1970.)

Hence, several further languages that show a general relationship between shorter vowel and closed syllable can be added to those that provide evidence for the widespread effects of CSVS. If CSVS is universal, there will be no languages in which it does not occur. Therefore, a search for possible counterexamples was conducted.

7. APPARENT COUNTEREXAMPLES TO CSVS

There are a small number of apparent counterexamples to CSVS. One of these, Japanese, is the only documented language that shows no difference in the length of the vowels preceding geminate and single consonants in word-medial position (Dalby & Port 1982; Han 1962; Homma 1981). However, Japanese has long been held to be organized temporally on the basis of the mora (see, e.g., Bloch 1950). That is, /kan/ is a two-mora word equivalent in this respect to /kana/, but /kana/ is not equivalent to /kanna/, which has three moras. Many analyses of Japanese treat the word-final consonants and the first element of the "geminates" as syllabic consonants (e.g., Jorden 1963). The first part of a geminate consonant in Japanese derives from a former CV syllable and is represented orthographically by a symbol that corresponds to such a syllable (Miller 1967:109). In an emphatic (facetious?) style of pronunciation this syllable may be pronounced in full (Akira Fukuyama, personal communication, March 1984). The two elements of a geminate are also separated in a pig latin-type secret language, reflecting a division such as /ka.n.na/. There is thus specific evidence in the case of Japanese to reject the general assumption made above that the first part of a geminate is the coda of the syllable containing the preceding vowel. Japanese is therefore not a genuine counterexample to CSVS. All other languages with geminates that have been studied show shorter vowels before them.

The other apparent counterexample to the relation between phonetic vowel length and consonant gemination arises from the conclusion of Delattre (1968) that "in distinguishing a geminate from a single consonant, the duration of the preceding vowel is a negligible factor" in English, French, Spanish, and German (p. 126). These are not languages that have geminates of the sort found in the languages surveyed above. Most of the examples used concern consonants that occur on either side of word boundaries. Delattre comments that "what is most striking as one looks at spectrograms of these utterances is the number of cases in which a vowel preserves its original length despite a practical doubling of the following consonant's duration, as in *The race ends* vs. *The race sends*" (p. 126). In these sentences [ei] is 170 msec long in each case but [s#] is 120 msec in the first while [s#s] in the second is 230 msec. But there is no reason to consider the final consonant of *race* in the first sentence to have been resyllabified as an onset to the word *ends;* in such circumstances many English speakers have a distinct word-initial onset to the vowel with glottalization. Hence there is no reason to anticipate a longer vowel in *race* in this sentence. Delattre's data do not address the issue of concern in this chapter.

As for counterexamples to the more general correlation of shorter vowel with closed syllable, there is a possible one in French. Standard descriptions of French (e.g., Martinet 1960) mention that there is a rather limited length contrast of /ã/ and /ã:/ on the basis of such contrasts as *grand–grande* (/grã/–grã:d/). The long vowel occurs in the form with the closed syllable. Malmberg (1964) challenges this account, suggesting that the longer vowel optionally occurs as an indication of the originally closed nature of the syllable when it is resyllabified, as in *la grande Adèle*, where the syllabification would be /la.grã.da.dεl/, but that it is otherwise absent. No other authorities seem to agree with Malmberg. In fact, the long vowel in forms like *grande* probably originally arose when the feminine became disyllabic with addition of /-e/ (Ewart 1943) and thus had two open syllables at a time when the masculine *grand* was a single closed syllable. Hence the /ã/–/ã:/ contrast derives from operation of CSVS, and Martinet's account of it as an underlying contrast (for those speakers who maintain it) is probably preferable.

Some languages have phonological rules that appear to run counter to CSVS. The Micronesian language Kusaiean (Lee 1975; Levin 1983) is reported to have a phonological rule that lengthens vowels in closed syllables. In one pattern of reduplication, a short vowel in the unredu-plicated form is repeated as a long vowel in a closed syllable; for example, the simple form /fule:/ has the derived form /fu:lfule:/. The reduplication process appears sensitive to the closed nature of the syllable because there is another reduplication pattern in which the medial consonant is not repeated, that is, the reduplicated syllable is CV rather than CVC. In this pattern, when the simple form has a short vowel, the reduplicated syllable also has a short vowel, giving, for example, /fufule:/. However, it should be noted that the lexically short vowels in this language are severely restricted in their distribution, and it is clear that vowels are normally long. The short vowels are only permitted in the first syllable of disyllabic or longer words (apart from a few derived forms including some reduplicates). All vowels in monosyllables and noninitial syllables are long. Moreover, only nonlow vowels may be short. Lee's grammar of Kusaiean does not include any evidence to suggest that the occurrence of the short vowels can be predicted, but their limited distribution does suggest that this might be a possibility. An account of Kusaiean in which all vowels are underlyingly long would replace the rule that lengthens vowels in closed reduplicated syllables with one that shortens vowels under certain conditions that are not tied to syllable structure. It is unclear that such an account can be successfully made, but, if it were, it would have the advantage of explicitly representing the fact that the long vowels are the normal variants.

According to Bloomfield (1939), Menomini has rules that both lengthen short vowels in closed syllables and shorten long vowels in open syllables under certain conditions. These rules are a part of a process that appears to be mainly concerned with establishing an alternating rythmic pattern that is in part tied in with stress (Pesetsky 1979). The rythmic pattern seems to evaluate CV and CVVC syllables as equivalents; the even-numbered syllables following the first long vowel in a word are changed minimally so that they conform to one or the other of these structures. On the other hand, the vowel in the second syllable of a word is lengthened regardless of whether it is in an open or closed syllable, and vowels in the odd-numbered syllables are unchanged in length. This set of rules taken as a whole does not produce any general association of length and syllable structure that is counter to CSVS.

The above are the possible counterexamples to CSVS that I am aware of. They do not seem to be such as to seriously challenge the validity of the claim that CSVS is found across the broad generality of languages.

8. DISCUSSION

CSVS seems to be present in the world's languages with sufficient uniformity that it can be used as a cue to the syllabic constituency of a string of segments. In addition, the demonstration of the generality of CSVS may have an important implication for the understanding of speech production and linguistic structure. CSVS is consistent with the view that the rhyme of a syllable is a unit of organization in speech production. This view is connected with, but not identical to, the view that -VC-sequences are units of timing organization. Many studies have drawn attention to the tendency for vowel duration to be longer and consonant duration to be shorter in VC sequences in which the following consonant is voiced compared to when it is voiceless. Walsh and Parker (1982) have used this inverse relationship as evidence for the unity of the VC portion of a CVC syllable (at least at some point in the derivation). Port (1981) also argues for a similar "macrounit" consisting of the vowel plus the following tautosyllabic consonant. However, much of the experimental data on vowel duration and consonant voicing demonstrates that voicing-related length variations occur whether or not there is an intervening syllable boundary. Chen (1970) provides examples from French and Russian that show these phenomena before both tautosyllabic and heterosyllabic consonants and Korean data in which all the consonants are heterosyllabic but which still show a mean vowel duration 28 msec shorter before voiceless (aspirated) stops than before voiced stops. In Balasubramanian's Tamil data, mean duration of long vowels before heterosyllabic voiced consonants is 30.3 msec longer than before voiceless ones; short vowels are 14 msec longer before voiced cononants than before voiceless ones (data recalculated from tables in Balasubramanian 1981).

None of the many studies on this question of vowel length before consonants that contrast in voicing reports data in a way that enables the possible effect of syllable boundary placement to be entirely separated from other factors that also affect duration (such as word length, consonant manner, or vowel quality). However, in Chen's Russian data, the five word pairs in which the vowel was measured before a heterosyllabic consonant have a mean difference of 27.2 msec, and the six word pairs with tautosyllabic consonants show a mean difference of 29.8 msec. These differences are obviously of similar magnitude. Consonants and vowels are not matched across these two sets of words, and the majority of tautosyllabic cases occur in monosyllables whereas the heterosyllabic cases in disyllables. Furthermore, there is a rule of final obstruent devoicing in Russian; hence the monosyllables examined by Chen show a contrast in which the phonetic presence of voicing is probably not a factor.[8] Nonetheless, there is some indication here that the length difference associated with the voicing contrast is the same in open syllables and in closed syllables.

Because of this, those who have argued that the vowel- (and consonant-) length adjustment associated with voicing contrast provides evidence for the unity of VC as a constituent of the syllable have yet to show that there is any basis for doing so. This influence on vowel length behaves like certain types of coarticulation such as anticipatory rounding of the lips, which has been shown to ignore word (Bell-Berti & Harris 1982) and syllable boundaries (to judge from McAllister 1978). Although data from coarticulation studies have sometimes been interpreted as throwing light on the syllabic organization of speech production (e.g., Song & Perkell 1983), these studies do not normally examine utterances that differ minimally in syllabification. Hence they also do not address the question of syllable structure in speech production and language representation.

CSVS, on the other hand, is (ex hypothesi) related to syllable structure and thus provides a basis for drawing conclusions about the role of the syllabic unit in languages and in the general human capacity for producing articulate speech. It also provides some support for those such as Kiparsky (1979) and Selkirk (1980) who wish to recognize the rhyme as an internal constituent of the syllable.

NOTES

1. This is implicit, for example, in Clements and Keyser's (1983) discussion of their Resyllabification Convention (RC), which states that "the output of every rule is resyllabified according to the syllable structure rules examined up to that point in the derivation" (p. 54). They go on to comment that "individual grammars may specify a point in the set of ordered rules at which the [RC] becomes inoperative; indeed, some languages may not make use of the [RC] at all. . . . Resyllabification across word boundaries . . . is normally optional, and may differ in some respects from initial syllabification."
2. Jones (1931/1972) asked a similar question about the phonetic reality of the word and drew attention to several features that serve to demarcate words in English, including marking the internal boundaries in compounds.
3. Even British English accents differ in this regard. For example, in Jenny Ladefoged's speech *holy* and *holey* rhyme, both being [hou.li]. Note that in my speech the lateral in *holey* could well be considered to be an ambisyllabic consonant. However, this means that it is still a constituent of the first syllable, which is the major point of interest here, so I do not argue for or against this interpretation.
4. Maddieson (1983) argues that this [p] is actually an underlying /b/.
5. Note that the example in Figure 14.2 shows /tsa:/ before underlying /b/ and /p/. If this underlying voicing difference made a contribution to the difference in vowel length in these two phrases, it would be expected to be in the opposite direction from that seen, i.e., vowels are commonly longer before voiced stops (for a brief discussion of the generality of this phenomenon see Javkin 1979: 53). Ohala (1981) suggests use of this length distribution as a tool to determine if [p] in words like *teamster* [timpstɚ] is underlying or intrusive. Such a use of phonetic patterning is similar to using the vowel-length difference as evidence for syllabification, as suggested here and in Maddieson (1983).
6. Another property of vowels, associated with the difference between closed and open syllables and possibly linked to the question of length, is the tendency for high and mid vowels to have lower and/or more central allophones in closed syllables than in open syllables. This may also help to determine whether a postvocalic consonant is closing the syllable in which the vowel occurs or is the onset to a following syllable. At this point the generality of this tendency is harder to establish than the generality of CSVS. Some effects of vowel lowering in closed syllables are reported in Kharia (Pinnow 1959), Kurukh (Pinnow 1964), Javanese (Herrfurth 1964), Danish (Basbøll 1974), Spanish (Navarro Tomás 1968), and French (Lennig 1978). Like CSVS, this tendency has also left its historical imprint in a number of languages. A well-known example is French (Ewart 1943: 42–48), where phonetic changes based on the open or closed nature of the syllable have occurred in several historical periods. One result of this is the kind of alternation seen in forms like *sot, sotte* [so, sɔt] and *espère, espérons* [ɛspɛr, ɛsperɔ̃]. CSVS and vowel lowering in closed syllables could be linked because of the general association between shortness and lower or more central quality in vowels that is found in language as diverse as Navaho, Kurdish, Arabic, and Somali. For some disussion of the relationship see Straka (1959).
7. No restriction of this kind operates in Tamil and Finnish, where we have already seen the phonetic shortening effect, nor in Hungarian, Malayalam, and various other languages where phonetic data are not readily to hand. Hegedüs (1958) published waveforms of words with geminates in Hungarian but provides no data on contrasting words with single consonants.
8. It is not clear if phonologically voiced obstruents that have been devoiced are actually phonetically the same as the phonologically voiceless obstruents in this position in Russian. It seems likely that they are not, just as the stops in pairs of English words like *rope* and *robe* are not.

REFERENCES

Abercrombie, D. (1967). *Elements of general phonetics*. Edinburgh: Edinburgh University Press.

Abraham, R. C. (1959). *The language of the Hausa people*. London: University of London Press.

Abramson, A. S. (1962). *The vowels and tones of standard Thai: Acoustical measurements and experiments*. Bloomington: Indiana University.

Al-Ani, S. H. (1970). *Arabic phonology*. The Hague: Mouton.

Antonetti, P., & Rossi, M. (1970). *Précis de phonétique italienne: Synchronie et diachronie*. Aix-en-Provence: La Pensée Universitaire.

Applegate, J. R. (1958). *An outline of the structure of Shilha*. New York: American Council of Learned Societies.

Balasubramanian, T. (1972). *The phonetics of colloquial Tamil*. Unpublished doctoral dissertation, University of Edinburgh.

Balasubramanian, T. (1981). Duration of vowels in Tamil. *Journal of Phonetics, 9*, 151–161.

Bannert, R. (1972). *Zur Stimmbehaftigkeit und Quantität in einem bairischen Dialect* (Working Papers 6). Phonetics Laboratory, University of Lund.

Basbøll, H. (1974). The phonological syllable with special reference to Danish. *Annual Report of the Institute of Phonetics, University of Copenhagen, 8*, 39–128.

Bell-Berti, F., & Harris, K. S. (1982). Temporal patterns of coarticulation: Lip rounding. *Journal of the Acoustical Society of America, 71*, 449–454.

Bertinetto, P. M., & Vivalda, E. (1978). Recherches sur la perception des oppositions de quantité en italien. *Journal of Italian Linguistics, 3*, 97–116.

Bloch, B. (1950). Studies in colloquial Japanese: IV phonemics. *Language, 26*, 86–125.

Bloomfield, L. (1939). Menomini morphophonemics. *Travaux du Cercle Linguistique de Prague, 8*, 105–115.

Bothorel, A. (1982). *Etude phonétique et phonologique du breton parlé à Argol (Finistere-sud)*. Lille: Atelier National Reproduction des Thèses, Université Lille III.

Buth, R. (1981). The twenty vowels of Dhe Luwo (Jur Luwo, Sudan). In T. Schadeberg & M. L. Bender (Eds.), *Proceedings of the First Nilo–Saharan Linguistics Colloquium*, Leiden (pp. 119–132). Foris.

Cairns, C. E., & Feinstein, M. H. (1982). Markedness and the theory of syllable structure. *Linguistic Inquiry, 13*, 193–226.

Chen, M. (1970). Vowel length variation as a function of the voicing of the consonant environment. *Phonetica, 22*, 129–159.

Clements, G. N., & Keyser, S. J. (1983). *CV Phonology: A generative theory of the syllable*. Cambridge, MA: MIT Press.

Dalby, J., & Port, R. F. (1981). Temporal structure of Japanese: Segment, mora and word. *Research in Phonetics* (Dept. of Linguistics, Indiana University, Bloomington), *2*, 149–172.

Delattre, P. (1968). Consonant gemination in four languages: An acoustic, perceptual and radiographic study. In *The general phonetic characteristics of languages* (Final report 1968) (pp. 105–163). Santa Barbara: University of California.

Elert, C-C. (1964). *Phonologic studies of quantity in Swedish*. Uppsala: Skriptor.

Ewart, A. (1943). *The French language* (2nd ed.). London: Faber.

Faure, G. (1972). Analyse acoustique de deux allophones du l final anglais. In A. Valdman (Ed.), *Papers in linguistics and phonetics to the memory of Pierre Delattre* (pp. 117–127). The Hague: Mouton.

Fintoft, K. (1961). The duration of some Norwegian speech sounds. *Phonetica, 7*, 19–39.

Ghai, V. K. (1980). Contributions to Dogri phonetics and phonology. *Annual report of the Institute of Phonetics, University of Copenhagen, 14*, 31–94.

Gill, H. S., & Gleason, H. A. (1963). *A reference grammar of Panjabi.* Hartford, CT: Hartford Seminary Foundation.

Goswami, G. C. (1966). *An introduction to Assamese phonology.* Poona: Deccan College.

Gowda, K. K. (1970). *Gowda Kannada.* Annamalainagar: Annamalai University.

Han, M. S. (1962). The feature of duration in Japanese. *The Study of Sounds* (Phonetic Society of Japan), *10*, 65–75.

Han, M. S. (1964). *Studies in the phonology of Asian languages 2: Duration of Korean vowels.* Los Angeles: University of Southern California.

Harris, J. W. (1983). *Syllable structure and stress in Spanish: A nonlinear analysis.* Cambridge, MA: MIT Press.

Hegedüs, L. (1959). Beitrag zur Frage der Geminanten. *Zeitschrift für Phonetik und Allgemeine Sprachwissenschaft, 12*, 68–106.

Herrfurth, H. (1964). *Lehrbuch der modernen Djawanischen.* Leipzig: VEB.

Homma, Y. (1981). Durational relationships between Japanese stops and vowels. *Journal of Phonetics, 9*, 273–281.

Javkin, H. R. (1979). *Phonetic universals and phonological change* (Rep. No. 4). Berkeley: University of California, Phonology Laboratory.

Jones, D. (1973). The "word" as a phonetic entity. In W. E. Jones & J. Laver (Eds.), *Phonetics in linguistics: A book of readings* (pp. 154–158). London: Longmans. (Transcribed from *Le Maître Phonétique*, 1931, *36*, 60–65).

Jones, D. (1950). *The phoneme: Its nature and use.* Cambridge: Heffer.

Jorden, E. H. (1963). *Beginning Japanese:* Part I. New Haven: Yale University Press.

Kahn, D. (1976). *Syllable-based generalizations in English phonology.* Doctoral dissertation, MIT, distributed by Indiana University Linguistics Club, Indiana University, Bloomington.

Kiparsky, P. (1979). Metrical structure assignment is cyclic. *Linguistic Inquiry, 10*, 421–442.

Ladefoged, P. L. (1982). *A course in phonetics* (2nd ed.). New York: Harcourt Brace Jovanovich.

Lee, K-D. (1975). *Kusaiean reference grammar.* Honolulu: University Press of Hawaii.

Lehiste, I. (1964). *Acoustical characteristics of selected English consonants.* Bloomington: Indiana University.

Lehiste, I. (1966). *Consonant quantity and phonological units in Estonian.* Bloomington: Indiana University.

Lennig, M. (1978). *Acoustic measurement of linguistic change: The modern parisian vowel system.* Doctoral dissertation, University of Pennsylvania. Distributed by U.S. Regional Survey, Philadelphia.

Levin, J. (1983). *Reduplication and prosodic structure.* Unpublished manuscript, MIT, Cambridge, MA. (Revised version of a paper presented at GLOW Colloquim, York, U.K., March 1983. Abstract in *GLOW Newsletter, 10*, 52–54.)

Lisker, L. (1958). The Tamil occlusives: Short vs. long or voiced vs. voiceless? *Indian Linguistics, Turner Jubilee Volume, 1*, 294–301.

Maddieson, I. (1980). Palato-alveolar affricates in several languages. *UCLA Working Papers in Phonetics, 51*, 120–126.

Maddieson, I. (1983). The analysis of complex phonetic elements in Bura and the syllable. *Studies in African Linguistics, 14*, 285–310.

Malmberg, B. (1967). The phonetic basis for syllable division. In I. Lehiste (Ed.), *Readings in acoustic phonetics* (pp. 293–300). Cambridge, MA: MIT Press. (Reprinted from *Studia Linguistica*, 1955, *9*, 80–87.)

Malmberg, B. (1964). Juncture and syllable division. In D. Abercrombie, *In honour of Daniel Jones* (pp. 116–119). London: Longmans.

Marlett, S. A., & Stemberger, J. P. (1983). Empty consonants in Seri. *Linguistic Inquiry, 14*, 617–639.

Martinet, A. (1960). *Eléments de linguistique générale*. Paris: Colin.

McAllister, R. (1978). Temporal asymmetry in labial coarticulation. *Papers from the Institute of Linguistics, University of Stockholm* 35.

McKay, G. R. (1980). Medial gemination in Rembarrnga: A spectrographic study. *Journal of Phonetics, 8*, 343–352.

Miller, R. A. (1967). *The Japanese language*. Chicago: University of Chicago Press.

Navarro Tomás, T. (1968). *Manuel de pronunciación Española* (14th ed.). Madrid: Consejo Superior de Investigaciones Cientificas.

Ohala, J. J. (1981). Speech timing as a tool in phonology. *Phonetica, 38*, 204–212.

Ohala, M. (1972). *Topics in Hindi–Urdu phonology*. Unpublished doctoral dissertation, University of California, Los Angeles.

Orešnik, J., & Pétursson, M. (1977). Quantity in modern Icelandic. *Arkiv för Nordisk Filologi, 92*, 155–171.

Pesetsky, D. (1979). Memomini quantity. *MIT Working Papers in Linguistics, 1*, 115–139.

Pike, K. L. (1943). *Phonetics*. Ann Arbor: University of Michigan Press.

Pinnow, H-J. (1959). *Versuch einer historischen Lautlehre der Kharia-Sprache*. Wiesbaden: Harrassowitz.

Pinnow, H-J. (1964). Bemerkungen zur phonetik und phonemik des Kurukh. *Indo-Iranian Journal, 8*, 32–55.

Port, R. F. (1981). Linguistic timing factors in combination. *Journal of the Acoustical Society of America, 69*, 262–274.

Schuh, R. G. (1978). Bade/Ngizim vowels and syllable structure. *Studies in African Linguistics, 9*, 247–283.

Selkirk, E. (1980). The role of prosodic categories in English word stress. *Linguistic Inquiry, 11*, 563–605.

Sohn, H-M., & Bender, B. W. (1973). *A Ulithian grammar* (Pacific Linguistics, Series C, 27). Canberra: Australian National University.

Song, S. S., & Perkell, J. S. (1983). A syllabic component of speech motor control? *Speech Communication Group Working Papers* (Research Laboratory of Electronics, MIT), *2*, 67–76.

Steriade, D. (1982). *Greek prosodies and the nature of syllabification*. Unpublished doctoral dissertation, MIT, Cambridge, MA.

Stetson, R. H. (1951). *Motor phonetics* (2nd ed.) Amsterdam: North Holland.

Straka, G. (1959). Durée et timbre vocalique. *Zeitschrift für Phonetik und Allgemeine Sprachwissenschaft, 12*, 276–300.

Strang, B. M. H. (1970). *A history of English*. London: Methuen.

Tyler, S. A. (1969). *Koya: An outline grammar*. Berkeley: University of California Press.

Velayudhan, S. (1971). *Vowel duration in Malayalam: An acoustic phonetic study*. Trivandrum: Dravidian Linguistic Association of India.

Walsh, T., & Parker, F. (1982). Consonant cluster abbreviation: An abstract analysis. *Journal of Phonetics, 10*, 423–438.

Wiik, K. (1965). *Finnish and English vowels*. Turku: University of Turku.

15

Around *Flat*

John J. Ohala

1. INTRODUCTION

In this chapter I first discuss some of the uses of the feature *flat* and then, using *flat* as an example, explore the role of phonological feature systems in general.

2. WHAT *FLAT* WAS AND IS

Although the term *flat* appears in phonetic descriptions as early as 1855 (Müller) as a characterization of nonfront vowels, it appears that Trubetzkoy (1939/1969:127ff.) was the first to employ the term *flat* to describe the auditory quality of retroflexes (and other sounds). Nevertheless, the concept itself can be found in impressionistic phonetic descriptions in many places and at many times in history, referred to by such colorful terms as "hollow," "dark," and "heavy." In its modern usage (in the Jakobsonian feature system), the feature *flat* is defined as sounds manifesting "a downward shift of a set of formants or even of all the formants in the spectrum (Jakobson, Fant, & Halle 1963:31) or, alternatively, as sounds "characterized by a downward shift or weakening of some of their upper frequency components" (Jakobson & Halle 1956: 31). In articulatory terms, the feature refers to sounds that are distinctively labialized, retroflexed, or pharyngealized (or, possibly, velarized or uvularized). In Jakobson's system all features are binary, and the opposite of *flat* is simply *plain* or *nonflat*. However, the exclusive binarity of features is imposed rather arbitrarily and artificially on this feature, and it is more realistic to view it as one end of a continuum: sounds having a downward shift of their higher resonances at one extreme and those having an upward shift, Jakobson's feature *sharp,* at the other. This continuum interacts with the features *grave–acute* (concentration of energy in low- versus high-frequency region) in interesting ways (detailed below),

PHONETIC LINGUISTICS

which suggests that in some cases it might be justified to regard all these features as being points on a single continuum.

3. SOME INTERESTING FEATURES OF THE FEATURE *FLAT*

Flat is interesting for a number of reasons. First, it is an example of a feature that started out as a completely impressionistic term, not even very rigorously defined, which has evolved to a point that plausible acoustic correlates can now be specified for it. Second, these acoustic correlates can to some extent be derived from, that is, shown to be natural consequences of, its articulatory correlates. Third, it demonstrates in an even more dramatic fashion than is possible with *grave,* another acoustically defined feature with discontinuous articulatory correlates (labial and velar but not the intervening apical and palatal places of articulation), how essential it is to keep not only the articulatory but also the acoustic correlates of speech sounds in mind when trying to figure out why speech sounds behave the way they do—a point insisted on by Ladefoged (1971a) but neglected by many other phonologists.

Fourth, there is an interesting sense in which *flat* is inherently non-orthogonal with respect to other features at the acoustic–auditory level. Assuming a feature system like the Jakobsonian one, *flat,* in general, does not need to be assigned to a segment until after values for *grave* and *diffuse* have been assigned. This, however, is not just an artifact of the Jakobsonian system; as Stevens (1980) has emphasized, there is a strong tendency for languages not to utilize distinctively labialized, ret-roflexed, or pharyngealized sounds until after they have gotten near-maximal use out of the features *grave* and *diffuse,* that is, the features that determine the primary places of articulation. One might at first think that this is a matter of definition: One cannot have distinctively labialized sounds unless there are nonlabialized ones to contrast with. But the tendency is phonetically true as well. In languages with small segmental inventories, the consonants present are not phonetically labialized or pharyngealized, and if a language has one apical stop, it is generally not retroflex. Stevens suggests that there is a relatively small number of ways in which speech sounds can differ from one another and that some of these ways are more robust than others; for example, the large abrupt amplitude modulations characterizing sounds labeled 'consonantal' are more salient than the rather slow and spread-out acoustic modulations typical of labialization, retroflexion, palatalization, pharyngealization, and voice quality. Languages, as it were, first utilize segments made from the robust set and only optionally use the less salient features. The same principles guide the construction of a snowman: fingers, bracelets, and earrings, are optional, but if one chooses to have them, one must have first chosen to make arms and ears. The implication of this is that speech sounds—some of them, at any rate—do not occupy a perceptual space with orthogonal dimensions.

3.1. *Flat* Permits Useful Phonological Generalizations

Since *flat* has a single acoustic–perceptual correlate but multiple articulatory correlates, Jakobson et al. (1963) were able to predict that no more than one of the articulatory phonetic manifestations of *flat* could be used distinctively in any given language. Although this prediction is apparently not absolutely true since there are languages (e.g., Abkhaz) that have contrasts between labialized and nonlabialized uvulars and pharyngeals (Catford 1977b; Colarusso 1974), it certainly is statistically true.

On the other hand, it would also be predicted that these secondary articulations made in quite distinct parts of the vocal tract would often be used together to enhance the "flatness" of some sounds vis-à-vis non*flat* sounds. In agreement with this, it has been noted that in some dialects of Arabic the pharyngealized or "emphatic" consonants are accompanied by lip rounding (Lehn 1963; however, see Ghazeli 1977:74ff.).

It may be for this reason or because of the inherent auditory similarity of all *flat* segments that Arabic pharyngealized sounds are often changed to labialized segments when Arabic words are borrowed by other languages (Jakobson 1962). Representative data (from Leslau 1957) showing borrowing into Argobba, a Semitic language of Ethiopia, are given in Table 15.1.

One of the most remarkable co-occurrences of labialization, retroflexion, and pharyngealization can be found in the American English vowel [ɚ] or in some versions of its associated glide [ɹ]. These segments are somewhat unusual in that their retroflex tongue configuration can apparently be

Table 15.1

ARABIC PHARYNGEALIZED SEGMENTS BORROWED AS LABIALIZED
SEGMENTS CONTRASTED WITH PLAIN SOUNDS BORROWED UNCHANGED[a]

	Standard Arabic	Argobba	Translation
Pharyngealized	*ṣabiǰǰ*	*sʷabiǰǰ*	'baby'
	ṣadaqa	*sʷadaqa*	'alms, charity; death commemoration'
Nonpharyngealized	*risala*	*risāla*	'letter'
	dʒism	*dʒism*	'body'

[a] Data from Leslau (1957).

substituted by an extreme bunching of the tongue near the palate in a region that is approximately halfway between the maximal constrictions of the vowels [i] and [u] (Uldall 1958; Delattre 1971). Not coincidentally, the most obvious acoustic correlate of [ɚ] or [ɹ] is an extremely low F_3 (Peterson & Barney 1952; Lehiste & Peterson 1961; Lehiste 1964).

Possible further evidence for the similar character of *flat* segments is that there is a certain amount of overlap in the effects they create on neighboring vowels. Labial or labialized consonants such as [w], often cause front vowels, especially [i], to become more or less backed, centralized, and/or rounded, for example, [i] → [y]; on the other hand, they have relatively little effect on back rounded vowels (Ohala 1979a, 1979b). Retroflex consonants can do the same: Kirton (1967) reports that retroflex consonants in Anyula shift /i/ to [e] but have no noticeable effect on /a/ or /u/. Hercus (1969) indicates that retroflex consonants in Wembawemba (and other languages of Victoria, Australia) shift /i/ and /e/ approximately to the vowels [y] and [ɜ], respectively, but cause only slight centralization to /u/. In Arabic, pharyngealization causes noticeable lowering of /i/ and backing of /a/ but has much less influence on /u/ (Ghazeli 1977; Card 1983).

The similar effect that *flat* segments have on vowels may be responsible in some way for the fact that in Ancient Chinese the retroflex initial consonants and labial final consonants both resulted in the merger of adjacent tense and lax vowels (Hashimoto 1973), although why labial initials and retroflex finals did not do the same is still to be explained.

The extreme effect that *flat* sounds have on segments like [i], that is, those with high F_2, is a reflection of the fact that *flat* segments are at the opposite end of the tonality scale from *acute* or *sharp* segments. Or, rather, to avoid circularity, this interaction is the motivation for opposing the phonological feature *flat* to these other features. This relation also gives rise to the prediction that the distinctiveness of *flat* would be most evident on or near *acute* segments. Accordingly, pharyngealization in Arabic seems to be distinctive primarily on apical consonants; claims that pharyngealized labials or postvelars exist in some dialects of Arabic are, at best, controversial (see arguments in Ghazeli 1977, chapter 7, against this latter view). For similar reasons, one would predict that if optimal segmental sequences should be made from sounds that are as different as possible from each other acoustically, then *flat* sounds should not be found adjacent to other sounds that have low tonality. Although this is not absolutely true, there is a strong tendency among languages in this direction. Thus, Kawasaki (1982) found that sequences of *labial* + [w] are often absent in languages that otherwise allow [w] as the second member of consonant clusters. English, for example, allows [w] after apicals and velars, for example, *dwarf, twin, swine, quality, Gwendolyn,* but not after labials (except in words that are obvious loans, e.g., *bwana)* (see also Ohala 1978; Ohala & Lorentz 1977).[1] High tonality segments can also induce *flatness* (phonetically, at least) in contrasting segments. In Russian (and other Slavic languages), as is well known, there are extensive contrasts of *sharp* versus non*sharp* segments. Phonetically, the non*sharp* segments are often velarized, that is, phonetically, if not phonologically, *flat* (Fant 1960). (The reverse can also happen: Nonpharyngealized consonants in Arabic have been shown to have a somewhat fronted tongue configuration, Ghazeli 1977:75–76.) High tonality segments also reveal their opposition to *flat* segments by inhibiting their assimilatory effects. In Arabic, the palatal or *acute* segments like /i/ and /j/ block the assimilation of pharyngealization (Ghazeli 1977; Card 1983). In the development from Proto-Dravidian to (modern) Koḍagu, the front unrounded vowels /i/ and /e/ underwent a backward shift due to the influence of following retroflexes or labials but not if the palatal consonant /c/ preceded (Emeneau 1970).

   In the preceding cases, the underlying unity of the diverse articulatory manifestations of *flat* segments are revealed first by the fact that they are all uniformly opposed to high tonality segments (those characterized as *sharp* or *acute)* and second by the observation that they often act in concert with or alternate with each other. These are, on the face of it, rather remarkable generalizations and should stimulate as much curiosity about their causes as would a generalization that high airflow segments such as voiceless fricatives, or affricates, or aspirated stops produce phonological effects similar to nasal consonants (which happens to be the case; see Ohala 1980, 1983b; Ohala & Amador 1981). How does the use of the feature *flat* and its defined physical correlates help to satisfy that curiosity? Before attempting to answer that question, let us take several paces back and examine in a more general way the explanatory task of phonology.

4. THE TASK OF PHONOLOGY

   The discipline of phonology seeks to understand the behavior of speech sounds. The behavior of interest includes variation in pronunciation due to speaking style, phonetic context, sound change (and the results of sound change: regional and social dialectal variation, morphologically conditioned variation, the patterns of selection of sounds in segment inventories, etc.), the order of acquisition and patterns of mistakes in first and second language acquisition, and so on. As Hermann Paul (1880) pointed out, given the comlex nature of language, we must look in three domains for answers to our questions: the physical, psychological, and social. In each of these domains we identify entities or features of these domains that help us to explain the behavior of interest.[2] These features are the substantive primitives of the theoretical system or explanatory model—henceforth, simply "theory"—that we construct. For example, in the physical domain, oral-cavity volume and the compliance of the vocal tract walls are good candidates for such substantive primitives. From these (and further theoretical machinery) one can explain to a satisfying extent why the back-articulated stops, for example, [G, g], are the voiced stops most often missing even in languages that possess their voiceless cognates (Ohala & Riordan 1979; Ohala 1983a). Substantive primitives by themselves, however, accomplish nothing. Alone, they are like the ingredients of a cake, flour, sugar, eggs, and so on, which, even if lined up side-by-side on the kitchen counter, will never assemble themselves into a cake. One also needs an indication of how these things are to be mixed together. These are the formal primitives. In chess, they are the rules of the game; in economics, the laws of how prices are a function of supply and demand; in physics, the equations or nomograms that show how one variable can be predicted from others. Thus the familiar equation $p_2 = p_1 (v_2/v_1)$, a version of Boyle-Mariotte's Law, shows how, if one takes starting pressure and starting and ending volume as primitives, one can predict the resulting pressure of a gas in an enclosure. This equation is also part of the theory the phonologist needs to predict some of the aerodynamic conditions that affect voicing, frication, and derivative phenomena such as voice onset time and fundamendal frequency (F_0) microstructure, which phenomena play an important role in precip- itating certain sound changes (Hombert, Ohala, & Ewan 1979; Ohala 1983a). Ultimately, all and every detail of the physical world that we find to be essential to an understanding of the behavior of speech sounds will have to be incorporated in the theory we construct. Naturally this will include neuromotor details, details on the structure and workings of the articulators, how the articulations get transformed into sound, how the sound is processed in the auditory system, and so on. Although it is necessary to limit the primitives in such a system to the absolute minimum, it does not seem to be a realistic expectation that the substantive primitives, that is, features, needed to explain the workings of speech can be limited to a mere 12 or 25 or even 50. Attempts to impose too small a limit on features could retard phonology in the same way Western chemistry was hampered by the premature theory that the primitive ingredients of all matter were earth, air, fire, and water.

The notion of primitive needs further qualification, however. In a complete, strictly logical system, for example Euclid's geometry, there is only one level of primitives, and all theorems or predictions are derived directly or indirectly from it. One might imagine, then, that in phonology we could simply set up primitives at one level, say the level at which the physical properties of the speech mechanism were represented, and then all the rest of speech behavior, including aerodynamic and acoustic, could be derived from that. In such a system, tissue compliance might not be a primitive but rather something derived by reference to more basic physical properties of the tissues. In principle one could do things this way, but it is not really a very practical thing to try. First of all, our knowledge of how speech sounds are produced is now and always will be incomplete. So if we had to put off making predictions of how sounds will behave due to the characteristics of the auditory system until we had worked out all relevant details back to the level of the physical properties of tissues, we might never venture any explanations at all. Second, even though we know how to explain the resonances of the vocal tract by reference to more basic physical principles, it is hardly practical to have to cite them, when all that is to be explained is why listeners tend to confuse [k^w] and [p]—namely, because their acoustic patterns are similar. In this case it is sufficient to prove the point to refer to nomograms (e.g., those in Fant 1960) or acoustic data derived from spectrograms. The level at which primitives are stated is therefore a matter of choice. In this we do not differ from other disciplines: Molecular biologists seldom refer to the principles of atomic physics in their work.

Aside from coming up with theories in the first place, one of the principal activities of scientists is the evaluation of theories. Some forms of evaluation can be done by examining the linguistic and logical structure of the theories; others require comparison of the predictions made by theories with observations of the behavior of the object the theory purports to represent. In the former category there is the requirement that a theory do what it was constructed to do: make familiar what was mysterious. This seems such an obvious requirement, but it is so difficult to achieve that scientists in all fields have shown great ingenuity in masking their failure to satisfy it. They may do this by positing as a primitive or input to their theory a disguised form of the behavior or output they are supposed to account for. Positing a "vital principle" to account for differences between living and nonliving things or attributing the mutual attraction of physical bodies to gravity are examples of this. Theories also have to be self-consistent and nonredundant. This latter requirement— violations of which are said to be subject to correction by Occam's Razor—means that not only must primitives not duplicate each other but they must also be independent or orthogonal of each other, that is, the value or presence of one must not depend on any other primitive. It would violate orthogonality to state that susceptibility to heart disease is a function of salt intake and incidence of high blood pressure, since the latter is dependent, in part, on the former. (Of course, if salt consumption contributed to heart disease independently of its effects on blood pressure, then it, too, could be used as a primitive.)

The ultimate and often the most difficult form of evaluation of a theory requires comparing its predictions with what happens in nature, that is, to evaluate a theory by experiment. As Popper (1959) has convincingly argued, experimental tests do not reveal whether a theory is true but only that competing theories do less well at predicting what one observes. Thus the history of science is replete with examples of theories once thought to be true but which eventually had to be revised or replaced entirely by newer, more "fit," theories.

5. FEATURE SYSTEMS AS THE MODE FOR EXPLANATION

How do the traditional feature systems offered as the formal mechanism for representing and explaining aspects of speech-sound behavior stand up under these forms of evaluation? An assessment of this sort is attempted here, although, given the limitation of space, it is rather cursory. Nevertheless, except where noted, the criticisms made apply equally to all the better-known features systems and to the less well known ones, too (Brücke 1863; Bell 1867; Techmer 1880; Jespersen 1889; Pike 1943; Jakobson et al. 1963; Ladefoged 1971b, 1980; Chomsky & Halle 1968).

A feature system consists of the substantive primitives, the features, and the definitions of the features. In all the cases I know of, the definitions are given in physical terms, either articulatory (including aerodynamic) or acoustic–auditory. The definitions for *flat*, cited above, are typical. Inherent contradictions in the definitions of features can occur but are not a major problem.[3] Lack of orthogonality, however, is a serious problem for all, as has been recognized previously. Because the Jakobsonian and the Chomsky and Halle system use two binary features for vowel height, it turns out, for example, to use the former system, a value of '+' for [diffuse] dictates a '−' value for [compact] and vice versa. Ladefoged's multivalued feature system avoids this awkwardness and as a result is capable of giving a more insightful representation to vowel-shift rules (Ladefoged 1970). Lack of independence is also seen when a feature like [strident] is irrelevant for nasals and vowels. Any system that uses a feature of [voice] in addition to manner of articulation features such as [sonorant] or [continuant] violates orthogonality since, as is well known, the value for voicing depends to some extent on whether there is a complete blocking of the airflow. If manner of articulation features are specified (they need not be; the primitives could have been chosen at a higher level), then voicing should be derived. In Ladefoged's (1980) system, the features [grave] and [sibilance] are dependent on the features for place of articulation. Such lack of orthogonality can be corrected by adopting primitives at a more basic level; on the other hand, the lack of orthogonality between *flat* and the features *grave* and *diffuse* (mentioned above) is apparently inherent in the makeup of speech and does not count as a defect of the system.

Inconsistency and redundancy are rather trivial imperfections, however. At most, they make the theories inelegant. A more important requirement is that these theories achieve their primary purpose of explaining speech-sound behavior. Most of the feature systems were designed to account for only a limited range of speech-sound behavior: the fact that speech sounds are different from each other and so can create semantically distinct utterances, and to give a common name to speech sounds that behave similarly. Although most feature systems need patching up as they are applied to a greater variety of languages, there does not seem to be any inherent flaw in them that would prevent them from achieving the first goal. The second goal, perhaps first articulated by Jespersen (1889:80–81), offers problems to virtually every feature system. By defining features in acoustic–auditory terms, the Jakobsonian system corrected an obvious deficiency of previous systems that were unable to deal with sounds that behaved similarly due to their shared acoustic–auditory properties. The feature *flat* that, as illustrated above, shows the similar phonological properties of labialization, retroflexion, and pharyngealization, is a prime example of this. But problems still remain. Some of these problems arise from failure to choose features at a sufficiently primitive level. For example, the glottal consonants [h ʔ] pattern like nonobstruents [j w l] in not blocking spreading nasalization (Schourup 1973), but they pattern like obstruents in creating F_0 perturbations (Hombert *et al.* 1979). Labial–velars such as [w k͡p g͡b] have a greater affinity to labials when they become or interact with fricatives or when they perturb the quality of adjacent vowels; however, they have greater affinity to velars when they become or interact with nasals (Ohala & Lorentz 1977; Ohala 1979a, b). Such problems will not be solved without an almost complete overhaul of most feature systems.

Feature systems used in generative phonology have adopted goals that go beyond the two just discussed; they are expected to reveal the naturalness of phonetically natural or expected sound patterns (Halle 1962;

Chomsky & Halle 1968:306–308, 400ff.). It is recognized that the feature systems in use fail to do this, that, as Chomsky and Halle note, their system fails to reflect the "intrinsic content" of the features. For example, there is nothing in the representations below to show that (1a) is more expected than (1b). Their proposed solution is a metarule, a marking convention (1c), which is used to interpret and evaluate the differences in naturalness of (1a) and (1b) (*u* is to be read as "the unmarked or expected value of").

(1)   a. [−sonorant] → [−voice]
       b. [−sonorant] → [+voice]
       c. [*u* voice]   → [−voice] / [_____]
                                     [−sonorant]

Unfortunately, the deficiency recognized is no more solved by the marking conventions (Chomsky & Halle 1968:chap. 9) than the introduction of further epicycles corrected the fundamental defect of the Ptolemaic model of the cosmos. The phonetic naturalness of sound patterns should be a product of the theory, that is, be derived from it; the marking conventions, on the contrary, decree it. This is an example of the fallacy whereby a restatement of a problem in a disguised way may be offered as a solution to the problem (Ohala 1971, 1972). None of the other feature systems would fare any better if adopted for the same task.

The problem is that there is more to creating a workable explanatory phonological theory than simply putting square brackets around adjectives. Stripped of the square brackets, arrows, and other typographical shorthand for ordinary verbal expressions such as "becomes," "in the environment of," these formal representations of phonological processes are virtually identical to the kinds of expressions used by Panini for the sandhi rules in Sanskrit, exemplified in (2).

(2)   "The letters [s] and dentals in contact with [ṣ] and retroflexes are changed to [ṣ] and retroflexes [with the same manner of articulation], respectively" (Vasu 1891/1962:1671; "cerebrals" in original changed to "retroflexes").

There have been some advances made since Panini's time—one would hope so after 2300 years!—in the selection and definition of features, especially in picking ones that adequately reflect the natural classes of speech sounds and in defining features that are based on acoustic–auditory factors, but the theoretical matrix these terms are inserted into has not evolved accordingly.

It is the failure to develop an appropriate set of formal primitives for these feature systems, that is, relations that show how the features interact to produce observed sound patterns, that hinders progress. This is not because we are ignorant of the factors responsible. True, there are many important gaps in our knowledge about the workings of speech, for example, why assimilation occurs, but the more crucial hindrance is that the feature systems used are incapable of representing what we do know. The basic factors that affect the voicing of obstruents, for example, have been common knowledge for a long time (Passy 1890:161; Chao 1936; Chomsky & Halle 1968:325ff.) but the feature systems used simply are not adapted to incorporate this knowledge.

There are, however, several very promising formal theories of the speech process or parts of it that meet all the criteria discussed so far, including orthogonality of features (or what is equivalent, a strict differentiation of things that are primitive from those that are derived), full attention to substantive and formal primitives, and the ability (demonstrated in some cases, potential in others) to explain facts of speech of interest to phonologists; see, for example, Fant (1960); Liljencrants and Lindblom (1972); Stevens (1971, 1972); Mermelstein (1973); Flanagan, Ishizaka, and Shipley (1975); Catford (1977a); Ladefoged, Harshman, Goldstein, and Rice (1978); Wright (1980); Muller and Brown (1980); Kawasaki (1982); Ohala (1983); Keating (1984); Lindblom (1984). If we take seriously the goal adopted by generative phonologists of creating a formal system that will reflect the naturalness of sound patterns, then I suggest that we invest our time and energies in creating systems such as these that can help us to achieve that goal. The effort spent in creating and refining feature systems will never give us the same return.

6. WHAT ARE FEATURE SYSTEMS GOOD FOR?

At this point one might draw the conclusion that feature systems play no useful role at all in the task of phonology. This conclusion may be countered in the following ways.

First, it might be claimed that the task of representing sound patterns in a way that reveals their naturalness is not something that should be attempted using features grounded in phonetic substance. Such, at least, seems to be Ladefoged's view (Ladefoged 1980; Ladefoged & Traill 1980). He would limit the task of the phonetic features to their traditional task of accounting for the differences in sounds used to convey differences of meaning. A loose mapping would relate phonetic features to a separate set of phonological features, the task of the latter being to reveal naturalness of sound patterns. As should be clear from the preceding discussion, I agree with him that a simple list of phonetic features by themselves has very little explanatory value. However, I believe that a phonetically grounded theory should offer explanations for natural sound patterns. My solution to the dilemma is not to abandon the work but to use the right tools, to augment our list of features (substantive primitives) with a full range of formal primitives that show how the primitive elements interact. There is no need to develop logical arguments that this is the way to proceed; there are numerous existence proofs, those cited earlier, that demonstrate this. Ladefoged seems rather to emphasize nonexistence proofs for his position, that is, phonological data that cannot (yet) be explained by any known phonetic principles. Of course he is right. There will always be things in phonology that cannot be explained by reference to known phonetic principles—either because we have not discovered these phonetic principles yet or because they do not have a phonetic causation. As Paul (1880) indicated, some aspects of language are due to psychological and social factors. But Ladefoged has not identified (as Gödel and Heisenberg have in their disciplines) a logically or empirically necessary constraint on our phonological understanding. So, let us continue to try as best we can to explain phonological data in terms of phonetics. We will never know the limits of our understanding until we press those limits.

Second, it might be claimed that the set of features that reflects the naturalness of sound patterns has primarily (or even exclusively) a psychological reality. Thus, marking conventions may very well be represented in speakers' brains in a way not unlike a list so that metarules of the sort in (1c) are the appropriate way to indicate phonological naturalness. There is little evidence that native speakers are aware of all the sound patterns that linguists are able to discover and even less evidence that the native speakers have a special skill in differentiating natural and unnatural patterns. Until further evidence is produced, there is no reason to give serious attention to this position. I do agree, though, that it is important to investigate the psychological aspect of speech to discover the mental factors that help us to explain the behavior of speech sounds, but this is not to be done by the kind of facile psychologizing that has characterized the field of phonology for the last 30 years or so. Several techniques for exploring what native speakers know about the sound patterns in their language have been developed, and they give results of far more validity than those developed in the armchair (Ohala 1974, 1984; Ohala & Ohala 1978; Jaeger 1980).

Third, and this is my own position, it can be claimed that the features that have been offered over the past two millennia play a very useful role in phonology in that they are the terms we use in an informal, quite ad hoc, way to talk about speech sounds and classes of sounds. Every scientific discipline makes use of such an informal, or less than rigorously defined, vocabulary. The terms "noble gas," "metal," and "semiconductor" have (or used to have) this status within chemistry. Terms such as "predator" and "altruism" serve a similar informal function in ethology. There is no need to think that every term finding its way into scientific descriptions has to be a primitive in a theoretical system or strictly orthogonal to every other term. An ad hoc label can even be applied to a class (defined by enumeration) whose underlying common composition has not yet been discovered. In this case it acts as a kind of flag alerting us to the need for further investigation; the label is not "carved in stone" and may be revised or dropped entirely as more information becomes available.[4] Needless to say, terms of this sort that can be casually invented should not be included in formal explanations unless they have been made to pass the kinds of tests discussed above. Feature systems, as they have traditionally been constructed and used, have this very useful but very limited function; the mistake made since the rise of generative phonology is to saddle them with a task that they are inherently incapable of accomplishing.

7. *FLAT* IS NOT AN ELEMENT IN A FORMAL SYSTEM

The feature *flat*, for example, is still primarily an informal term. It is defined by enumerating the class of segments that are included under it. Although some of the acoustic correlates of this class of sounds can be derived from the articulatory specification of members of the set, that is, labialization, retroflexion, and pharyngealization, not all of them can, and, more to the point, the common auditory effect of these sounds cannot yet be accounted for.

7.1. Where *Flat* Comes From

An appreciation of how vocal tract configurations give rise to some of the acoustic characteristics of *flat*, especially as this involves a lowering of F_3, may be obtained from the following oversimplified account (adapted from Chiba & Kajiyama 1958:149ff.; Fant 1960:86–87; Lieberman 1977).

Figure 15.1 shows, on the left, the standing wave patterns[5] of the volume–velocity waveforms of the lowest three resonances, R_1, R_2, and R_3, of a uniform tube closed at one end and open at the other. This is an analogue of the vocal tract, with the closed end representing the glottal region and the open end, the lips. The location of the minima and maxima in the waveform are marked by the letters "N" and "A,"

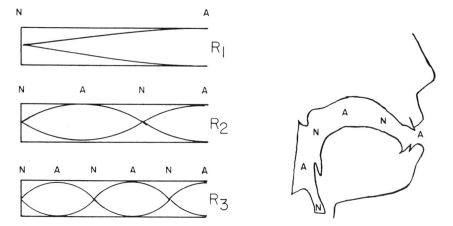

Figure 15.1   Left: schematic representation of the volume–velocity standing wave patterns of the lowest three resonant frequencies of a uniform tube closed at one end and open at the other. Right: the position of the nodes and antinodes of the standing wave pattern in the vocal tract of the third resonant frequency.

respectively (for "node" and "antinode"). The resonant frequencies of a vibrating body (in this case the air confined inside the tube) are those frequencies whose standing wave patterns optimally conform to the boundary conditions of the body. In this case the boundary conditions demand a velocity minimum at the closed end—where the movement of the air is most constrained—and a velocity maximum at the open end—where the movement of the air is least constrained. The standing waves shown are the lowest three that meet these conditions. The lowest resonant frequency has a wavelength equal to 4 times l (l = the length of the tube), the second to $\frac{4}{3}$ times l and the third to $\frac{4}{5}$ times l. Given that frequency = speed of sound/wavelength, it follows that for a 17.5 cm long tube (a typical value for an adult male speaker), and given the speed of sound as 35,000 cm/sec, the lowest three resonances will be 500, 1500, and 2500 Hz, which are roughly those of [ɜ], the vowel most closely approximating a uniform tube. Resonant frequencies higher or lower than these are obtained by introducing one or more constrictions. A constriction at a velocity maximum for a given resonant frequency's standing wave will lower the frequency, and a constriction at a velocity minimum will raise it. Conversely, a larger-than-normal dilation of the vocal tract at a velocity maximum will help to raise the frequency and at velocity minimum to lower it. In the right of Figure 15.1 is rough indication of where the velocity maxima and minima for the third resonance's standing wave are located in the vocal tract. Thus, a constriction at the antinodes, that is, at the lips, in the midpalatal region, and/or in the pharyngeal region, will help to lower the third resonance. It should be emphasized that this is a considerably oversimplified account of the conversion from articulation to sound, but it does serve to indicate very roughly how the acoustic characteristics of *flat* might ultimately be related in a systematic way to its articulatory correlates.

This helps to make less mysterious the fact that articulations as distant as those at the lips and in the pharynx have similar effects. It also suggests why one variant of American English [ɚ], the vowel with the maximally low F_3, has three constrictions, one at the lips, one in the pharynx, and one in the midpalatal region. This still leaves unexplained, however, how the midpalatal constriction for this vowel can be substituted by a retroflex tongue shape, what is usually thought of as the canonical configuration for [ɚ]. Also unexplained is why a lowering or a weakening of the higher formants gives rise to the same auditory effect and why a lowering and/or weakening of either F_3 and/or F_2 or (in the case of labialization) all three of the lowest formants have the same auditory effect. Until we have answers to all these questions through a formal theory of the speech apparatus, the use of the feature *flat* is the only way—an informal way—we have to call attention to the natural class constituted by the segment types to which we attach that label. Nevertheless, it should not be assumed that the informal terminological system that includes *flat* is any substitute for the eventual explanatory formal theory of the speech process that is the ultimate goal of phonology.

NOTES

1. It might seem, at first glance, that the many instances of co-occurrence of labialization with velars or of sequences of velars plus [w], for example, [kʷ] or [kw], are obvious counterexamples to the above prediction, since velars as well as labials are [+grave]. Velars, however, can be front or back; only back velars properly should be considered [+grave], that is, near the low end of the tonality scale. Front velars, that is, those at the beginning of English, *key, cape,* and *cash,* actually have quite high center frequencies in their noise burst and high F_2 (Lehiste & Peterson 1961; Liberman, Delattre, Cooper, & Gerstman 1954). In accord with the prediction given, back velars do not often exhibit a labialized–nonlabialized contrast. In fact, labialization is frequently found to accompany back velars, conceivably to enhance a contrast between them and front velars.

2. It should not be supposed—but unfortunately it often is—that these explanations can be completely lawlike, that is, nomological. They will instead be partial, probabilistic, explanations. So, in fact, are all explanations in every scientific discipline with the exception of mathematics, which has the advantage of dealing with manmade structures rather than the real world (Ohala forthcoming).

3. An inherent contradiction appeared, for example, in Halle's (1964) definitions of the Jakobson, Fant, and Halle featural characterizations of the major class segments (pointed out by Peter Ladefoged, personal communication). Halle recognized four degrees of narrowing in the vocal tract, from greater to lesser: contact, occlusion, obstruction, and constriction. Segments that are [+consonantal] have occlusion or contact; [+vocalic] segments have no narrowing closer than constriction. Given this, the characterization of liquids as [+consonantal] and [+vocalic] was inherently contradictory.

4. A good example of this is the replacement in many cases of the poorly defined terms "tense" versus "lax," "fortis" versus "lenis," and so on, by terms describing voice onset time (Lisker & Abramson 1964).

5. A standing wave is created when two waves having the same frequency and amplitude pass through each other going in opposite directions, as happens when a wave reflects off some acoustic interface, for example, the glottis end of the vocal tract. The summation of the two waves forms a wave that seems to oscillate in one spot in such a way that in certain regions (nodes) there is no net movement (these are found at intervals one-half wavelength apart) and at one-fourth wavelength away from the nodes there are areas where there is maximum movement of the wave (antinodes).

REFERENCES

Bell, A. M. (1867). *Visible speech: The science of universal alphabetics*. London: Simpkin, Marshall.

Brücke, E. W. von. (1863). Über eine neue Methode der phonetischen Transcription. *Sitzungsberichte der Philosophische-Historischen Classe der Kaiserlichen Akademie der Wissenschaften Wien, 41*, 223–285.

Card, E. A. (1983). *A phonetic and phonological study of Arabic emphasis*. Unpublished doctoral dissertation, Cornell University.

Catford, J. (1977a). *Fundamental problems in phonetics*. Bloomington: Indiana University Press.

Catford, J. (1977b). Mountain of tongues: The languages of the Caucasus. *Annual Review of Anthropology, 6*, 283–314.

Chao, Y. R. (1936). Types of plosives in Chinese. In D. Jones & D. B. Fry (Eds.), *Proceedings of the 2nd International Congress of Phonetic Sciences* (pp. 106–110). Cambridge: Cambridge University Press.

Chiba, T., & Kajiyama, M. (1958). *The vowel, its nature and structure*. Tokyo: The Phonetic Society of Japan.

Chomsky, N., & Halle, M. (1968). *The sound pattern of English*. New York: Harper & Row.

Colarusso, J. (1974). Consonants with advanced tongue root in the Northwest Caucasian languages. *Papers from the Annual Meeting of the North Eastern Linguistic Society, 5*, 153–161.

Delattre, P. (1971). Pharyngeal features in the consonants of Arabic, German, Spanish, French, and American English. *Phonetica, 23*, 129–155.

Emeneau, M. B. (1970). Koḍagu vowels. *Journal of the American Oriental Society, 90*, 145–158.

Fant, G. (1960). *Acoustic theory of speech production*. 's-Gravenhage: Mouton.

Flanagan, J. L., Ishizaka, K., & Shipley, K. L. (1975). Synthesis of speech from a dynamic model of the vocal cords and vocal tract. *Bell System Technical Journal, 54*, 485–506.

Ghazeli, S. (1977). *Back consonants and backing coarticulation in Arabic*. Unpublished doctoral dissertation, University of Texas at Austin.

Halle, M. (1962). Phonology in generative grammar. *Word, 18*, 54–72.

Halle, M. (1964). On the bases of phonology. In J. Fodor & J. Katz (Eds.), *The structure of language* (pp. 324–333). Englewood Cliffs, NJ: Prentice-Hall.

Hashimoto, M. J. (1973). Retroflex endings in Ancient Chinese. *Journal of Chinese Linguistics, 1,* 183–207.

Hercus, L. A. (1969). *The languages of Victoria: A late survey* (Australian Aboriginal Studies No. 17; Linguistic Series No. 6). Canberra: Australian Institute of Aboriginal Studies.

Hombert, J.-M., Ohala, J. J., & Ewan, W. G. (1979). Phonetic explanations for the development of tones. *Language, 55,* 37–58.

Jaeger, J. J. (1980). Testing the psychological reality of phonemes. *Language & Speech, 23,* 233–253.

Jakobson, R. (1962). Mufaxxama, the 'emphatic' phonemes in Arabic. In *R. Jakobson, Selected Writings, Vol. 1: Phonological studies* (pp. 510–522). 's-Gravenhage: Mouton.

Jakobson, R., Fant, C. G. M., & Halle, M. (1963). *Preliminaries to speech analysis* (sixth ed.). Cambridge: MIT Press.

Jakobson, R., & Halle, M. (1956). *Fundamentals of language.* 's-Gravenhage: Mouton.

Jespersen, O. (1889). *Articulation of speech sounds, represented by means of analphabetic symbols.* Marburg in Hesse: N. G. Elwert.

Kawasaki, H. (1982). An acoustical basis for universal constraints on sound sequences. Unpublished doctoral dissertation, University of California, Berkeley.

Keating, P. (1984). Aerodynamic modeling at UCLA. *UCLA Working Papers in Phonetics, 59,* 18–28.

Kirton, J. F. (1967). Anyula phonology. *Pacific Linguistics, Series A, 10,* 15–28.

Ladefoged, P. (1970). An alternative set of vowel shift rules. *UCLA Working Papers in Phonetics, 17,* 25–28.

Ladefoged, P. (1971a). The limits of phonology. In L. L. Hammerich, R. Jakobson, & E. Zwirner (Eds.), *Form and substance. Phonetic and linguistic papers presented to Eli Fischer-Jørgensen* (pp. 47–56). Copenhagen: Akademisk Forlag.

Ladefoged, P. (1971b). *Preliminaries to linguistic phonetics.* Chicago: University of Chicago Press.

Ladefoged, P. (1980). What are linguistic sounds made of? *Language, 55,* 485–502.

Ladefoged, P., Harshman, R., Goldstein, L., & Rice, L. (1978). Generating vocal tract shapes from formant frequencies. *Journal of the Acoustical Society of America, 64,* 1027–1035.

Ladefoged, P., & Traill, T. (1980). The phonetic inadequacy of phonological specifications of clicks. *UCLA Working Papers in Phonetics, 49,* 1–27.

Lehiste, I. (1964). Acoustical characteristics of selected English consonants. *International Journal of American Linguistics,* Publication 34.

Lehiste, I., & Peterson, G. E. (1961). Transitions, glides, and diphthongs. *Journal of the Acoustical Society of America, 33,* 268–277.

Lehn, W. (1963). *Emphasis in Cairo Arabic. Language, 39,* 29–39.

Leslau, W. (1957). The phonetic treatment of the Arabic loanwords in Ethiopic. *Word, 13,* 100–123.

Liberman, A. M., Delattre, P. C., Cooper, F. S., & Gerstman, L. J. (1954). The role of consonant–vowel transitions in the perception of stop and nasal consonants. *Psychological Monographs, 68,* no. 8 (whole no. 379), pp. 1–13.

Lieberman, P. (1977). Speech physiology and acoustic phonetics: An introduction. New York: Macmillan.

Liljencrants, J., & Lindblom, B. (1972). Numerical simulation of vowel quality systems: The role of perceptual contrast. *Language, 48,* 839–862.

Lindblom, B. (1984). Can the models of evolutionary biology be applied to phonetic problems? In M. P. R. v. d. Broecke & A. Cohen (Eds.), *Proceedings, 10th International Congress of Phonetic Sciences* (pp. 67–81). Dordrecht: Foris.

Lisker, L., & Abramson, A. S. (1964). A cross-language study of voicing in initial stops: Acoustical measurements. *Word, 20*, 384–422.

Mermelstein, P. (1973). Articulatory model for the study of speech production. *Journal of the Acoustical Society of America, 53*, 1070–1082.

Muller, E. M., & Brown, W. S., Jr. (1980). Variations in the supraglottal air pressure waveform and their articulatory interpretation. In N. J. Lass (Ed.), *Speech and language: Advances in basic research and practice* (Vol. 4) (pp. 317–389). New York: Academic Press.

Müller, M. (1855). *The languages of the seat of war in the East* (2nd ed.). London: Williams & Norgate.

Ohala, J. J. (1971). The role of physiological and acoustic models in explaining the direction of sound change. In *Project on Linguistic Analysis Reports* (No. 15, pp. 25–40). Berkeley: University of California.

Ohala, J. J. (1972). Physical models in phonology. In A. Rigault & R. Charbonneau (Eds.), *Proceedings, 7th International Congress of Phonetic Sciences, Montreal, 1971* (pp. 1166–1171). The Hague: Mouton.

Ohala, J. J. (1974). Experimental historical linguistics. In J. M. Anderson & C. Jones (Eds.), *Historical linguistics II: Theory and description in phonology* (pp. 353–389). Amsterdam: North Holland.

Ohala, J. J. (1978). Southern Bantu vs. the world: The case of palatalization of labials. *Proceedings, Annual Meeting of the Berkeley Linguistics Society, 4*, 370–386.

Ohala, J. J. (1979a). The contribution of acoustic phonetics to phonology. In B. Lindblom & S. Ohman (Eds.), *Frontiers of speech communication research* (pp. 355–363). London: Academic Press.

Ohala, J. J. (1979b). Universals of labial velars and de Saussure's chess analogy. *Proceedings of the Ninth International Congress of Phonetic Sciences* (Vol. 2) (pp. 41–47). Copenhagen: Institute of Phonetics.

Ohala, J. J. (1980). The application of phonological universals in speech pathology. In N. Lass (Ed.), *Speech and language: Advances in basic research and practice* (Vol. 3) (pp. 75–97). New York: Academic Press.

Ohala, J. J. (1983a). The origin of sound patterns in vocal tract constraints. In P. F. MacNeilage (Ed.), *The production of speech* (pp. 189–216). New York: Springer Verlag.

Ohala, J. J. (1983b). The phonological end justifies any means. *Proceedings of the XIIIth International Congress of Linguists, Tokyo* (pp. 232–243). Tokyo: ICL Editorial Committee.

Ohala, J. J. (1984). *Consumer's guide to evidence in phonology.* Berkeley (Cognitive Science Report No. 17). Berkeley, University of California. Forthcoming in R. Rhodes (Ed.), *Evidence in phonology.* Ann Arbor: Karoma Press.

Ohala, J. J. (Forthcoming). Explanation, evidence, and experiment in phonology. *Proceedings, Fifth International Phonology Meeting, Eisenstadt.*

Ohala, J. J., & Amador, M. (1981). Spontaneous nasalization. *Journal of the Acoustical Society of America, 69*, 954–955.

Ohala, J. J., & Lorentz, J. (1977). The story of [w]: An exercise in the phonetic explanation for sound patterns. *Proceedings, Annual Meeting of the Berkeley Linguistics Society, 3*, 577–599.

Ohala, J. J., & Ohala, M. (1978). Experimental methods in phonology. *Acta Linguistica Hafniensia, 16*, 229–230.

Ohala, J. J., & Riordan, C. J. (1979). Passive vocal tract enlargement during voiced stops.

In J. J. Wolf & D. H. Klatt (Eds.), *Speech communication papers* (pp. 89–92). New York: Acoustical Society of America.

Paul, H. (1880). *Prinzipien der Sprachgeschichte*. Halle: Max Niemeyer.

Passy, P. (1890). *Étude sur les changements phonétiques*. Paris: Librairie Firmin-Didot.

Peterson, G. E., & Barney, H. L. (1952). Control methods used in a study of the vowels. *Journal of the Acoustical Society of America, 24*, 175–184.

Pike, K. L. (1943). *Phonetics*. Ann Arbor: University of Michigan Press.

Popper, K. R. (1959). *The logic of scientific discovery*. London: Hutchinson.

Schourup, L. C. (1973). A cross-language study of vowel nasalization. *Working Papers in Linguistics* [Ohio State University], *15*, 190–221.

Stevens, K. N. (1971). Airflow and turbulence noise for fricative and stop consonants: Static considerations. *Journal of the Acoustical Society of America, 50*, 1180–1192.

Stevens, K. N. (1972). The quantal nature of speech: Evidence from articulatory-acoustic data. In E. E. David & P. B. Denes (Eds.), *Human communication: A unified view* (pp. 51–66). New York: McGraw Hill.

Stevens, K. N. (1980). Discussion during symposium on phonetic universals in phonological systems and their explanation. *Proceedings, 9th International Congress of Phonetic Sciences* (Vol. 3) (pp. 185–186). Copenhagen: Institute of Phonetics.

Techmer, F. H. H. (1880). *Phonetik; zur vergleichenden Physiologie der Stimme und Sprache*. Leipzig.

Trubetzkoy, N. S. (1969). *Principles of phonology* (C. A. M. Baltaxe, Trans.). Berkeley: University of California Press. (Original work published 1939.)

Uldall, E. T. (1958). American 'molar' *r* and 'flapped' *r*. *Revista do Laboratorio de Fonetica Experimental* (Coimbra), *4*, 103–106.

Vasu, S. C. (1962). *The Ashṭādhyāyī of Pāṇini* (Vol. 2). Delhi: Motilal Banarsidass. (Original work published in 1891.)

Wright, J. T. (1980). The behavior of nasalized vowels in the perceptual vowel space. *Report of the Phonology Laboratory* (Berkeley), *5*, 127–163.

16

Evidence for the Role of Acoustic Boundaries in the Perception of Speech Sounds*

Kenneth N. Stevens

1. INTRODUCTION

During the production of an utterance, there are frequently times when abrupt changes occur in the amplitude or spectrum of the sound. These events are often regarded as boundaries between speech sounds, and the identification and marking of these points in time is sometimes viewed as a process of segmenting the sound stream into units. The properties of the sound between these events are considered to provide the requisite information for identification of the phonetic segments.

There is a growing body of data to indicate that a great deal of information concerning the phonetic features of segments is carried by various properties of the sound in the time interval that lies within 10 to 30 msec of these so-called boundaries. Rather than considering these regions as boundaries between segments, it may be appropriate to regard them as intervals that provide cues for a number of the phonetic features of the segments in an utterance.

Examples of acoustic properties that occur within these brief time intervals are the acoustic properties that identify place of articulation for stop and nasal consonants. Acoustic data and evidence from perceptual experiments suggest that place of articulation can be identified on the basis of the gross shape of the short-time spectrum sampled at the consonantal release (Blumstein & Stevens 1979), the way this spectrum

* This work was supported in part by Grant NS-04332 from the National Institute of Neurological and Communicative Disorders and Stroke and by Grant MCS-81-12899 from the National Science Foundation. The help of Sheila Blumstein and the advice of Dennis Klatt in the synthesis of appropriate nasal stimuli are gratefully acknowledged.

PHONETIC LINGUISTICS

changes in the 10–20 msec following release (Lahiri, Gewirth, & Blumstein 1984; Kewley-Port 1980; Stevens 1975), or possibly some other attributes such as the starting frequencies of the second and third formants (Delattre, Liberman & Cooper 1955; Hoffman 1958; Lehiste & Peterson 1961; Stevens, House, & Paul 1966). Another example where information near an acoustic discontinuity helps to identify a phonetic feature is the voiced–voiceless contrast for stop consonants in English. It is well known that if vocal-fold vibration occurs within about 20 msec of a stop-consonant release in syllable-initial position preceding a stressed vowel, a listener judges the consonant to be voiced; otherwise, if there is no evidence for vocal-fold vibration within this time window, the consonant is voiceless (Lisker & Abramson 1964). Still another example is the distinction between the stop consonant [b] and the glide [w] in syllable-initial position. When the onset of the amplitude in a frequency band in the vicinity of the first formant is sufficiently abrupt that it occurs within about 30 msec, the syllable is judged as a stop, whereas when the onset is slower it is identified as a glide (Liberman, Delattre, Gerstman, & Cooper 1956; Miller & Liberman 1979). In the case of the stop–glide continuum, the different rates of amplitude onset are achieved by manipulating the rate of increase of the freqency of the first formant.

In this chapter we present the results of some perception experiments that provide further evidence that acoustic events in the vicinity of these boundaries signal particular phonetic features. The phonetic oppositions we examine are strident–nonstrident ([s] versus [θ]), anterior–nonanterior for fricatives ([s] versus [š]), and the nasal–stop opposition ([m] or [n] versus [b] or [d]). In each case we have synthesized a series of stimuli spanning the range from one member of the pair to the other, and we attempt to show that, at the point in this series where listeners hear a shift from one member of the pair to the other, the change in the acoustic attributes can be described in terms of a simple property in a 20-msec time window close to a so-called consonant–vowel boundary.

2. THE STRIDENT–NONSTRIDENT DISTINCTION

We examine first the distinction between the strident alveolar consonant [s] and the nonstrident dental in English [θ]. Both of these consonants are *coronals* and both are *anterior,* using the features of Chomsky and Halle (1968) for purposes of classification. That is, they are both produced by raising the tongue blade, and the tongue blade is in a relatively fronted position. For the strident [s], the airstream from the consonantal constriction is directed against the lower incisors, producing an enhanced amplitude

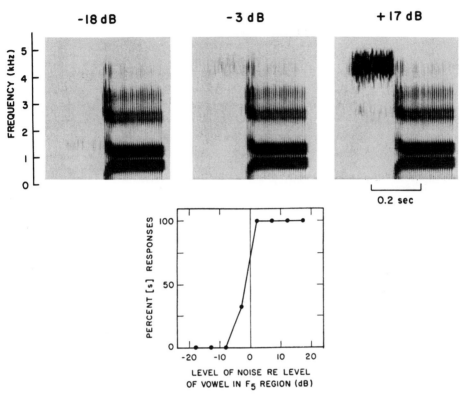

Figure 16.1   Top: Spectrograms of three of the stimuli used in the [θ]–[s] identification test. The level of the noise in the fifth-formant region relative to that of the vowel in the same region is indicated above each stimulus. Bottom: Results of [θ]–[s] identification test.

of turbulence noise, whereas for the nonstrident [θ], the airstream is directed in such a way as to avoid impinging on an obstacle.

A series of eight fricative–vowel syllables (with the vowel [ɑ]) was synthesized in such a way that the amplitude of the turbulence noise at high frequencies (in the F_5–F_6 region) was gradually reduced from one stimulus to the next in the series. (A slight increase was made in the spectrum amplitude of the noise in the F_2 region in order to obtain more natural [θ] stimuli.) Spectrograms of three stimuli in the series—the endpoint stimuli and a middle stimulus—are shown at the top of Figure 16.1. The figure shows that for the stimulus at the right the spectrum amplitude of the noise in the F_5–F_6 region is well above the same spectrum amplitude for the stimulus at the left. In the case of the middle stimulus, the high-frequency amplitude is comparable to or slightly less than that at the onset of voicing for the vowel. The change in spectrum amplitude in this region from one stimulus to the next was 5 dB. The first three formants underwent transitions during the initial 30–40 msec following the onset of voicing. The F_1 transition was rising, and the starting frequencies of the F_1, F_2, and F_3 transitions were 450, 1500, and 2700 Hz, respectively. These starting frequencies were selected to be intermediate between the values expected for [sɑ] and [θɑ] on the basis of acoustic data. The F_2 starting frequency is usually higher for the alveolar than for the dental consonant, presumably reflecting the fact that the tongue body is more backed for the dental. (See, e.g., Lehiste & Peterson 1961; Stevens, House, & Paul 1966; or Stevens, Keyser, & Kawasaki in press.) The frequencies of the first three formants for the vowel were 720, 1240, and 2500 Hz.

A number of replications of these synthetic syllables were presented in random order to four American English listeners, who identified the consonant as either *th* or *s*. The results, shown at the bottom of Figure 16.1, are plotted with percentage of *s* responses as the ordinate and the level of the noise in the F_5 region relative to the amplitude of the F_5 spectral peak within the vowel as the abscissa. There is a rather abrupt shift from *th* responses to *s* responses very close to the point where the noise amplitude is equal to the amplitude of the vowel formant. In fact, there was only one stimulus that was not identified unanimously as [s] or [θ] by all listeners. In other words, the listeners appear to identify the consonant as *th* if the high-frequency noise amplitude increases at the fricative–vowel boundary and as *s* if there is a drop in amplitude as the frication noise ends and voicing for the vowel begins.

3. THE ANTERIOR–NONANTERIOR DISTINCTION FOR FRICATIVES

In the next experiment, a series of synthetic syllables that spanned the range from [sɑ] to [šɑ] was generated. Three of the stimuli in this series are shown in Figure 16.2. To generate the fricative consonants in this continuum, noise was passed through three formant filters corresponding to F_3, F_5, and F_6. The amplitude of the noise in the two high-frequency filters was kept the same for all stimuli. Falling transitions were produced in F_2 and F_3 at the onset of the vowel, similar to those for [θ–s] continuum in Figure 16.1, and these transitions were the same for all stimuli. The only variable in the series was the amplitude of noise in the third formant. From one stimulus to the next in this eight-member continuum, this amplitude was increased in steps of about 4 dB.

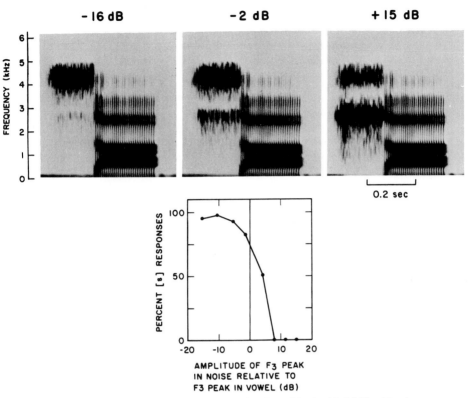

Figure 16.2 Spectrograms of three of the stimuli used in the [s]–[š] identification test. The level of the noise in the third-formant region relative to that of the vowel in ine same frequency region is indicated above each stimulus. Bottom: Results of [s]–[š] identification test.

These stimuli were appropriately replicated and randomized and were presented to four listeners who were instructed to identify each item as beginning with *s* or *sh*. The results of this identification test are shown at the bottom of Figure 16.2, with the abscissa indicating the amplitude of F_3 in the noise relative to the amplitude of the F_3 peak at the onset of the vowel. The identification function in this case is not quite so sharp as that in Figure 16.1 (there were slight differences among listeners), but on the average the crossover occurs near the 0-dB point. That is, listeners identify the consonant as the anterior coronal [s] if there is a rise in amplitude in the F_3 region going from the consonant into the vowel, but the consonant is identified as nonanterior [š] if the amplitude in this region falls. The lack of an abrupt identification function in this case can probably be attributed to the fact that fixed transitions were placed on the formants for all stimuli, whereas it is known that [š], being normally produced with a higher and more fronted tongue body position, has a higher F_2 starting frequency in the following vowel than does [s]. (See, e.g., Lehiste & Peterson 1961 and Stevens et al. 1966.) Thus, for stimuli for which the F_3 noise amplitude is close to the boundary, listeners may resort to transition information but may differ in the degree to which they use this acoustic attribute.

Informal observation of spectra and spectrograms of real speech support the results of the perception experiments summarized in Figures 16.1 and 16.2. The spectrograms of Figure 16.3 show examples of the utterances *a thin, a sin,* and *a shin,* and the relevant properties can be observed: high-frequency noise that is weaker than the high-frequency spectrum for the vowel for [θ] and stronger for [s]; amplitude of the third-formant energy that is greater than (or comparable to) that for the vowel for [š] and weaker for [s]. These observations must, of course, be substantiated by detailed measurements for utterances in English and in other languages that utilize these consonants.

There is also evidence from the [s]–[f] distinction in Spanish (Gurlenkian 1981) and English (McCasland 1979) that the spectrum of the noise alone does not determine the identity of a fricative consonant, but that the spectrum amplitude of the noise in relation to the vowel can influence listener judgments. Similar influences of noise amplitude on perception of place of articulation for the bursts in stop consonants have been observed by Ohde and Stevens (1983). Results of this kind indicate the importance of carefully describing the spectrum and amplitude characteristics of consonantal stimuli used in perception experiments, especially the relative amplitudes of frication noise and vowel.

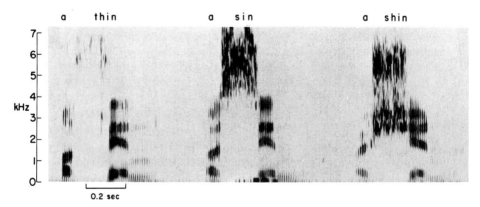

Figure 16.3 Spectrograms of *a thin, a sin,* and *a shin,* produced by an adult male speaker.

All of this evidence suggests that the vowel is used as some kind of anchor against which the spectrum of the fricative noise is judged or evaluated. This hypothesis needs to be examined more thoroughly for a wider variety of vowels and fricatives and for fricatives in different languages. It is recognized that other factors may also come into play as cues for fricative consonants, such as the transitions of the formants. There may also be fine details of fricative spectra that vary from language to language (Nartey 1982) and may not be distinctive in a given language but that can often be detected by listeners.

4. THE NASAL–STOP DISTINCTION

In another experiment that was designed to provide insight into the perceptual importance of acoustic events in the vicinity of a rapid change in amplitude or spectrum, we examined the responses of listeners to four different consonant–vowel stimulus series spanning the range from a nasal consonant to a stop consonant. Two of the series ranged from [ma] to [ba], and the other two from [na] to [da]. The nasal murmur was produced with a lowest resonance at 250 Hz and with appropriate higher-frequency resonances corresponding to a bilabial [m] or an alveolar [n]. At the release of the nasal, the transitions of formants F_2 and F_3 into the vowel were rising for [m] and falling for [n] and had durations of 40 msec. Details of the control parameters for the synthesizer in the F_1 region are shown in Figure 16.4. A pole–zero pair simulated nasalization

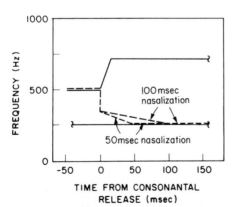

Figure 16.4 Parameters used to control the formant synthesizer in the first formant region for the stimuli in the nasal series. The solid lines represent the trajectories of two poles of the synthesizer; the dashed line represents the trajectory of a zero. Two trajectories of the zero are shown, corresponding to two different durations of nasalization following the release. In regions where a pole and zero coincide, there is cancellation.

that gradually decreased to zero during the initial 50 or 100 msec of the vowel onset depending on the stimulus series. The frequencies of the additional pole and zero at the consonant release (or vowel onset) were 250 and 350 Hz, respectively, and the frequency of F_1 at this point was 500 Hz. The additional pole remained at 250 Hz throughout the vowel, and the zero moved downward to cancel the pole in the above–mentioned time interval of 50 or 100 msec for the different series. The first formant rose to 720 Hz (F_1 for the steady vowel) in 15 msec. Different items in each series were produced by successively cutting back on the duration of the nasal murmur, as shown in the spectrograms in Figure 16.5. There

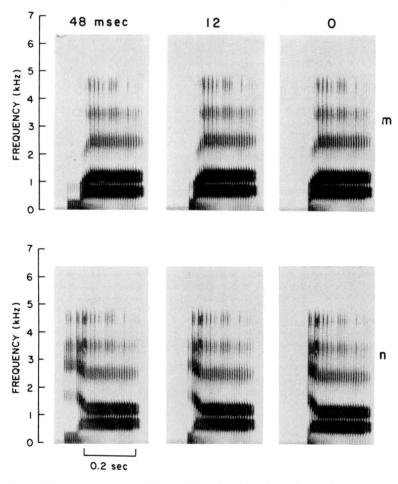

Figure 16.5 Spectrograms of three of the stimuli in a [mɑ]–[bɑ] series (top) and in a [nɑ]–[dɑ] series (bottom).

were five stimuli in each series. The top row shows three of the members of the [ma–ba] series (the one with a 100-msec interval of nasalization following the release) and the bottom row shows three items in the corresponding [na–da] series. The first item (at the left in Figure 16.5) had six pitch periods (about 48 msec) before release, and the last item (right in Figure 16.5) had no voicing before release but the complete formant transitions were maintained. All of these 20 stimuli (four series, five stimuli in each) were replicated and randomized and were presented to four American English listeners who were instructed to identify the initial consonant as *b, d, m,* or *n.*

There are other ways of producing a series of stimuli ranging from a voiced stop consonant to a nasal consonant by manipulating certain parameters of a speech synthesizer (e.g., Miller & Eimas 1977). This method was selected in order to draw attention to the role of events near the consonantal release as cues for this distinction, which involves both the nasal–nonnasal and the sonorant–nonsonorant opposition.

As an incidental point relating to the role played by events at acoustic discontinuities, we observe in Figure 16.5 the substantial high-frequency spectral energy in the first two or three periods following the release of the synthetic coronal nasal consonant [n] compared with the weak high-frequency energy in this region for the [m]. This difference in spectrum balance at consonantal release for the two places of articulation is a consequence of the different starting frequencies for F_2 and F_3 and has been noted before (Fant 1956, 1960; Stevens & Blumstein 1978). That is, the higher frequencies of F_2 and F_3 at the release for the coronal lead to a greater spectrum amplitude at frequencies at and above F_3, whereas the lower frequencies of F_2 and F_3 for the labial give rise to a reduced spectrum amplitude at these high frequencies.

Identification functions for the different nasal–stop series, based on the responses of the four listeners to eight replications of each stimulus, are displayed in Figure 16.6. These functions show that as the duration of the murmur drops below about 20 msec, a stop consonant tends to be heard. There is a small effect (bigger for [m] than for [n]) of the duration of nasalization in the vowel, with the longer duration leading to more nasal responses. One way of stating these results is the following: If the onset of the low-frequency murmur and the release of the consonant occur within 20-odd msec of each other, then these two onsets merge to form a single onset perceptually, and the consonant tends to be heard as a stop. If the onset of the murmur occurs more than 20 msec before the consonantal release, then the murmur and the release are perceived separately, and the consonant is interpreted as a nasal.

The identification functions in Figure 16.6 are not very sharp, indicating that there is a range of murmur durations over which listeners give

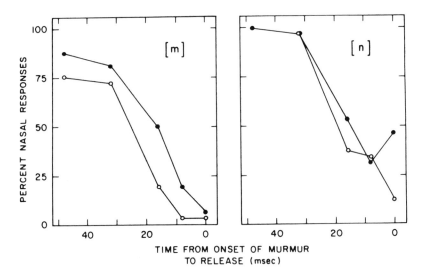

Figure 16.6 Results of identification tests for the various nasal–stop series. Open circles represent data from stimuli with a 50-msec duration of nasalization following release; closed circles represent a 100-msec duration of nasalization.

equivocal responses. This lack of a sharp boundary in the responses, together with the influence of duration of nasalization in the vowel following the release, can perhaps be attributed to the fact that two phonetic features are involved in distinguishing a nasal from a stop consonant, and each of these has an acoustic correlate to which the listeners are responding. One of these is the nasal–nonnasal distinction and the other is the sonorant–nonsonorant distinction. The acoustic correlate of the feature [+nasal] appears to be modification of the spectral prominence in the vicinity of the first formant in the vowel immediately following the release—a consequence of introduction of a pole–zero pair at low frequencies. For the feature [−sonorant], the acoustic correlate is introduction of some aperiodicity in the vicinity of the release. While there is no frication noise at the release in these stimuli to provide a cue for the [−sonorant] feature, the abruptness of the onset, coupled with the rapid movement of the formants occurring in the vicinity of the onset, could lead to perception of an aperiodicity in the sound at the release. All of the stimuli in all of the tests contain the modification of the low-frequency prominence immediately following the release, and hence the cue for the feature [+nasal] is always present, but to different degrees depending on the duration of nasalization. However, the abruptness of onset in the vicinity of the rapid formant motions for small values of delay time from onset to release could provide a cue for the feature

[− sonorant], thus leading to a conflict with the feature [+ nasal] (which is inherently [+ sonorant]). This conflicting information could lead to variability in the responses of the listeners, since they are attempting to respond to a combination of acoustic properties that they do not normally hear. More experiments are clearly needed to provide a better understanding of the perceptual correlates of these features and how they interact.

5. GENERAL DISCUSSION

We have illustrated several different phonetic distinctions for which acoustic events near a rapid change in amplitude or spectrum appear to contribute to a listener's identification of some phonetic feature. In the case of the strident–nonstrident distinction, exemplified by the [s]–[θ] distinction in English, the strident consonant is heard when there is a drop in the high-frequency spectrum amplitude at the time when the frication noise ends and glottal excitation begins. The nonstrident consonant is heard when there is an increase in the high-frequency spectrum amplitude at this boundary. The distinction between [s] and [š] in English can be characterized by a similar rise or fall in spectrum amplitude at this boundary, but in this case the part of the spectrum that is of interest is the midfrequency range, in the vicinity of the third formant. In both of these stimulus series, the adjacent vowel appears to provide some kind of anchor against which the noise spectrum is assessed. For the nasal–stop distinction as produced in this study, a stop is heard if the onset of the nasal murmur and the consonant release are within about 20 msec. The data also show that the presence of nasalization in the few tens of msec following the release can influence the responses of the listeners.

These and other data, then, lead us to the conclusion that these brief time intervals when there is a rapid change in spectrum or amplitude create regions that are rich in information concerning the phonetic features in an utterance. Either the acoustic correlates of phonetic features consist of specification of how the spectrum is changing in this region, or the region provides a landmark that indicates where nearby spectral or temporal information is to be sampled.

On the basis of these observations it would appear that a great deal of information is carried by these one-eighth-inch time slots in the spectrogram—much more than one would expect on the basis of the space they occupy in linear time. The auditory-perception system seems to give special attention to these events that are packed with properties that identify a number of consonantal features.

It is, of course, dangerous to generalize about acoustic and perceptual correlates of features based on data from just one language—a point that Peter Ladefoged has emphasized. His influence and painstaking efforts to obtain careful descriptions of phonetic events for a variety of diverse languages provides a rich source of information that can be used to test hypotheses of the kind proposed in this paper.

REFERENCES

Blumstein, S. E., & Stevens, K. N. (1979). Acoustic invariance in speech production: Evidence from measurements of the spectral characteristics of stop consonants. *Journal of the Acoustic Society of America, 66,* 1001–1017.

Chomsky, N., & Halle, M. (1968). *The sound pattern of English.* New York: Harper and Row.

Delattre, P. C., Liberman, A. M., & Cooper, F. S. (1955). Acoustic loci and transitional cues for consonants. *Journal of the Acoustic Society of America, 27,* 769–773.

Fant, G. C. M. (1956). On the predictability of formant levels and spectrum envelope from formant frequencies. In *For Roman Jakobson* (pp. 109–128). The Hague: Mouton.

Fant, G. C. M. (1960). *Acoustic theory of speech production.* The Hague: Mouton.

Gurlenkian, J. A. (1981). Recognition of the Spanish fricatives /s/ and /f/. *Journal of the Acoustical Society of America, 70,* 1624–1627.

Hoffman, H. S. (1958). Study of some cues in the perception of the voiced stop consonants. *Journal of the Acoustic Society of America, 30,* 1035–1041.

Kewley-Port, D. (1980). Representation of spectral change as cues to place of articulation in stop consonants. In *Research on speech perception* (Tech. Rep. No. 3). Bloomington: Indiana University, Department of Psychology.

Lahiri, A., Grewirth, L., & Blumstein, S. E. (1984). A reconsideration of acoustic invariance for place of articulation in diffuse stop consonants: Evidence from a cross-language study. *Journal of the Acoustical Society of America, 76,* 391–404.

Lehiste, I., & Peterson, G. (1961). Transitions, glides, and diphthongs. *Journal of the Acoustical Society of America, 33,* 268–277.

Liberman, A. M., Delattre, P. C., Gerstman, L. J., & Cooper, F. S. (1956). Tempo of frequency change as a cue for distinguishing classes of speech sounds. *Journal of Experimental Psychology, 52,* 127–137.

Lisker, L., & Abramson, A. S. (1964). A cross-language study of voicing in initial stops: Acoustical measurements. *Word, 20,* 384–422.

McCasland, G. P. (1979). Noise intensity and spectrum cues for spoken fricatives. *Journal of the Acoustical Society of America, 65,* Suppl 1, S78–S79.

Miller, J. L., & Eimas, P. D. (1977). Studies on the perception of place and manner of articulation: A comparison of the labial-alveolar and nasal-stop distinctions. *Journal of the Acoustical Society of America, 61,* 835–845.

Miller, J. L., & Liberman, A. M. (1979). Some effects of later-occurring information on the perception of stop consonant and semivowel. *Perception & Psychophysics, 25,* 457–465.

Nartey, J. N. A. (1982). On fricative phones and phonemes. *UCLA Working Papers in Phonetics* No. 55.

Ohde, R. N., & Stevens, K. N. (1983). Effect of burst amplitude on the perception of stop consonant place of articulation. *Journal of the Acoustical Society of America, 74,* 706–714.

Stevens, K. N. (1975). The potential role of property detectors in the perception of consonants. In G. Fant & M. A. A. Tatham (Eds.), *Auditory analysis and perception of speech* (pp. 303–330). New York: Academic Press.

Stevens, K. N., & Blumstein, S. E. (1978). Invariant cues for place of articulation in stop consonants. *Journal of the Acoustical Society of America, 64,* 1358–1368.

Stevens, K. N., House, A. S., & Paul, A. P. (1966). Acoustical description of syllabic nuclei: An interpretation in terms of a dynamic model of articulation. *Journal of the Acoustical Society of America, 40,* 123–132.

Stevens, K. N., Keyser, S. J., & Kawasaki, H. (in press). Toward a phonetic and phonological investigation of redundant features. In J. Perkell & D. H. Klatt (Eds.), *Symposium on invariance and variability of speech processes.* Hillsdale, NJ: Erlbaum.

Index